CAE Testbuilder

WITH ANSWER KEY

Amanda French

MACMILLAN

Macmillan Education
Between Towns Road, Oxford OX4 3PP
A division of Macmillan Publishers Limited
Companies and representatives throughout the world

ISBN 1 405 01400 8 (with key)
ISBN 1 405 01401 6 (without key)

Original design by Xen Media Ltd
Page layout by eMC Design, www.emcdesign.org.uk
Illustrated by Paul Collicutt and Gary Rees
Cover design by Xen Media Ltd

The author would like to thank Liam Keane, Jeanette Barsdell and Keith
Harding for their help and support.

The author and publishers would like to thank the following for
permission to reproduce their material:
Extracts from 'The Inspiration Flows' from 'Jazz Albums: Pick of the
Month' first published in BBC Music Magazine May 2002, reprinted by
permission of the publisher and extracts from book review of Llynne
Arriale Trio: Inspiration by Ian Carr, reprinted by permission of Barbara
Levy Literary Agency on behalf of the author; Extracts from 'No dodo' by
Stephanie Pain, first published in New Scientist 01.06.02, reprinted by
permission of the publisher; Book reviews of Earthshaking Science
reviewed by Sue Bowler, Small Wonder reviewed by Maggie McDonald,
Zoo: A History of Zoological Gardens In The West reviewed by Adrian
Barnett and Solar Flair reviewed by Ben Longstaff, all taken from
www.newscientist.com/opbooks 04.07.02, reprinted by permission of the
publisher; Extracts from book review of The Man Who Stopped The
Planet reviewed by Robert Mc Farlane, copyright © Robert McFarlane
2002 from 'Giving a sense of shape to our world' first published in The
Guardian Weekly 04.07.02, reprinted by permission of the publisher;
Extracts from 'On the other hand…' by Robert Fulford, copyright ©
Robert Fulford 2002, first published in National Post 25.06.02, reprinted
by permission of the author; Extracts from 'Getting the pack mentality'
by Gerry Volgenau, copyright © Gerry Volgenau, first published in The
Detroit Free Press 09.07.02, reprinted by permission of the author;
Extracts from 'No more heroes' by Nicola Jones, first published in New
Scientist 01.06.02, reprinted by permission of the publisher; Extracts
from 'Oh for the arms of Morpheus' by Alan Judd taken from
www.arts.telegraph.co.uk 23.06.02 copyright © Telegraph Group
Limited 2002, reprinted by permission of the publisher; Extracts from
'Waltzing in the midnight sun' copyright © Fran Weaver 2002, first
published in The Guardian Weekly 4–10.07.02, reprinted by permission
of the author; Extracts from 'Capsize? I try not to in three metre waves'
by Mark Mackenzie, first published in The Independent on Sunday
14.07.02, reprinted by permission of the publisher; Extracts from 'The
Brain Gain' by Sharon Stephenson, first published in She Magazine July
2002, reprinted by permission of the publisher; Extracts from 'Lamb's
Tales' by Stephanie Pain, first published in New Scientist Magazine
15.06.02, reprinted by permission of the publisher; Extracts from
'Virtuous Nature' by Mark Bekoff first published in New Scientist
Magazine 13.07.02; Extracts from 'Let's Dance' by Rupert Mellor and
friends, copyright © News International Newspaper Limited, London
2002 first published in The Times 03.08.02, reprinted by permission of
the publisher; Extracts from 'Britain goes bananas' by Robert McKie,
copyright © Robert McKie, first published in The Guardian Weekly
25.07.02, reprinted by permission of the publisher; Extracts from 'Silent
Blessings' by Giles Tremlett copyright © Giles Tremlett 2002, first
published in The Guardian Weekly 01.08.02, reprinted by permission of
the author; Extracts from 'Most languages face silent death' by David
Ward, copyright © The Guardian 2002, first published in The Guardian
Weekly 01.08.02, reprinted by permission of the publisher; Extracts
from 'I'm a 11 bag man myself' by Mark Mackenzie and Simon
O'Hagan, first published in The Independent on Sunday 14.07.02,
reprinted by permission of the publisher; Extracts from 'Face of
yesterday' by Henry Gee, copyright © Henry Gee 2002, first published
in The Guardian Weekly July 2002, reprinted by permission of the
publisher; Book reviews of Everything is Illuminated: Back in the Totally
Awesome U.S.S.R by Francine Prose taken from New York Times on
the Web 14.04.02; By The Lake: Coming Home to Ireland by John
Sutherland taken from New York Times on the Web 17.03.02; Crow
Lake: The Girl She Left Behind by Janet Burroway taken from New York
Times on the Web 24.03.02 and The Bondwoman's Narrative: An
1850's Account of Slave Life by Mia Bay taken from New York Times on
the Web 12.05.02, all copyright © The New York Times Co 2002,

reprinted by permission of the publisher; Extracts from 'What's the best
way to climb Mont Blanc?' by Alex Wade, first published in The
Independent on Sunday 11.08.02, reprinted by permission of the
publisher; Extracts from 'A Bundle of cash for writing jokes' by Veronica
Lee, first published in The Independent 04.08.02, reprinted by
permission of the publisher; Extracts from 'More than a breath of fresh
air' first published in New Zealand Wilderness Magazine September
2002, reprinted by permission of the publisher; Extracts from 'Venice
gets that sinking feeling' by Paul Brown, copyright © The Guardian
2002, first published in The Guardian 20.06.02, reprinted by permission
of the publisher; Extracts from 'Astronauts deafened by space station
motorway roar' copyright © The Guardian 2002, first published in The
Guardian Weekly 18.07.02, reprinted by permission of the publisher;
Extracts from 'They're jumping, skating, flying, riding and biking' by
Jonathan Thompson, first published in The Independent on Sunday
14.07.02, reprinted by permission of the publisher; Extracts from 'Sweet
and Sour is the new tikka masala' by Robert Mendick, first published in
The Independent 08.08.02, reprinted by permission of the publisher;
Extracts from 'Not just a pretty face' by Maureen Freely, copyright ©
Maureen Freely 2002, first published in The Observer 01.09.02,
reprinted by permission of the publisher; Extracts from 'Are you a tourist
or a traveller' by Dea Birkett, copyright © Dea Birkett 2002, first
published in The Guardian 24.08.02, reprinted by permission of the
publisher; Extracts from 'Sorry sweetie, it's certainly not adfab' by Mary
O'Hara, copyright © The Guardian 2002, first published in The Guardian
31.08.02, reprinted by permission of the publisher; Extracts from 'What
does every corporate boss need? Lego' by David Rowan, copyright ©
The Observer 2002, first published in The Observer 01.09.02, reprinted
by permission of the publisher; Extracts from 'Finding that extra bit of
Income' by Margaret Hughes, copyright © The Guardian 2002, first
published in The Guardian 31.08.02, reprinted by permission of the
publisher; Extracts from 'Basement home for medieval ship' by David
Ward, copyright © The Guardian 2002, first published in The Guardian
Weekly 29.08.02, reprinted by permission of the publisher; Extracts
from 'How peach turned me into a blue cow' by Mark Dapin, copyright ©
Mark Dapin 2002, first published in The Observer 07.04.02, reprinted by
permission of the publisher; Extracts from 'Ad firms adrift in grey area'
by Ben Summerskill, first published in The Guardian, copyright © The
Guardian 2002, reprinted by permission of the publisher.

The author and publishers would like to thank the University of
Cambridge Local Examinations Syndicate for the sample answer
sheets.

The author and publishers would like to thank the following for
permission to reproduce their material on cassette:
Extracts from 'Waltzing in the midnight sun' copyright © Fran Weaver
2002, first published in The Guardian Weekly 4–10.07.02, reprinted by
permission of the author; Extracts from 'Capsize? I try not to in three
metre waves' by Mark Mackenzie, first published in The Independent on
Sunday 14.07.02, reprinted by permission of the publisher; Extracts
from 'Face of yesterday' by Henry Gee, copyright © Henry Gee 2002,
first published in The Guardian Weekly July 2002, reprinted by
permission of the publisher; Extracts from 'They're jumping, skating,
flying, riding and biking' by Jonathan Thompson, first published in The
Independent on Sunday 14.07.02, reprinted by permission of the
publisher; Extracts from 'Sweet and Sour is the new tikka masala' by
Robert Mendick, first published in The Independent 08.08.02, reprinted
by permission of the publisher; Extracts from 'Ad firms adrift in grey
area' by Ben Summerskill, first published in The Guardian, copyright ©
The Guardian 2002, reprinted by permission of the publisher.

The author and publishers would like to thank the following for
permission to reproduce their photographs:
Alamy p148(b,m); Ardea p155(m); Corbis pp146(t), 151(b), 154(m);
Getty Images p151(t); Masterfile p148(t); Mirror Syndication
International p155(b); Oxford Scientific Films p155(t); PBPA/Libby
Welch p154(b); PA Photos p146(b); Rex p154(t)

Printed and bound by Scotprint, Haddington

2007   2006   2005   2004
10 9 8 7 6 5 4 3 2

With Answer Key

10 9 8 7 6 5 4 3

CONTENTS

Introduction   4

TEST ONE

Paper 1
Part 1   6
Further Practice   8
   Paper 1 Part 1   9
Part 2   10
Part 3   12
Further Practice
   Paper 1 Part 3   14
Part 4   16

Paper 2
Part 1   19
Further Practice   20
   Paper 2 formal letter   21
Part 2   23

Paper 3
Part 1   24
Part 2   26
Further Practice
   Paper 3 Part 2   27
Part 3   29
Part 4   30
Further Practice
   Paper 3 Part 4   32
Part 5   34
Part 6   35

Paper 4
Part 1   36
Further Practice
   Paper 4 Parts 1 & 2   37
Part 2   38
Part 3   39
Part 4   40
Further Practice
   Paper 4 Part 4   41

Paper 5
Parts 1 and 2   43
Parts 3 and 4   44
Further Practice   45
   Paper 5 Part 1   46
   Paper 5 Part 2   47

TEST TWO

Paper 1
Part 1   48
Part 2   50
Further Practice
   Paper 1 Part 2   52
Part 3   53
Part 4   55
Further Practice
   Paper 1 Part 4   58

Paper 2
Part 1   60
Part 2   61
Further Practice
   Paper 2 entry/article   62

Paper 3
Part 1   64
Further Practice
   Paper 3 Part 1   66
Part 2   69
Part 3   70
Part 4   71
Part 5   73
Part 6   74
Further Practice
   Paper 3 Part 6   75

Paper 4
Part 1   76
Part 2   77
Part 3   78
Further Practice
   Paper 4 Part 3   79
Part 4   81

Paper 5
Parts 2 to 4   82
Further Practice
   Paper 5 Parts 3 and 4   83

TEST THREE

Paper 1
Part 1   84
Part 2   86
Further Practice
   Paper 1 Part 2   88
Part 3   90
Part 4   92

Paper 2
Part 1   95
Further Practice
   Paper 2 report   96
Part 2   98

Paper 3
Part 1   99
Part 2   101
Part 3   102
Further Practice
   Paper 3 Part 3   103
Part 4   104
Part 5   106
Further Practice
   Paper 3 Part 5   107
Part 6   109

Paper 4
Part 1   110
Part 2   111
Part 3   112
Part 4   113
Further Practice
   Paper 4 Part 4   114

Paper 5
Parts 2 to 4   115
Further Practice
   Paper 5 Part 2   116

TEST FOUR

Paper 1
Part 1   117
Part 2   119
Part 3   121
Part 4   123

Paper 2
Part 1   126
Further Practice
   *Paper 2 letter of
   application*   127
Part 2   128
Further Practice
   Paper 2 leaflet   129
General Impression
   Mark Scheme   131

Paper 3
Part 1   132
Part 2   134
Part 3   135
Part 4   136
Part 5   138
Part 6   139

Paper 4
Part 1   140
Part 2   141
Part 3   142
Part 4   143

Paper 5
Parts 2 to 4   144

Writing Mark Scheme   131

Paper 5 Visual material   145

Sample answer sheets   155

Key and explanation   161

Listening scripts   182

INTRODUCTION

The Certificate in Advanced English Testbuilder is more than a book of practice tests; it offers students 'tests that teach'. This teaching function is achieved in part through sections of further practice and guidance. These sections review the questions in the practice tests, helping students to reconsider their answers and increasing their chance of getting the answers correct. The tests are designed to reflect the actual CAE examination as closely as possible.

The edition with the answer key helps to further the learning process. Answers are often accompanied by an explanation of why they are correct, and why others are wrong.

Using the Certificate in Advanced English Testbuilder

Either:

- Do each part of a Paper under 'exam conditions'. This means that you cannot use a dictionary and you limit the time you spend on it. Then check your answers or do the further practice and guidance section. When you have answered the questions in this section, you can reconsider your answers to the original questions in the test before checking the final answers.

Or:

- You may wish to do some of the further practice and guidance questions before answering the questions in the test that they relate to. Alternatively, teachers may wish to do the further practice and guidance pages as discussion or pairwork, or ask students to prepare them before class.

The Certificate in Advanced English

Paper 1 Reading (1 hour 15 minutes)

There are between 40–50 questions in total.
- The paper consists of four parts.
- The tasks for Part 1 and Part 4 are multiple matching. Candidates may have to read one long text, a text divided into sections or a set of short texts connected by a similar theme.
- Part 2 is a gapped text. Candidates need to choose the correct extract to fill each gap.
- Part 3 is multiple choice. Candidates need to choose from four answers.

Paper 2 Writing (2 hours)

- The paper consists of two parts.
- There is only one question in Part 1 and this is compulsory.
- There are four questions in Part 2 and you must answer one of them.
- Each question must be completed in approximately 250 words. Aim to write no fewer than 230 and no more than 270 words.
- The compulsory task will involve responding to a text you have read. Your reply may be a letter, a note, a memo or any other document providing information. The question will tell you who you are writing to and the purpose of your response. You will need to include specific points in your answer which will be mentioned in the input text.
- For the second task, candidates also need to respond to a specific situation and target reader, but the content is less specific. Question 5 is always connected to business or a work situation.
- For both tasks, candidates will need to consider who they are writing to or for (imagined target reader), the register/style of their writing, organisation and cohesion (how ideas are connected), their range of vocabulary and grammar and their accuracy. Candidates may have to write one or two of a range of writing types: see page 20 for a full list.

Paper 3 English in Use (1 hour 30 minutes)

- The paper consists of six parts:
- a cloze with 15 gaps. The text will be followed by 15 four-option multiple-choice questions. The emphasis will be on vocabulary.

- a cloze with 15 gaps. This will differ from the previous cloze in providing candidates with 'open' choices; there are no words from which to select. The emphasis will be on grammar and vocabulary.

- a correction exercise with 16 lines. Candidates will have to either identify and correct spelling and punctuation mistakes, or identify extra unwanted words. Correct lines must be marked with a tick.

- a word formation exercise based on two texts with 15 gaps. Candidates must fill each gap by forming a word from a given 'base word'. The emphasis will be on vocabulary.

- a transformational exercise where candidates must change the register: from formal to informal, informal to informal.

- a sentence-fill text. Candidates need to decide which extract logically and grammatically completes each gap.

Paper 4 Listening (about 45 minutes)

There are between 30–40 questions in total.
- This paper consists of four parts.
- Each part will be heard twice except for Part 2.
- Texts will include monologues (such as people making speeches, giving information or expressing opinions by themselves) or exchanges (such as people agreeing/disagreeing with one another or interviewing one another.)
- Parts 1 and 2 will involve note-taking or sentence completion.
- Part 3 is either multiple choice, where you need to choose from four answers, or sentence completion.
- Part 4 is multiple matching, where you will need to match 'list A' to 'list B' – perhaps a list of people to attitudes, a list of occupations to experiences, etc.
- The approximate time of 45 minutes includes time for candidates to transfer their answers to the answer sheet.

Paper 5 Speaking (about 15 minutes)

Two examiners will be at the interview: an interlocutor who asks the questions and guides your discussions and an assessor who is listening to the English you produce. You will have a partner in the exam – either someone you do or do not know – it does not matter. The important thing is that you include your partner in the discussions.
For more information on the speaking test see page 45.

Marking the Practice Tests

In the actual examination all five papers have equal weighting (40 marks each) giving a total of 200. You should aim to get 60 – 65% in each paper, but if you do not achieve 60% in one paper, and you do very well in another paper, you may still pass.

The following advice is designed to help students or teachers to assess the practice tests in a similar way:

Paper 1 (approximately 45 questions): Give 1 mark for answers in Parts 1 and 4; 2 marks for answers in Parts 2 and 3.
Paper 2 (two tasks): Mark each task out of 5.
Paper 3 (80 questions): Give 1 mark for each correct answer.
Paper 4 (between 30–40 questions): Give 1 mark for each correct answer.
Paper 5 The maximum mark is 30. Grammar and Vocabulary, Discourse Management, Pronunciation, and Interactive Communication are all assessed.

TEST ONE

PAPER 1 READING   1 hour 15 minutes

Part 1

Answer questions **1–13** by referring to the magazine article on page **7** in which four critics review newly-released jazz albums. In the exam, you will mark your answers on a separate answer sheet.

For questions **1–13**, answer by choosing from the list (**A–D**) on the right below. Some of the choices may be required more than once.

Which critic		
feels that the group's current album proves they now have a clearer sense of musical identity?	**1**	
says that the album affected his mood in an extremely positive way?	**2**	
praises the album for its sense of drama and deeper meaning?	**3**	
believes that it is the result which is important, not the process through which it was achieved?	**4**	
believes this album lives up to expectations?	**5**	**A** Ian Carr
suggests that the group has taken a very free approach in their adaptation of certain established musical pieces?	**6**	
mentions that the music featured on the album has been chosen due to the impression the original artists had made?	**7**	**B** Richard Cook
expresses surprise that all the performers can successfully create a reasonable sound together?	**8**	**C** Chris Parker
feels that two musicians' very different approaches to musical performance are complementary?	**9**	**D** Stuart Nicholson
praises a previously unknown musician for standing out as an extraordinary performer?	**10**	
states that one musician in particular has become the symbol for a musical trend?	**11**	
mentions a musician's decision to take up jazz in order to invent and play music without preparation?	**12**	
expresses uncertainty as to what reaction the music is supposed to provoke?	**13**	

Before you check your answers, go to page 8.

Jazz Albums: Pick of the Month

BBC Music Magazine reviews this month's new jazz releases

A Ian Carr Lynne Arriale Trio: *Inspiration*

It's always thrilling when a new star shines in the 'jazz universe', but pianist Lynne Arriale is an exceptional talent. After training in classical piano, she turned to jazz because she wanted 'the challenge of combining performance and composition on the spot'. She says she was mainly influenced by artist Keith Jarrett, but it's clear she has her own concept of how jazz music can be played to an audience and this is what lies behind the frequent creative surprise of her work. Not only this, there's often a magical rapport between Arriale and her trio colleagues, Anderson and Davis. *Inspiration* is a celebratory investigation of the songs, composers and performers that have made their mark on them over the years. They take a few daring liberties with some of the pieces: *It Don't Mean a Thing* by legendary musician Duke Ellington is given a slow, tender performance, but over a reggae beat; Thelonious Monk's *Bemsha Swing* begins with the whole trio making up the music as they go along, during which fragments of the original melody gradually emerge, a rhythm is established and the crazily inventive piano phrases magnify Monk's peculiar style. This is a great album.

B Richard Cook Instant Composers Pool Orchestra: *Oh, My Dog!*

Dutch jazz artists have been stereotyped by some music critics as very theatrical and this image is largely a result of the light-hearted approach of Han Bennick, Misha Mengelberg and Willem Breuker, the three musicians who founded the Instant Composers Pool Orchestra concept nearly 40 years ago. The three have now been joined by six others, and their album, *Oh, My Dog!* will not confound their reputation: it's comic and theatrical, as well as urgent and rather profound. The opening four-minute improvisation, *Write Down Exactly*, is a little miracle of nine people making a decent noise without getting in each other's way. Musician Ab Baars pays peculiar homage to the composer Charles Ives with *A Close Encounter with Charles's Country Band*, while Misha Mengelberg's *A la Russe* starts as a stately Russian folk-tune before gradually transforming into mild disharmony. Michael Moore plays his pieces with a tight delivery that is an excellent counter to Baars' gloomy style. It is a bizarre world, where you're never sure whether you should be grinning or flinching in alarm. Serious fun!

C Chris Parker Bobby Previte & Bump: *Just Add Water*

Since rising to prominence on the crest of the 'downtown-style' wave in the early eighties, drummer/composer Bobby Previte has epitomised that influential movement's open-eared adventurousness: in other words, its restless search for inspiration from diverse music styles. His own projects, ranging from the electronically oriented Empty Suits, to the futuristic sounding rock band Latin for Travellers, draw on everything from minimalism to film music, as well as jazz and rock. But whatever the genre in which his widely disparate bands operate, Previte himself is right at the centre of the action. *Just Add Water* is thoughtful and carefully constructed, yet I also found it infectiously exuberant and irresistibly uplifting. All the band members, save the peerless electric bassist Steve Swallow, are long-time Previte associates, and the rapport between them – particularly on such vigorous pieces as the lengthy, rousing *Put Away Your Crayons* – is the key to the album's considerable subtlety and power.

D Stuart Nicholson Wibutee: *Eight Domestic Challenges*

Wibutee made its debut album in 1999, but it has taken until this, the ensemble's second album, to define its voice. Wibutee has dropped the keyboards and vocals heard on its first album and replaced them with a sampling machine. This modern piece of technology has given many previously 'traditional' jazz artists the opportunity to explore a whole new world of sounds. Hakon Kornstad, the group's leader, clearly demonstrates that he is well up to the challenge on this album. A prodigiously gifted young man, he also leads his own Kornstad Trio, but with Wibutee, however, all the members of the group are equal and are all concerned to focus their considerable individual talent into making an integrated collective sound. As might be expected from a contemporary jazz group, there is a certain amount of eclecticism; a broad selection from, for instance, contemporary classical music, house music and free jazz. But of course it is the end not the means that counts, and on a track like *First There Was Jazz*, the group achieves its artistic purpose through its insistence on perfection and clarity.

WHAT'S TESTED

The Reading Paper has four parts: four different texts and three different types of comprehension task. The texts come from a variety of sources, e.g. newspapers, magazines, brochures and journals, and may deal with a range of general interest topics. You will need a high level of vocabulary to understand the texts so it is important that you read English language newspapers and/or magazines. The texts never come from fiction books so while reading fiction may improve your general level of vocabulary, it may not be the type of vocabulary that you will see in Paper 1 texts.

Multiple matching (1 mark for each correct answer)
Parts 1 and 4 test your ability to find specific information in a long text or a series of short texts connected by theme. There will be a set of questions which you will need to match to the relevant information in the text. Some examples of matching tasks are:

- matching a list of attitudes to a set of people
- matching a list of opinions to a set of book or film reviews
- matching a list of statements to different sections of a text.

The text for Part 1 covers a single page and the text for Part 4 covers two pages.

TIPS

- Read the questions first and highlight any key words. The questions are written in a very precise way, which means that wrong answers will not match them. By reading the questions first, you will also have an idea of what to look for while you are reading. If you start by reading the text first, you may waste time trying to understand part of the text or some vocabulary that is not being tested.
- Beware of choosing an answer just because you notice a word in the question that is a synonym for a word in the text.

A DETAILED STUDY

The exercise below will help you to make sure that you have chosen the correct options for the questions on *Jazz Albums: Pick of the Month*. Match the words or phrases on the left (which appear in the questions) with the words or phrases on the right (which appear in the four reviews). Do **not** look back at the texts to help you.

Language in the questions	Language in the texts
1 to have a clearer sense of musical identity *f*	**a** profound (adj.)
2 to affect someone's mood in a positive way	**b** this album will not confound the group's reputation
3 deep (adj.)	**c** to be uplifting
4 the process you use to achieve something	**d** to do something on the spot
5 this album lives up to expectations	**e** to make a mark on someone
6 to take a free approach with something	**f** to define its (the group's) voice
7 to make an impression on someone	**g** (this style) is an excellent counter to (this style)
8 a reasonable sound	**h** a decent noise
9 the different approaches are complementary	**i** to epitomise
10 to be an extraordinary performer	**j** to take daring liberties
11 to become the symbol for something	**k** you're never sure whether you should be grinning or flinching
12 to do something without preparation	**l** the means (by which something is done)
13 to express uncertainty as to what reaction the music is supposed to provoke	**m** to have exceptional talent

Now check your answers to Part 1 of the test.

Part 2

For questions **14–19** choose which of the paragraphs **A–G** on page **11** fit into the numbered gaps in the following magazine article. There is one extra paragraph which does not fit in any of the gaps. In the exam, you will mark your answers on a separate answer sheet.

The fight to save New Zealand's giant parrot

For the past 28 years Don Merton has battled to save the kakapo, New Zealand's extraordinary green parrot. In 1995, when numbers fell to 50, it looked like the end for this bird. But this year they staged a comeback. The last survivors of this unique species have produced 26 chicks – more than in the whole of the past two decades. Instead of having no future at all, the kakapo suddenly has prospects.

14	

Males gather at an arena to compete for females. After mating, the females leave and raise their young alone. 'The kakapo is important because it has combinations of features found in no other bird,' says Merton, the longest serving member of the National Kakapo team. Unfortunately, its peculiarities have also made it vulnerable. A thousand years ago, there were millions of kakapo. Their only enemies were predatory birds and the kakapo's green plumage provided perfect camouflage against the vegetation.

15	

Then after years of searching, Merton and a team from the New Zealand Wildlife Service discovered a single bird in a valley in Fjordland in the far south. It was an old male. Search parties found seventeen more – all old males. Three years later, when many had written the species off, Merton's team uncovered signs of kakapo in the south of Stewart Island. It turned out to be a colony of 200 birds and some were breeding. 'We thought the kakapo was safe then,' says Merton. They were wrong. Cats were killing them at an alarming rate.

16	

Merton knew what he had to do. The birds had to breed before it was too late and nothing could jeopardise this. From now on, the team would manage almost every aspect of kakapo life. They laid traps for kiore and watched nests 24 hours a day. If anything other than a kakapo entered the nest, a watcher set off a tiny explosive charge that made a small bang and a flash, enough to startle any intruder. By 1999, all the kakapo had been successfully moved to two islands – Maud Island, and Codfish Island, both free of kiore.

17	

'The challenge was to work out a diet and persuade them to eat it,' says Merton. The team eventually found that kakapo were especially partial to nuts. The birds thrived on the extra food, but still wouldn't breed. They seemed to be waiting for some special cue. On Maud Island it wasn't clear what that cue was, but on Codfish island there was no doubt that the birds bred in response to some signal from the rimu tree that alerts them to a coming mast.

18	

Armed with this new knowledge, the team was ready to swing into action as soon as they spotted signs of masting on Codfish Island. Last year, it became obvious that the rimu were going to produce a large crop of seeds the next autumn. Merton moved all the adult females to Codfish Island. As the breeding season drew nearer, the kakapo rescue team arrived with electronic monitoring equipment, and spent the next months watching nests throughout the long, cold nights.

19	

The result was a large batch of chicks, a remarkable breakthrough, but there are still only 86 kakapo in the world. Do they really have good prospects? Merton is confident they do. 'As long as we keep using the same techniques, the population will steadily rise,' he says. 'The kakapo won't be extinct in our lifetime.'

A   What followed was an intensive rescue operation. During the following fifteen years all the kakapo were moved to islands free from cats, stoats or possums. 'We thought we'd put them out of reach of predators,' says Merton. Again they were mistaken. They hadn't realised how dangerous the kiore were. Not only did they compete with kakapo for food, they also ate eggs and chicks. It finally came to the point where only 50 kakapo remained.

B   In September the team began to fill up the food hoppers. 'We had to provide enough so the birds could breed but not so much that they'd get fat,' says Merton. 'We wanted to keep their weight down to encourage them to produce female chicks.' In December the males began their booming noises, and the females trekked to the courtship areas to choose a mate, unaware that electronic eyes were watching them.

C   The kakapo is nocturnal, looks like an owl, smells sweet and fruity and makes some very odd noises – from growls and metallic 'chings' to deep resonant booms. Kakapo can't fly, but they are excellent climbers. They live a very long time and are the world's biggest parrots. The kakapo also has a unique breeding system.

D   Persuading the birds to breed was the next harder step as this only occurs when certain plants produce large crops of fruit and seeds, an event known as *masting*. At other times, the birds manage on very little. It's enough to support their metabolism, but not enough to raise a family. In the past, the kakapo from Fjordland and Stewart Island bred in response to masting by a range of plants including rimu trees. The team hoped with extra food the birds might breed.

E   Merton estimates this could take at least 15 years, less if they can trick the birds into breeding more often. 'We're looking for whatever it is in rimu that triggers breeding. It's probably chemical – perhaps one of the terpenes the tree is packed with,' says Merton. 'Or it might be nutritional.' The team is currently testing an improved food pellet to see if that works.

F   There was nothing the team could do but patiently wait for nature to take its course. They continued with the food programme to ensure the females were in top condition and monitored the males to keep an eye on their numbers. The population remained stable but the team recognised the fact that it was only the rimu tree that would turn things around.

G   Once man arrived, bringing with him not only his dogs but kiore – Polynesian rats – that could sniff out nests, it was a different story. The rats went for eggs, chicks and even adults. The decline in numbers accelerated once European settlers arrived. They cleared large areas of kakapo habitat and brought more predators – cats, rats, stoats, and possums. By the late 1960s the kakapo was feared extinct.

Part 3

Read the following magazine article and then answer questions **20–25** on page **13**. Indicate the letter **A**, **B**, **C** or **D** against the number of each question. Give only one answer to each question **20–25**. In the exam, you will mark your answers on a separate answer sheet.

How will advertisers reach us?

It's Superbowl live in 2020. Record-setting numbers of viewers are tuned in to watch the game by using handheld devices that allow them to project the transmissions onto any flat surface. And in 2020, not unlike today, viewers are interested in the game, but they're actually more absorbed by the advertising. The commercials on screen are far better than they are now. Directors make sure they are moving, exciting, entertaining and technicians make sure the effects are breathtaking. It's not the commercials on screen that are the most interesting part, though: the really crucial advertising is hiding in plain sight on the field. Brand names blaze from each player's shirt. The game is held at U-tech Stadium in U-tech town – formerly known as Philadelphia. Corporations will pay big money for the right to digitize logos onto the T-shirts of the fans in the stands. Logos of sponsors won't be painted on stadium signs or on the field any more. Thanks to technology that is already emerging, logos of sponsors will be digitally embedded in the image on your screen. The logos you see will be chosen depending on your personal interests and profile, and they'll be different from the ones aimed at your next-door neighbours.

Advertising will change profoundly over the next couple of decades, although there's a good chance you won't notice the difference, since the most meaningful changes won't be visible to the casual observer. It's the changes that are happening underground that will count, and they're the ones we should be aware of. Advertising in the future will be stealthily and eerily targeted, disturbingly omnipresent and inescapable. Technology, naturally, will be the engine. User-tracking software that records your TV and Internet viewing habits in minute detail – and crosses it with your purchasing history – will allow the advertiser to know that you have children, that you eat meat, that your native tongue is Spanish and that your dishwasher is however many years old. That way you will be shown commercials for mini-vans, cheeseburgers and replacement dishwashers, all in Spanish, and not for sports cars, tofu and replacement refrigerators, in English. In fact, this technology already exists. Refined with data that track what kinds of online ads you tend to click on – funny, sentimental, fact-laden – every commercial will hit home.

Say what you will, that's a nifty trick. In the future, people won't be bothered with advertising messages irrelevant to them. They'll tend to like advertising better because it's so carefully tailored to their tastes and will begin to feel less like an intrusion. This works for the advertiser too because fewer dollars will be wasted. While it's a little dispiriting to think we can be so predictably manipulated, maybe that's a fair price to pay to avoid the pollution of messages you don't care about.

Nevertheless, it seems clear that the advertising outlets that exist today – TV and radio commercials, prints ads, billboards and taxi tops – will be inadequate for accommodating all the commercial messages that are agitating to get out. Advertising will therefore inevitably slip beyond the boundaries of the 30-second commercial and the full-page ad and migrate to the rest of the world, including entertainment, journalism and art. You can glimpse the future now. Product placement in movies is an obvious instance of where advertising has slipped outside its traditional container into entertainment. The music channels which are an entertainment medium designed expressly to sell records are another classic example. Every time an artist mentions a brand in their lyrics, advertising slips into art. If you have a tattoo of your team's name, you're already there. If you wear a T-shirt with a logo on it, you're also there but with less pain. Eventually, every surface that can display a message will be appropriated for advertising. A backlash is inevitable. Perhaps people will pay a premium to live in advertising-free zones.

People get very nervous when they see the line blurring between advertising and other forms of content; they think advertising is some kind of infection that pollutes the purity of art, ruins objectivity and distracts from the pleasure of entertainment. Yet this is missing the point. Surely consumers are smart and perfectly aware when they're being sold something; surely people who go to company websites are happy to find worthwhile information there and are capable of distinguishing between a commercial message and an editorial one? Art and journalism, until they became pretentious in the late 20th century, always relied on direct subsidy from private sources. Don't think for a minute that commercial interests didn't enter into it. The genuinely disturbing aspect of the ubiquity of advertising is that it has begun to supplant what was formally civic. Even the parks are gradually being renamed after corporations. The venerable Boston Garden was replaced not so long ago by the Fleet Centre: a city erased, its role played by a bank. A little town in the Pacific Northwest just renamed itself after a dotcom company in return for a generous donation. I won't mention the name here, since I figure advertising should be paid for. That's when advertising has gone too far: when it's become something we are, rather than something we see.

20   According to the writer, the greatest difference about TV audiences in 2020 is that they will

   A   require spectacular special effects to be persuaded to purchase anything.

   B   have the right to choose the kind of commercials they wish to receive.

   C   be exposed to different mediums of advertising than are common today.

   D   appreciate certain programmes to a lesser extent than current audiences.

21   The writer suggests that over the next couple of decades, viewers will probably

   A   be unaware of the effect that advertising has on them.

   B   fail to realise how advertisers are promoting products.

   C   resent the lack of privacy they have in their own homes.

   D   feel pressurised to consume more disposable products.

22   In paragraph 3, what does the writer feel about the consumer being 'predictably manipulated'?

   A   He condemns it as a form of deception.

   B   He believes people will be indignant at the removal of choice.

   C   He suggests that this is a cost-effective approach for the consumer.

   D   He states that consumers will appreciate the precision of this approach.

23   What does the writer state about the future of advertising outlets?

   A   Current outlets will no longer be used for promotional purposes.

   B   Advertisements will take on a globally similar style and approach.

   C   Advertising will overtake the importance of artistic value in music channels.

   D   The high level of outlets will result in some people turning against advertising.

24   In paragraph 5, the writer warns that

   A   advertising has turned what belonged to the public into commercial enterprise.

   B   some consumers are not able to discriminate between truth and subjectivity.

   C   journalists have always regarded their readers as kinds of consumers.

   D   people should be more wary about the invasion of advertising into art.

25   In writing this article, the writer's aim is to

   A   highlight which consumers will be most vulnerable.

   B   dispel unnecessary fear about the impact of advertising.

   C   warn people against becoming part of an advertising culture.

   D   discredit certain companies and expose their tactics.

Before you check your answers, go to page 14.

WHAT'S TESTED

Part 3 Multiple choice

This part tests detailed understanding of the text. The text is on a single page, followed by the questions on the next page. The order of the questions follows the same order as the corresponding information in the text. The final question may test your overall understanding of the text, e.g. you may need to interpret the writer's purpose for writing the text, or their attitude or opinion towards the subject matter.

TIPS

* Read the text first to get a general understanding. The information in the text is very detailed and often contains opinions, reasons or ideas which are very similar to one another. You need a reasonable understanding of the text before you look at the questions. If you look at the questions first, you may choose an answer because you think it 'looks right' or is 'the most likely answer'. This doesn't always work!
* After reading the text, highlight the key words in the question and the four possible answers. The questions and answers are written in a very precise way. Only one answer can be correct; the other answers contain ideas or vocabulary which make them wrong.

A DETAILED STUDY

The questions below will help you to make sure that you have chosen the correct options for questions **20–25** on page 13. Use a dictionary to help you where necessary.

20   Look at the first paragraph.

   A   Does it say that viewers in 2020 would be persuaded to buy products because of special effects?

   B   Who will choose the advertisements? Think about the grammatical structure and meaning of *'the logos you see <u>will be chosen</u> depending on your personal interests and profile, and they'll be different from the ones <u>aimed</u> at your next-door neighbours'*.

   C   What does the word *'medium'* mean? Can you find any *'mediums of advertising'* mentioned in the text?

   D   Does the text mention some different types of programmes? Does it say that people are less interested in the Superbowl than before?

21   Look at the second paragraph.

   A   What does *'there's a good chance you won't see the difference'* refer to? The effect of advertising or the way viewers are exposed to advertising?

   B   What do you understand by the terms *'targeted'*, *'omnipresent'* and *'inescapable'*? What connection do these words have with the previous sentence in the text?

   C   The text states that technology will allow advertisers to track or discover what kind of advertisements viewers prefer to watch. Does it mention how viewers will react to this?

   D   The text mentions some disposable products: dishwashers and refrigerators. Does the text state anywhere that viewers will feel forced to buy them?

22 Look at the third paragraph.

  A   What do you understand by the word *'condemn'*? What does *'nifty'* mean? Does each word have a positive or a negative connotation?

  B   What does *'indignant'* mean? Are there any words in the text that show the attitude of the viewers?

  C   What does *'cost-effective'* mean? Who will be saving money?

  D   What does a *'tailor'* do? What does *'to tailor something to somebody's taste'* mean? If something was tailored exactly to your taste, would you appreciate or dislike it?

23 Look at the fourth paragraph.

  A   Does the text say that advertisers will stop using current outlets, e.g. TV and radio commercials and taxi tops?

  B   *'The rest of the world'* is used idiomatically here. What does it actually refer to?

  C   Does the text say that advertising will become more important than musical creativity?

  D   What does the phrase *'a backlash is inevitable'* mean?

24 Look at the fifth paragraph.

  A   Can you find examples of how something public has been turned into something which advertises companies?

  B   Does the writer contradict the idea that *'consumers are not able to discriminate between truth and subjectivity'*?

  C   What does the text say about journalists and finance?

  D   Does the writer agree with people who think *'advertising is some kind of infection that pollutes … art'*?

25 This question covers the whole text.

  A   What does *'vulnerable'* mean? Does the writer especially refer to any group he thinks will be at risk?

  B   What does *'to dispel'* mean? Is the writer afraid of the impact of advertising in any way?

  C   Which sentence in paragraph five shows the writer's true feelings about the advertising culture?

  D   Does the writer accuse any company of dishonesty?

Now check your answers to Part 3 of the test.

Part 4

Answer questions **26–42** by referring to the reviews of science books on pages **17–18**. In the exam, you will mark your answers on a separate answer sheet.

For questions **26–42**, answer by choosing from the reviews (**A–D**). Some of the choices may be required more than once.

In which review are the following mentioned?

the warning that the author does not always simplify the subject matter for the reader	**26** ....
an admission of past ignorance on the reviewer's part	**27** ....
the subject matter being dealt with in unparalleled detail	**28** ....
the book having both a narrative and simple academic approach	**29** ....
the depressing revelations the book makes about certain areas of its subject matter	**30** ....
the book's combination of established fact and doubt about the subject	**31** ....
a sense of satisfaction at the reviewer's personal achievement	**32** ....
the reviewer's appreciation of the pace and breadth of the content of the book	**33** ....
a comparison between two very different causes of anxiety	**34** ....
praise for the author's clarity of thinking and enthusiasm for the subject	**35** ....
a mild criticism about some of the style and content of the book	**36** ....
the reviewer's implication that the subject matter deserves more consideration	**37** ....
the book's neutral approach to its subject matter	**38** ....
a warning that the conclusions the author draws may be frustrating	**39** ....
the fact that opinions on the subject were once based on guesswork	**40** ....
the revealing of the real reason behind a particular institution	**41** ....
the suggestion that this book would be a good starting point for readers	**42** ....

A   Small Wonder

B   Earthshaking Science

C   Zoo

D   Journey from the Center of the Earth

Review: This month's new science books

A   Maggie McDonald: *Small Wonder* by Barbara Kingsolver

White letters chalked on a blackboard in Sri Lanka are the first things I remember reading. The pleasure of deciphering that first word (C-A-T, of course) remains with me to this day. By age 11, I read a book a day, and at 14 I was being tested by an irritated teacher and school librarian who demanded proof that I was actually reading my library books.

But there are only so many authors even the most avid of readers can digest, and some evaded me. Barbara Kingsolver was one. I had her filed in a 'sentimental nature-lover: must avoid' category. Friends kept recommending her and a few years ago, I read my first Kingsolver and ditched my ill-founded prejudice. She's a biologist by training and a wonderful writer. Possessed of an analytical mind, she's capable of putting it all down with real passion: a rare find. If you haven't tried her yet, do! *Small Wonder* is Kingsolver the essayist, elegant and insightful, and a great place to set out from before you tackle her backlist. Here you'll find the San Pedro river on the edge of survival, the energy bill behind the production of a five-calorie strawberry, and Darwin in all his complexity summed up in a mere four clear paragraphs.

B   Sue Bowler: *Earthshaking Science* by Susan Elizabeth Hough

Anyone who has ever driven an elderly, ailing car knows the feeling: it's going to break down, but who knows when, where and what part of the system will fail? Predicting earthquakes is much the same. Tidy forecasts of what, when, where and how much it will cost are as rare for quakes as for car repairs, and about as reliable. Have earthquake seismologists failed, then? Susan Elizabeth Hough says not, and *Earthshaking Science* sets out her case. This book gives us an excellent outline of how, why and where earthquakes happen together with a clear-eyed look at the subject's inherent uncertainties. This is not a book that proposes simplistic answers. It presents a real picture of a lively research field in all its gritty glory, written with a sharp eye for the absurdities of scientific life.

The focus on uncertainty paradoxically has the effect of highlighting the areas in which seismologists are confident, which makes it easier to deal with the ambiguities. Hough includes a careful and informative discussion of the earthquake risk across the US. Although her findings do not make easy reading, given the vagaries of intraplate quakes, it is an excellent analysis of what to worry about and where. Overall, this is an intelligent look at a broad field of science that affects many lives. Anyone heading for an earthquake area should buy a copy.

C   Adrian Barnett: *Zoo* by Eric Baratay

What's the attraction of gazing at captive animals? It's a good question and others have often sketched out an answer. But in *Zoo*, Eric Baratay gives us an unprecedented, in-depth answer. He explains why zoos lodge in the human psyche, their place in society, and how they developed over time. Placing them in their social and cultural context, *Zoo* traces the development of animal collections from medieval bear fights through the menagerie of the French king Louis XIVth to modern captive breeding centres. Combining architectural analysis and political history, the author shows that the desire to display our domination over nature has long been a hidden feature of zoos.

The text has been translated from the French and in places retains a certain unnatural clunkiness. A trained biologist on the translation team might have weeded out appalling zoological errors such as describing the gannet as 'rare and much sought after.' But these are forgivable oversights in a wonderful book that is acute at tracing themes of modern animal husbandry. While the book neither apologises for nor criticises the modern zoo, the extensive appendices tell a grim story. They contain a wealth of statistics on the death rate in collections, and the success rate of captive breeding. An absolute must for those interested in zoo history – or anyone fascinated by homo sapiens's changing relationship with our fellow creatures.

D   Ben Longstaff: *Journey from the Center of the Sun* by Jack B. Zirker

Up, down, in or out. If that's about as much attention as you pay the Sun, you're ignoring something mind-boggling. Did you know that it loses a million tonnes every second in the form of light alone? That's just for starters. In *Journey from the Center of the Sun*, Jack Zirker goes on a breakneck trip from its hellish core out into the realm of the planets, explaining as much as possible about our star on the way. His story-meets-textbook approach mainly avoids confusing scientific equations, but enables him to delve into lots of physics from massive sound waves to exploding pieces of Sun the size of Asia.

Zirker's explanations are clear and sharp, although don't expect him to lead you by the hand. You do need to find the stomach for a few serious doses of physics and daunting diagrams, but that's just great news if you want plenty of juicy details as well as the grand view. His informal style keeps things moving along swiftly, while balancing the latest findings with background on the pioneers of the field. He shows how solar research has progressed from inspired speculation into a flourishing science.

PAPER 2 WRITING 2 hours

Part 1

You **must** answer this question.

1   You recently attended the opening night of a restaurant which belongs to a friend of yours, David Vaylet. Now, a week later, you have received a letter from David and a copy of a review of the restaurant's opening night which appeared in the local newspaper.

Read part of David's letter below and an extract from the review he has sent you on which you have made some notes. Then, **using the information appropriately**, write a **letter** to the editor of the newspaper explaining why you think the review has unfairly criticised the restaurant.

> The critic obviously didn't notice the party room downstairs and he doesn't seem to know the first thing about French food either! The chef, Marc, actually grew up in the Perigord region of France and has worked in many top restaurants there, so he knows what he's doing!
>
> I'd really appreciate it if you could write to the paper and give them your view.
>
> Many thanks
>
> David

yes – 7–8pm at bar / not with meal

It was their opening night and according to the promotional advertisement, drinks were free. You can imagine then, how annoyed we were to see them on the bill! The so-called authentic food was nothing like French food I have ever tasted, the service slow and the owner never once showed his face. Café Perigord also boasts that parties can be catered for. What? With only ten tables? Fine if you only have a few friends! 2/10
Mike Champion

mention customers' tips

not true! each table visited!

Now write your **letter** to the editor as outlined above (about 250 words). You should use your own words as far as possible.

Before you write your letter, go to page 20.

WHAT'S TESTED?

There are two parts in the Writing Paper: Part 1 (one compulsory question) and Part 2 (one question from a choice of four). You have two hours to do both questions. Each question carries equal marks. You need to write a total of 250 words for each part.

Part 1: Types of task

Part 1 requires candidates to respond to a text or texts, notes and/or visual prompts such as diagrams. This response may involve writing any of the following kinds of texts:

- **a formal letter:** you may need to complain, request information, give information, correct information or make suggestions.
- **an informal letter:** this involves writing to someone you know well. The content will depend on the input text, but you may have to explain something, make suggestions, give directions or instructions, give or ask for advice.
- **an article or a feature:** this would be written for a magazine or newspaper. The content would focus on a general issue such as 'Changes in Eating Habits' or 'Environmental Problems: Now and in the Future'.
- **a report:** this would be written for a specific person or specific group of people who already have some knowledge or interest in the subject you are writing about. It is generally more formal than an article.
- **a proposal:** this is similar to a report in that it would need a clear heading and clearly separate paragraphs for each point. Although it is written in a formal way like a report, it is also different because you will have to give your opinion and make recommendations. In your conclusion you will probably use language like *I feel we should… , I recommend that we… , I propose that the company… .* A report may not ask you to give your personal opinion.
- **a note:** a short, informal piece of writing in which the writer leaves a message for the reader, for example, making an arrangement, explaining what the writer has done, leaving instructions, etc.
- **a review:** this would usually appear in a newspaper or magazine when the writer gives his or her opinion on a book, play, film, TV programme, video or music album. For Paper 2, you might be asked to describe one or more of these, comment on the quality and say whether you would recommend it/them to others.
- **a leaflet:** this is usually a single-sided sheet of paper used to advertise or give information about a product, event or service. In order to attract attention and interest, you need a heading and an attractive layout. You can see an example of a leaflet on page 129.
- **a contribution to a brochure:** a brochure is a magazine containing photographs and information, usually about holidays or travel. You might be asked to write a **contribution**, in other words, **part** of a brochure.
- **an entry:** this could be something you write for a competition: an **article**, a **story** or a **description**, or **a** small section in a **reference** or **guidebook.**
- **an information sheet:** this would provide the reader with useful information about a company or other organisation, or an event that is taking place. The register of an information sheet is neutral and factual. Because all the information will be important, you need a clear title and each point should be separated by a number or a space.
- **a series of directions:** you might be asked to write a short set of directions from one place to another.
- **a set of instructions:** you might be asked to write some instructions for a friend or acquaintance. The instructions will be quite general. You will not be expected to know very technical words!
- **an account:** this is usually a factual **description** of a previous event. The register depends on the question. 'Write an account of your best ever holiday for a competition' will be far more informal than 'You recently witnessed a theft in the street. Write an account of what you saw.' An **account** should have a clear title for a serious subject. For a non-serious subject, the title could be more intriguing.
- **a guide:** this is often connected with tourism. It gives visitors to the area some details and information about what to see, where to stay, etc. A guide can also be any written text which gives people advice: for example, 'Write a guide for new employees about the rules and conduct of the company' or 'Your college magazine has asked you to write a guide for new students about the best ways to manage their money.'
- **a draft:** this is a first version which may later be edited. For example: 'Draft a leaflet to advertise a new club': this just means that you have to write a leaflet as you would normally in the exam. (In 'real life' your leaflet may be checked and altered by someone else.) In the exam, you may possibly be asked to draft (write) a **report**, a **leaflet** or a **letter.**

- **a memo:** the word *memo* is a short form of *memorandum*. Memos are sent to employees, colleagues or agents working for the same company or institution. At the top of the memo you need to write and fill in the details for these headings below.

To: **Subject:**

From: **Date:**

Do not put your signature on a memo, but you can write your initials at the bottom.

For Part 1, you may have to write **one or more** of the above, for example, a note and a set of instructions, or a short formal letter and a short informal letter, but the total will still be 250 words.

What are the examiners looking for in your writing?

- **Content:** make sure the content of your answer responds to the question exactly. Read the question carefully and be sure you understand and mention all the necessary points.
- **Effect on the target reader:** make sure your answer has the right effect on the intended reader. How do you want the reader to feel: pleased/encouraged/comforted, etc.?
- **Range of appropriate vocabulary and structures:** a wide range of vocabulary and grammatical structures can increase your score.
- **Register:** the language you use might need to be formal or informal/persuasive/exciting/humorous/academic, etc. It depends on why and to whom you are writing.
- **Format:** this means using suitable headings and sub-headings for reports, making sure that the layout in leaflets is eye-catching and using the correct phrases to begin and finish letters, etc.
- **Organisation and cohesion:** organisation requires you to order your points or ideas so that they appear in a logical sequence. Similar points should be in the same or following paragraph, different points in a different paragraph, etc. 'Cohesion' means you need to use connecting words and phrases to show the relationship between your ideas, sentences and paragraphs.
- **Accuracy:** avoid making basic errors or errors that prevent the reader from understanding.

For the **General Impresion Mark Scheme** to page 131.

A DETAILED STUDY

Look again at Part 1 of the test on page 19 and answer the questions below.

Content
What five points need to be referred to in the letter to the editor? Find them in David's letter and Mike's review.

Effect on target reader
What is the purpose of this letter? How can you make sure your letter has a positive effect on the target reader/the editor?

Read the following sample answer to Part 1 Question 1 on page 19. Use the verbs in (brackets) to complete the letter, changing the form where necessary.

Organisation and cohesion
What is the purpose of paragraph 1? What two points does paragraph 4 contain? What linking words or phrases are used?

Range of language
Find an example of the passive, the third conditional and a past modal. Underline the reporting verbs which are used instead of *say*.

---

                                                      19 Corrington Street
                                                      Highgate
                                                      London
                                                      N6 5QR

The Editor   9/5/02
The Islington Press

Dear Sir/Madam,

I **(1)** .... (write) **to take issue with*** Mike Champion's review of the
Café Perigord, **(2)** .... (publish) in last week's Islington Press. I
(3) .... (also dine) there on the opening night and in my opinion,
Mr Champion's observations were completely inaccurate.

First of all, Mr Champion complains that drinks were added onto his bill. If he **(4)**
.... (look)* at the promotional advertisement properly, he
(5) .... (see) that free drinks **(6)** .... (serve) at the bar between
seven and eight o'clock, and not as part of the meal.

Mr Champion also suggests that the food was inauthentic and that the chef was not
French. This is completely untrue. **In fact***, the chef is highly experienced and is
from the Perigord region itself.

He further states that customers were dissatisfied with the service. **This was not the
case at all***. Perhaps Mr Champion **should have*** **looked** around more carefully as I
saw many generous tips **(7)** .... (leave). Customers also **(8)** ....˜..............
(seem) delighted that the owner, Mr Vaylet, personally **(9)** .... (visit)
every table.

Finally, if Mr Champion **(10)** .... (ask), he **(11)** .... (find out)
that **actually*** there is a large room downstairs for parties and private functions.

I **hope you will print*** this letter and I recommend that readers try the wonderful
Café Perigord as soon as possible.

Yours faithfully,

K. Wittwer

Karen Wittwer

* = to disagree with/to argue about

*3rd conditional often used in this type of letter

*shows the reality

*shows the reality
*should have + past participle – used to criticise past action / non-action

*shows the reality

*ask for a correction/an apology, etc.

Part 2

Choose **one** of the following writing tasks. Your answer should follow exactly the instructions given. Write approximately 250 words.

2   You have seen the following competition advertised by a British tour operator and decide to enter it.

Win flights to any international destination!

Send us a description of a traditional festival or event in your country.

Write about:

- its historical origins
- how people celebrate it today
- why it might be interesting for foreign visitors.

Write your **competition entry**.

3   You are going away on holiday and an Australian friend and his family are coming to stay in your house during your absence. Write to your friend describing two or three local places they could visit, and explain the best means of getting there.

Write your **letter**.

4   Your college magazine has asked you to write a report called 'Changing Ambitions'. Write about the way in which young people's ambitions have changed during the last twenty years and how you think they may continue to change in the future.

Write your **report**.

5   You work for an international company that often sends its employees to work in overseas branches. You have been asked to write an article for the in-house magazine on business customs in your country.

Write your **article**.

PAPER 3 ENGLISH IN USE   1 hour 30 minutes

Part 1

For questions **1–15**, read the text below and then decide which word on page **25** best fits each space. The exercise begins with an example **(0)**. In the exam you will put the letter for each question on a separate answer sheet.

Example: | **0** | *A* |

Gerard Mercator: The Man Who Mapped the Planet

When Gerard Mercator was born in 1512, the geography of the globe still **(0)** ..*remained*.. a

mystery. It was unclear whether America was part of Asia, if there was a vast **(1)** .... of sea at

the top of the world or if Australia was **(2)** .... to Antarctica.

Mercator's childhood was spent chiefly in Rupelmonde, a Flemish trading town on the river, and it

was here that his geographical imagination was **(3)** .... by the ships which passed to and from

the rest of the world. Alongside imagination, he developed two very different skills. The first was the

ability to gather, **(4)** .... and co-ordinate the geographical information **(5)** .... by explorers

and sailors who frequented the margins of the known. He also had to be able to imagine himself

(6) .... from the heavens, to achieve the visionary **(7)** .... of gods in the skies, **(8)** ....

down on the world. The main reason why Mercator's name is **(9)** .... to us is because of the

Mercator Projection: the solution he **(10)** .... to represent the spheroidal surface of the globe on

a two-dimensional plane. It is less well known that Mercator was the first man to conceive of

mapping the **(11)** .... surface of the planet or that he **(12)** .... the idea of multiple maps

being presented in bound books, to which he gave the name 'Atlas'.

It is difficult for us now to be surprised by maps, so many are there, and of such detail and

coverage, but we should **(13)** .... in mind that Mercator lived at a time when such knowledge

was far from **(14)** .... He was the man who **(15)** .... our worldview for ever.

0	**A**	remained	**B**	continued	**C**	maintained	**D**	endured
1	**A**	territory	**B**	distance	**C**	range	**D**	expanse
2	**A**	connected	**B**	coupled	**C**	united	**D**	integrated
3	**A**	raised	**B**	reared	**C**	supplied	**D**	nourished
4	**A**	congregate	**B**	amass	**C**	assimilate	**D**	construct
5	**A**	granted	**B**	conferred	**C**	contributed	**D**	provided
6	**A**	suspended	**B**	located	**C**	situated	**D**	attached
7	**A**	inspection	**B**	observation	**C**	perspective	**D**	assessment
8	**A**	glimpsing	**B**	scrutinizing	**C**	watching	**D**	gazing
9	**A**	familiar	**B**	famous	**C**	memorable	**D**	recognizable
10	**A**	invented	**B**	contrived	**C**	devised	**D**	schemed
11	**A**	sheer	**B**	full	**C**	entire	**D**	utter
12	**A**	pioneered	**B**	initiated	**C**	lead	**D**	prepared
13	**A**	carry	**B**	hold	**C**	take	**D**	bear
14	**A**	typical	**B**	common	**C**	routine	**D**	normal
15	**A**	converted	**B**	substituted	**C**	distorted	**D**	altered

13/5

Part 2

For questions **16–30**, read the text below and think of the word which best fits each space. **Use only one word in each space.** The exercise begins with an example **(0)**. In the exam you will mark your answers on a separate answer sheet.

Example: | **0** | *just* |

On the other hand?

We left-handed people lack collective pride. We **(0)** ..*just*... try to get by, in our clumsy way. We

make **(16)** .... demands and we avoid a fuss. I used to say whenever someone watched me

sign my name and remarked that he or she was also left-handed: 'You and me and Leonardo da

Vinci!' That was a weak joke, **(17)** .... it contained my often unconscious desire to belong to

Left Pride, a social movement that **(18)** .... far doesn't exist but I hope may one day come.

There are many false stories about the left-handed **(19)** .... circulation: for example, a few

decades ago someone wrote that Picasso was left-handed, and others kept repeating it, but the

proof is all **(20)** .... the contrary. The great genius Einstein **(21)** .... often still claimed as

one of ours, also **(22)** .... proof. And sadly there is also no truth **(23)** .... the myth that the

left-handed tend to be smarter and more creative.

(24) .... the amount of research that has been carried out, researchers in the field still find it

hard to decide precisely what we mean **(25)** .... left-handed. Apparently a third of those

(26) .... write with their left hand throw a ball with their right. **(27)** .... , those using their

right hand for writing rarely throw with their left. A difficult skill that becomes crucial at a most

impressionable age, writing defines **(28)** .... you will call yourself. I have never used scissors,

baseball bat, hockey stick or computer mouse with anything but my right; **(29)** .... so, I think I'm

left-handed as **(30)** .... everyone else.

Before you check your answers, go to page 27.

WHAT'S TESTED

Part 2 of the English in Use Paper is primarily a test of structural control, with many questions involving the completion of grammatical structures. Missing words can include articles, conjunctions, prepositions. Some questions may involve completing collocations and fixed phrases.

TIPS

- Always read through the text for general understanding before you begin to fill the gaps.
- Before you decide what the word should be, read the whole sentence including the sentences before and after it.

A DETAILED STUDY

1   Before you check your answers to Part 2 of Test 1, choose from the following:

16	**a**	some	**b**	few	**c**	little	**d**	any
17	**a**	yet	**b**	while	**c**	still	**d**	even
18	**a**	so	**b**	as	**c**	this	**d**	by
19	**a**	on	**b**	by	**c**	in	**d**	under
20	**a**	for	**b**	at	**c**	to	**d**	on
21	**a**	is	**b**	has	**c**	was	**d**	had
22	**a**	despite	**b**	without	**c**	lacking	**d**	beyond
23	**a**	with	**b**	from	**c**	in	**d**	for
24	**a**	Although	**b**	However	**c**	Nevertheless	**d**	Despite
25	**a**	as	**b**	for	**c**	by	**d**	with
26	**a**	can	**b**	people	**c**	types	**d**	who
27	**a**	However	**b**	Whereas	**c**	Despite	**d**	Unlike
28	**a**	what	**b**	how	**c**	this	**d**	which
29	**a**	more	**b**	yet	**c**	even	**d**	and
30	**a**	is	**b**	does	**c**	was	**d**	has

2   Now read the following information on conjunctions.

However

There are three ways to use *however*:
1 Jane doesn't have much money. **However**, she bought an expensive car last week.
   - We can use *However* for <u>one subject</u>: *Jane + she.*
2 Jane doesn't have much money. **However**, her sister, Mary, is quite rich.
   - We can use *However* for <u>two subjects</u>: *Jane + Mary.*
   - *However* starts the second sentence.
   - Notice the position of the comma.
3 Jane doesn't have much money, **however**, she bought an expensive car last week.
   - *however* can be placed between two clauses.
   - Notice the position of the two commas.

Nevertheless

Jane doesn't have much money. **Nevertheless**, she bought an expensive car last week.
- We can use *Nevertheless* for <u>one subject</u>: *Jane + she*
- *Nevertheless* starts the second sentence.
- Notice the position of the comma.

Despite/In spite of
There are four ways to use *despite* or *in spite of*:
1 Jane doesn't have much money. **Despite** this, she bought an expensive car last week. (*Despite + this*)
2 **Despite** the fact that Jane doesn't have much money, she bought an expensive car last week. (*Despite the fact that...*)
3 **Despite** her lack of money, Jane bought an expensive car last week. (*Despite + noun*)
4 **Despite** not having much money, Jane bought an expensive car last week. (*Despite + -ing*)
In spite of can be used in the same way as *despite* in all four sentences.

Although/Even though/Though
1 **Although/Even though** Jane doesn't have much money, she bought an expensive car last week.
   • *Although/Even though* start the first clause.
   • Notice the position of the comma.
2 Jane doesn't have much money. She bought an expensive car last week, **though.**
   • *though* is informal and used in spoken English and in informal letters.

Whereas
There are two ways to use *whereas*:
1 **Whereas** Jane doesn't have much money, her sister is quite rich.
2 Jane doesn't have much money **whereas** her sister is quite rich.
   • *Whereas* is used to contrast two subjects: *Jane + her sister*
   • Notice the position of the comma in the first sentence.

3   Use the correct conjunctions to fill the gaps in the following sentences. There may be more than one possible answer.

1 .... rising unemployment, the government still feel confident of winning the next election.

2 .... the position requires experience, we would consider hiring a graduate with excellent qualifications.

3 We were told that the price was all-inclusive. .... , we then found out we had to pay for our meals.

4 .... some journalists are keen to expose the truth, others seem keener on making up lies.

5 A healthy diet can prolong life .... a diet of junk food can be harmful to your health.

6 People say 'travel broadens the mind', ... , it might depend on how open-minded you already are.

7 .... working longer hours, some workers are actually taking fewer holidays.

8 Learning Italian was a real challenge for me. .... , the lessons were interesting and useful.

9 .... the fact that I enjoy working for my present company, I would welcome the chance to work abroad.

Now check your answers to Part 2 of the test.

Part 3

In **most** lines of the following text, there is one unnecessary word. It is either grammatically incorrect or does not fit in with the sense of the text. For each numbered line **31–46**, find this word. Some lines are correct. Indicate these with a tick (✓). The exercise begins with two examples **(0)** and **(00)**. In the exam you will write your answers on a separate answer sheet.

Examples:

0	✓
00	these

PACKING

0	How you pack can have as big an impact on your holiday as your
00	destination. There are two kinds of these packers: in terms of how
31	much they carry stuff, some believe less is more and others that more is
32	best. Some go even more further and say that you need only two
33	things for a trip which are your toothbrush and a credit card. Add a
34	passport if you are heading to overseas, but anything needed along the
35	way can be bought. In the 'more' category are there people who can't
36	leave home without a trunk filled with items to meet every contingency,
37	from some floods to sandstorms to afternoon tea with the local mayor. But
38	I would suggest you that anyone can happily get by with one suitcase, and
39	even if you do, you'll find you feel freer, pay fewer tips, have fewer back
40	pains and move with greater security because you only have one bag to
41	keep track of. If you remember the following tips for travelling light, so
42	you can manage a one-suitcase trip whatever is your destination or
43	how long you plan on staying there. First if you could lay out everything
44	you intend to take, this will give you a good picture of what you are trying to
45	carry and what you might have forgotten. Should you doubt you might not
46	need it, leave it behind. If you think you can't survive without it, pack it.

Part 4

For questions **47–61**, read the two texts on pages **30** and **31**. Use the words in the boxes to the right of the two texts to form **one** word which fits in the same numbered space in the text. The exercise begins with an example **(0)**. In the exam you will write your answers on a separate answer sheet.

Example: | **0** | *improvement* |

ARTICLE

IS THIS THE END FOR RECORD-BREAKING?

According to researchers, we have reached the limits for some sports. No matter how hard we train or whatever the **(0)** ....*improvements*.... in the design of our running shoes, they say we're just not going to get any better. A mathematical **(47)** ...*analysis*... was carried out to show that most of our track and field records are in fact being broken by chance. The researchers looked at the best annual performances in 22 events in German athletics **(48)** ...*championship*... over the last 20 years. Only four events showed any kind of **(49)** ...*systematic*... increase over that time and the record-breaking times fitted the **(50)** ...*statistically*... distribution you would expect if the overall level of performance had stayed the same. The researchers concluded that the **(51)** ...*existence*... of record breakers is not **(52)** ...*miraculous*... . Record breakers are just **(53)** ...*exceptional*... rare.

0	**IMPROVE**
47	ANALYSE
48	CHAMPION
49	SYSTEM
50	STATISTIC
51	EXIST
52	MIRACLE
53	EXCEPT

ADVERTISEMENT

AROUND NEW ZEALAND

Auckland's Sky Tower has opened a new **(54)** .... called
Vertigo which will take you up to some 300 metres above sea-
level. If bungee-jumping off the tower isn't enough, you can now
take an **(55)** .... two-hour guided tour up inside the mast to the
highest public viewing platform in the southern hemisphere.
Climbers wear a special helmet and body harness that's attached
to a safety-approved cable system which runs up the ladder. You
start with a practice climb and **(56)** .... video and then it's up in
the lift to Sky Deck on level 60 where you begin the 44-metre
(57) ....

Vertigo's spokesperson Sonya Haggie says it is an **(58)** ....
experience 'combining breathtaking views with the most
(59) .... sense of exhilaration and **(60)** ....'.

Vertigo is open daily from 9am–9pm and anyone who is
(61) .... fit can do it!

54	ATTRACT
55	ADD
56	EDUCATE
57	ASCEND
58	MISS
59	BELIEVE
60	ACHIEVE
61	REASON

Before you check your answers, go to page 32.

WHAT'S TESTED

Part 4 of the English in Use Paper is primarily a test of your ability to form words from different parts of speech given. Questions may involve:
• forming nouns from verbs, and adjectives from nouns.
• using prefixes to make words negative, or suffixes.

TIPS

• For each question, decide which part of speech you have to form for each gap – a noun, an adjective, an adverb, a verb?
• Next, decide what the meaning of the gap is likely to be and think how the given word can be changed to be the required part of speech.

A DETAILED STUDY

1 Look again at the first text on page 30. Think about the parts of speech that are needed, and the meaning of each gap.
2 Decide which of the words listed below could fill the gap for that question. Some of the words listed do not exist at all. Identify the words that **do** exist and try to match them to the meanings **a–d** given.
3 You may wish to change some of the answers you gave in the test after you have done this exercise.
4 Look at the second text. Think about the parts of speech that are needed, and the meaning of each gap.

Question 0
improvable
improvements
improver
improvisation

a a person who improves things
b the performance of a task or act without preparation
c things which improve
d having the possibility to be improved

Question 47
analyticant
analysis
analytical
analyst

a a person who analyses
b the subject which is analysed
c capable of analysing
d the careful study of a subject

Question 48
championhood
championer
championships
championality

a the state of being a winner
b the trainer of winners
c the quality needed to be a winner
d the contests held to find the winner

Question 49
systematically
systematic
systemise
systemate

a change to a new system
b in order and carefully planned
c arrange in a system
d in an ordered way

Question 50

statisary   a relating to a numerical approach to analysing data
statistical   b mathematically
staticism   c over-reliance on data
statistically   d a person who presents statistics

Question 51

existable   a to be living/real
existence   b the creation of life
existent   c the state of existing
existation   d having the potential to live

Question 52

miraculous   a like a miracle
miraculise   b happening in a very surprising way
miraculously   c to perform a miracle
miraculer   d a person who performs miracles

Question 53

exception   a making you feeling angry or offended
exceptionable   b not being included in a group
exceptionally   c unusually or outstandingly
exceptive   d something or someone not included in a rule, pattern or group

Now check your answers to Part 4 of the test.

Part 5

For questions **62–74**, read the following information sheet. Use the information in this text to complete the numbered gaps in the informal letter which follows. The words you need **do not occur** in the information sheet. **Use no more than two words for each gap.** The exercise begins with an example (0). In the exam you will write your answers on a separate answer sheet.

Example:	0	*worry*

INFORMATION SHEET

> # Driving Advice
>
> Many drivers are anxious about hiring or buying a car in order to travel across the country as they are unfamiliar with driving in remote areas and are unsure about costs. We recommend you bear the following points in mind.
>
> - Many backpackers prefer to buy a cheap car to explore the country and then sell it again before leaving for other destinations. This has its advantages such as greater freedom of route and if you buy a car at a reasonable rate, it can be cost-effective if you are planning to stay for a length of time.
>
> - We suggest you share the driving, when possible, amongst all the travellers in the car to avoid exhaustion.
>
> - There are many places where a cheap car can be found, ranging from private sales through the local newspaper to car auctions. However, you should beware of buying a car in a small town and then trying to sell it in a big city where prices and demand are considerably lower.
>
> - As the roads can be rather treacherous due to broken surfaces, there is a speed limit on the open road of 100 kilometres per hour, with a lower speed of 50km for the city and built-up areas.

LETTER

Hi Alex!

Glad to hear you're coming over and don't (0) ...worry... that you're not (62) .... driving long distances!

If I were you, I'd buy a car and have a (63) .... around the country that way before you (64) .... for Asia. One (65) .... for doing this is that it'll (66) .... you quite a bit of money in the (67) .... as
it works out as more of a (68) .... than buying loads of bus tickets. Having your own car also means you can (69) ....yourself where you want to go. If there's a group of you coming over, you could always take
(70) .... so no-one gets too tired driving and doesn't see any scenery.

There are (71) .... of places where you can pick up a car but it would be best to re-sell it out in the countryside where you can get a (72) .... price and where decent cars are in short (73) ....

Finally, don't forget that the roads outside the city are a bit (74) .... so keep it under 100kmph to be on the safe side!

See you soon!

Mike

Part 6

For questions **75–80**, read the following text and then choose from the list **A–J** given below the best phrase to fill each of the spaces. Each correct phrase may only be used once. **Some of the suggested answers do not fit at all.** The exercise begins with an example **(0)**. In the exam you will write your answers on a separate answer sheet.

Example: | 0 | *J* |

THE IMPORTANCE OF SLEEP

What happens during the 'dark third' of our lives? This is one way to describe the time with which we are so familiar **(0)** .....*J*..... . The point about sleep is that it is not waking time wasted **(75)** ....*E* . Most of us actually need the traditional eight hours **(76)** ....*B* . These include slower driving reactions, declining memory and proneness to conditions ranging from digestive problems to the inability to pay attention. Dreaming takes up about two hours a night **(77)** ....*I* . About two-thirds of rapid-eye movement dreams, that is, proper dreams as opposed to the brief, confusing mental videos we often get during the onset of sleep, **(78)** .... , tend to be unpleasant. Some people have 'lucid' dreams, which are the ones in which you know you are dreaming. These tend to be more pleasant **(79)** .... we might be able to direct them. As for the function of dreams, they often relate to waking experiences but not in the sense of symbolising anything else. As for the idea that some people may predict the future through dreams, this cannot be taken seriously **(80)** .... , it is unsurprising that some should feature things that happen the next day.

A   and there is at least a degree of evidence
B   because our mental state starts to deteriorate more rapidly
C   and those who claim not to are merely forgetful
D   which comprises two stages of light sleep and two of deep
E   but a positive activity essential to our physical, physic and emotional well-being
F   because given the millions of dreams dreamt nightly in this country alone
G   and we often surface between them but rarely remember
H   and the consequences of an accumulated deficit are far-reaching
I   which are known in the field as 'hypnagogic' dreams

J   but about which we know only a very little

PAPER 4 LISTENING approximately 45 minutes

Part 1

You will hear a courier on a package holiday talking about an event in Finland. For questions **1–8**, fill in the missing information.

You will hear the recording **twice**.

Finland: The Johannus festival

The Johannus festival dates back to pagan times.

Nowadays the festivities are associated with the Christian [**1**] of St John.

People often go back to their [**2**] in the countryside for midsummer.

During the festivities, towns and cities become almost [**3**]

To get from Helsinki to Hirvensalmi requires a [**4**] coach journey.

The local dance takes place on a [**5**]

The fire is set alight at [**6**]

People usually visit [**7**] the next day.

Anyone planning to go fishing should wear [**8**]

Before you check your answers, go to page 37.

WHAT'S TESTED?

For Parts 1 and 2 of the Listening Paper, you will hear a monologue for about two minutes. This monologue may be an announcement, a radio broadcast, a lecture, a speech, a talk or a telephone message. You will have to either complete a series of sentences or complete a set of notes. You will hear Part 1 **twice** and Part 2 **once**. (Part 3 of the Listening Test may also require sentence completion based on a conversation, not a monologue or it may be a multiple-choice exercise. See notes on multiple choice on page 79.)

TIPS

Note-taking

- Use the pause before each piece is heard to predict the kind of information that is required.
- The focus in this type of task is listening for specific detail so you will usually only need to write a single word – a noun, or a noun group.
- Because the task is note-taking, you will not be penalised if you omit articles or prepositions, unless these are essential to convey meaning.

Sentence completion

- Use the pause before each piece is heard to predict the kind of information that is required.
- The focus in this type of task can be both listening for specific points of information and listening for abstract ideas, feelings and attitudes that the speakers express. Sometimes the question may require you to summarise feelings.
- The answers are usually single words or noun groups.
- You should check that your answer completes the sentence in a way that is grammatically correct.
- Spelling should be correct in Part 1 and Part 2.

A DETAILED STUDY

Finland: The Johannus Festival

Question 1: The missing word(s) must be a noun/noun group. The topic in this sentence is religion. What words do you know that are associated with religious festivals? Write them down.

Question 2: What places might people go back to in the summertime? Notice the use of *'their'*: the answer is unlikely to be a beach/lake/forest, etc. because these places do not belong to individual people.

Question 3: You are being asked to describe cities, so an adjective is required. From the previous sentence, we know that the Finns return to the countryside, so what effect will that have on the cities? What adjectives can you think of that might be possible?

Question 4: What kind of information is required to complete the sentence?

Question 5: What does the preposition *'on'* tell us about the location of the dance? What places does it exclude?

Question 6: What kind of information do you think will follow the preposition *'at'*?

Question 7: Who might people visit during the festival?

Question 8: This question obviously requires a description of clothing. What advice about clothing would you give someone who was planning to go fishing?

Now, check your answers to Part 1 of the test.

Part 2

You will hear the director of a theatre company announcing changes to a production. For questions **9–17**, complete the notes.

Listen very carefully as you will hear the recording ONCE only.

MACBETH

Points to deal with:

Rehearsals in [＿＿＿＿＿＿＿＿＿＿＿＿＿ **9**]

at 7pm on [＿＿＿＿＿＿＿＿＿＿＿ **10**]

Winton Arts Council money to cover costs for

[＿＿＿＿＿＿ and ＿＿＿＿ **11**]

Finance still required for [＿＿＿＿＿＿＿＿＿＿＿ **12**]

Need ideas for [＿＿＿＿＿＿＿＿＿＿ **13**] events.

Replacement needed for [＿＿＿＿＿＿＿＿＿＿＿＿ **14**] actor.

Auditions also for part of [＿＿＿＿＿＿＿＿＿＿ **15**]

Price per ticket: [＿＿＿＿＿＿＿＿＿ **16**]

Website: www. [＿＿＿＿＿＿＿＿ **17**]

4

Part 3

You will hear a man on a radio programme interviewing Amelia Bryant who was the first British woman to complete the Arctic Sea Kayak Race in Norway. For questions **18–24**, choose the correct answer **A**, **B**, **C** or **D**.

You will hear the recording **twice**.

18 Amelia says that she started kayaking

    A   through people connected to her job.

    B   on the recommendation of her boyfriend.

    <u>**C**</u>   after she had tried a few other activities.

    D   when she moved to a new location.

19 Why did Amelia decide to enter the world championship?

    A   She was confident in her physical ability.

    B   She felt frustrated by the limitations of river kayaking.

    C   She was encouraged to by her kayaking trainer.

    D   She hoped to gain an international reputation.

20 Amelia thinks that few women take part in the Norway race because they

    A   feel the male competitors discourage them.

    <u>**B**</u>   perceive the event as too risky.

    C   can take part in races in the UK.

    D   are unable to maintain the same pace as the men.

21 Amelia recommends that effective marathon training means

    A   avoiding damage to the back.

    B   limiting practice to the sea.

    C   developing a 'touring style'.

    <u>**D**</u>   working on all the basic muscle groups.

22 According to Amelia, the vital skill competitors need is

    A   a sense of the distance they have covered.

    B   knowledge of how to use the islands for shelter.

    C   the ability to memorise the most time-saving route.

    D   the ability to recognise the direction of the tide.

23 What does Amelia mention can be a problem during the race?

    A   The decline in her physical strength.

    B   The risk of her kayak ending up on the shore.

    <u>**C**</u>   The high waves that could turn the kayak over.

    D   The sense of panic that makes her lose control.

24 According to Amelia, if a kayak turns over during the race,

    A   the competitor is disqualified from winning the race.

    B   it is likely that another competitor will come to the rescue.

    C   rescue teams will only come to assist in extreme circumstances.

    D   it is not in the interests of another competitor to help.

Part 4

You will hear five short extracts in which various people are talking about embarrassing situations. While you listen, you must complete **both** tasks. You will hear the recording **twice**.

TASK ONE

For questions **25–29**, match the extracts as you hear them with the people, listed **A–H**.

A interpreter

B student   25

C party organiser   26

D chef   27

E manager   28

F office worker

G photographer   29

H old school friend

TASK TWO

For questions **30–34**, match the extracts as you hear them with each speaker's concern, listed **A–H**.

A being unaware of social etiquette

B losing customers   30

C making introductions   31

D meeting childhood rivals   32

E getting lost abroad   33

F being in unnatural social situations

G feeling inferior   34

H impressing possible employers

In the exam you will have 10 minutes at the end of the test to copy your answers onto a separate answer sheet.

Before you check your answers, go to page 41.

WHAT'S TESTED

Multiple-matching and multiple-choice

In Part 4 of the Listening Paper you will either have a multiple-matching or a multiple-choice task. You may be required to identify the speakers (e.g. a salesman/a school teacher), interpret their attitudes or opinions (e.g. anger/irritation), recognise the function of their monologue (e.g. complaining/apologising), and recognise the context (e.g. traffic problems/rudeness).

Multiple-matching

There are two tasks: you are required to choose five correct options in the correct order from a list of eight for both tasks. You will hear the text **twice**.

Multiple-choice

There are ten questions with two questions each for the five speakers. You are required to choose the correct option from a choice of three. You will hear the text **twice**.

TIPS

Multiple-matching

- Remember – you will hear the tape **twice**. You need to do **both tasks** while the tape is played.
- Read both Task 1 and Task 2 before the tape begins so you can anticipate the kind of vocabulary or functional language you are going to hear. For example, if one of the options is 'expressing disappointment', you might expect to hear 'What a pity' or 'It wasn't as good as I'd hoped for'.
- When you read Tasks 1 and 2, do not automatically assume that an option in Task 1 matches an option in Task 2. For example, 'an airline pilot' in Task 1 may not be talking about 'long flights' in Task 2.

A DETAILED STUDY

Listen to the recording again and fill in the gaps below. Answer the questions that follow each extract.

Speaker 1

1 … when I'm supposed to be showing .... around, I can never ....

2 It doesn't come across as .... for someone in my ....

3 I'd find myself saying things like '........... .... ?'

4 My .... actually suggested I rehearse the whole thing.

What does the information in 1–4 tell you about the speaker and what he finds embarrassing?

Speaker 2

5 … they come along and I'm setting up the ....

6 I just hide behind the ....

7 They feel .... and they're .... to have their kid's .... taken.

8 It's not exactly good for .... or personal ....

What does the information in 5–8 tell you about the speaker and what she finds embarrassing?

Speaker 3

9 *I don't have much ....-........... in general.*

10 *I'm the new girl in the ....*

11 *I'm fed up with them all .... me.*

12 *It makes me feel really .... at times.*

What does the information in 9–12 tell you about the speaker and what she finds embarrassing?

Speaker 4

13 *I didn't spend a lot of time there, a couple of .... I think.*

14 *Nobody had .... to anybody and the few conversations we had were utterly ....*

15 *What do you expect after a ....-odd years?*

16 *…everybody remembered hating the ....*

What does the information in 13–16 tell you about the speaker and what he finds embarrassing?

Speaker 5

17 *I'm going out there again in a month's time and .... to a couple of ....*

18 *At least my .... skills are alright.*

19 *There won't be many people prepared to .... unless I have some idea of the language.*

What does the information in 17–19 tell you about the speaker and what he finds embarrassing?

Now check your answers to Part 4 of the test.

PAPER 5 SPEAKING about 15 minutes

Part 1 (3 minutes)

General and social
Questions that may be addressed to either candidate:

- Where do you live?
- What do you enjoy about living here/there?
- How long have you been studying English?
- Have you been studying English in the same class?

Topics that candidates may be asked to discuss:

- your interests and free time
- your opinions or feelings about life in this country
- your reasons for studying English
- places of interest you have visited in this country
- your future plans
- what you have both enjoyed/disliked most about studying English.
- interesting things you have done recently.

For Further Practice and Guidance, see page 46.

Part 2 (4 minutes)

1 Ambition

For both candidates
Look at the photographs on page 146. They both show people with different ambitions.

Candidate A: Compare and contrast these photographs, saying what ambitions these people might have, what they might be doing to achieve their ambitions, and what problems they might be be facing. (*1 minute*)

Candidate B: Say who you think is more likely to achieve their ambition? (*20 seconds*)

2 Holiday destinations

For both candidates
Look at the pictures on page 147. They show holiday destinations in different countries.

Candidate B: Compare and contrast two of these pictures, saying what reasons people might have for going there and what effect spending time in these places might have on them. (*1 minute*)

Candidate A: Say which destination you would choose and why. (*20 seconds*)

For Further Practice and Guidance, see page 47.

Part 3 (4 minutes) The written word

For both candidates

Look below at some examples of different texts that people read. Talk to each other and discuss what you feel these texts can each tell us about the different aspects of life today. Decide which three texts you would choose to put in a museum for future generations to see.

a book of modern poetry   a newspaper   a film script   children's fiction

an up-to-date dictionary   an entertainment guide   a comic   a collection of song lyrics

a book of contemporary jokes

Part 4 (4 minutes) Further discussion

For both candidates

- Is there any other text you would choose to put in the museum?
- What book or magazine have you read recently that you would recommend to others?
- How do you think reading compares to watching films as a form of entertainment?
- What role do you think newspapers should play in today's society?
- How important is it to encourage young people to read?
- How do you think written language might change in the next thirty years?

WHAT'S TESTED

In the Speaking Paper, students speak together in pairs or sometimes in a group of three. There will be two examiners: the *Interlocutor*, the examiner who asks the questions and gives you your tasks, and the *Assessor* who will listen and take notes. The test takes approximately 15 minutes and is divided into four parts:

Part 1	about 3 minutes	The interlocutor asks both/all students some general questions, e.g. about their families, home town, job, free time, future plans, etc. The interlocutor suggests similar general questions the students can ask each other.
Part 2	about 4 minutes	The interlocutor gives each student a set of two or more photographs or pictures to discuss, comment on or compare. The other student(s) are then asked to make a brief comment or response.
Part 3	about 4 minutes	The interlocutor gives the students a problem-solving or opinion activity which they negotiate or discuss together.
Part 4	about 4 minutes	The interlocutor asks questions which allow the students to further discuss some of the issues or themes raised in Part 3.

TIPS

Your performance in the Speaking Paper is judged according to the following criteria:

Grammar and vocabulary: your ability to use grammatical structures and vocabulary accurately and appropriately. At CAE level, you are expected to have sufficient grammar and vocabulary to express yourself without pausing too many times.

Discourse management: your ability to express your ideas and opinions in a coherent, connected manner. To achieve this, you will need a range of grammatical structures and phrases or linking words which show the relationship between ideas or sentences.

Pronunciation: your ability to produce individual sounds correctly, to use stress and intonation in a way that aids communication, and to link words together so that your spoken English sounds natural. You are not expected to have a perfect native-speaker accent, but your own accent should not interfere with communication.

Interactive communication: your ability to interact with the interlocutor and the other student(s) by asking questions, responding in a suitable way, and taking turns in the conversation. If you are asked a question, you shouldn't hesitate too much and you should be able to respond and develop the conversation. You should ask your partner(s) questions and allow them time to respond, without interrupting them.

Global achievement scale: your general performance in the Paper as a whole.

Part 1: General and Social

1 In this part of the test, you are required to demonstrate your ability to use interactional and social language. In one way, this might be considered the easiest part of the test – since you will either be talking about yourself and your life or asking your partner(s) questions about their lives. It is not a good idea to prepare a fixed speech; your intonation will sound unnatural and your presentation may not be a suitable response to the exact questions the interlocutor has asked you. However, you could make sure you are confident in using some correct grammatical forms. Read the following examples and add two more sentences which are true for you.

Your usual lifestyle/situation: *Present Simple*
*I **live** in Ticino, which as you probably know, is in the Italian-speaking part of Switzerland, and I **work** in a bank, in the personal loans department. I **don't have** much free time, but at weekends, I **try** to get out and do some sport, either tennis or golf.*

Your temporary lifestyle/situation: *Present Continuous*
*At the moment, I'**m living** in Oxford with a host family while I'**m doing** my English course.*
*I work during the day so I'**m studying** English part-time in the evenings.*

Talking about a situation or activity which started in the past and is still true: *Present Perfect*
*I'**ve been** in Cambridge, on this English course, for about three months, but I'**ve been learning** English since I was 13.*

*I was born in Thailand but I'**ve lived** in Paris since I was a child. I'**ve got** used to the French way of life and I feel quite at home there.*

Talking about experiences where the exact time isn't important or mentioned: *Present Perfect*
*Since I've been in London, I'**ve visited** loads of museums and galleries. Most of them were quite interesting and the best thing is that they're free. But I'**ve** also **spent** a lot of money on eating out and going to clubs.*
*I **haven't travelled** outside of London yet – but I hope to.*

Talking about the past: *Past Continuous, Past Simple, Past Perfect, used to*
*Before I **came** here, I **was working** as an assistant in a nursery school. I **used** to help the young children with their reading, but after four years, I got a bit fed up with it. So, I **decided** to quit and to learn English to get a better job. My friend Carina **had** already **studied** English in Dublin and she **recommended** that I went to the same school. That's why I'm here.*

Talking about future plans: *going to/Present Continuous/will*
*After this course finishes, I'**m going to hire** a car and travel around Australia. (for plans/intentions)*
*I'**m starting** work as soon as the course finishes. (arrangements)*
*I'**m not sure** what I'll do … **I think I'll** probably **look** for a new job. (uncertainty/spontaneous decisions)*

Comparing
*I think English is **easier than** French because French grammar is **much more** complicated.*
*In Barcelona, the bars and the cafés are open **later than** in the UK so I think the nightlife is **better** there.*

2 The interlocutor is likely to ask questions similar to those on page 43. With a partner, take turns to be the interlocutor and the student. Ask each other the questions and use your sentences above to help you. Try to respond from memory and don't just read your answers.

Part 2: Talking about pictures

Students may be given a combination of the following tasks:

Identify and eliminate

Both students have a similar set of pictures but in a different order, or with just one picture that is different. One student describes his/her set of pictures in detail and the other student suggests which picture has not been described.

Compare and contrast

One student is given two or more pictures to compare and contrast. For this type of task, it is important to use comparing words and phrases to demonstrate your range of structure and vocabulary. It would not be adequate to say 'This picture shows an old man who looks happy. This picture shows an old man who looks worried'. It would be better to say 'The old man in this picture seems to be quite happy, **whereas** the man in this picture looks rather worried **in comparison**.'

Comment on, speculate and hypothesise

One student is given one or more pictures and is asked to suggest what the picture/s may be showing. Students need to use a range of structures which are used to speculate and hypothesize, e.g. 'In my opinion, these children **seem/appear** to be ...'; 'He looks really excited ... **as if** he's just won a lot of money'; 'She looks very disappointed ... I think she **might have** just **failed** her driving test!'

But beware – if you can clearly see something, e.g. a street full of traffic, do not say 'This might be a street full of traffic'. Instead, you could say 'This street is full of traffic so it **must be** in a capital city ... **perhaps** it's somewhere in Italy because the shops have that kind of architecture and style'.

Using the phrases below for comparing and contrasting, practise Part 2 'Ambition' and 'Holiday Destinations' on page 43. Take turns to be the interlocutor and the student.

---

whereas   while   but   although   however   both   in comparison to
unlike   more/much more/slightly more, etc   comparative: *-er + than*   in contrast to

---

TEST TWO

PAPER 1 READING 1 hour 15 minutes

Part 1

Answer questions **1–16** by referring to the magazine article on page **49**, in which four successful career women talk about emigrating to New Zealand. In the exam, you will mark your answers on a separate answer sheet.

For questions **1–16**, answer by choosing from the list (**A–D**) on the right below. Some of the choices may be required more than once

Which woman…		
mentions the way in which she was disadvantaged in the country she left?	**1** ....C......	
mentions a negative point about a job she has had?	**2**	
explains an advantage of choosing to pursue her career in New Zealand?	**3** .....C.....	
mentions an aspect of living in New Zealand that she can find frustrating?	**4**	
appreciates the approach to achieving goals in New Zealand?	**5** .....C......	**A** Nicky Meiring
expresses a sense of regret about leaving her country?	**6** ....A.....	
appreciates the honesty she feels exists in New Zealand?	**7** ....C......	**B** Jenny Orr
states the fact she is happy to make an impression?	**8**	
denies conforming to a certain stereotype?	**9**	**C** Sarah Hodgett
appreciates New Zealand for its sense of calm and normality?	**10** ....A......	
mentions a feature of New Zealand which requires special consideration in her work?	**11** ....A......	**D** Lucy Kramer
mentions her move to a different area in the same field?	**12** ....A......	
states that her original nationality puts her in an advantageous position?	**13** ....b......	
recognises the fact that conflicting opinions can lead to improvements?	**14** ....b......	
recommends that New Zealanders take more pride in their country?	**15** .....C......	
appreciates working in a friendly environment?	**16** .....C......	

The Brain Gain

With New Zealand becoming renowned as a great place to live, it was the first-choice destination for a new generation of talented migrants looking for a better life. Sharon Stephenson talks to four of them.

A Nicky Meiring, Architect

Listen to Nicky Meiring talk about South Africa and it soon becomes evident that she's mourning for a country she once called home. 'The current economic situation has made South Africa quite a hard place to live in,' she says, 'but I do miss it.' Nicky first arrived in Auckland in 1994 and got a job in an architectural practice in Auckland where she soon settled in. She says 'New Zealand often feels like utopia. I just love the tranquillity and the fact you can lead a safe and ordinary life.' She lives and works from a renovated factory where her mantelpiece is littered with awards for the design of her summer house on Great Barrier Island. 'Although the design of buildings is fairly universal, houses here are generally constructed of timber as opposed to brick and when it comes to the engineering of buildings, I have to take great heed of earthquakes which isn't an issue in South Africa,' she says. 'But the very fact that my training and points of reference are different means I have something to offer. And I'm so glad I have the opportunity to leave my stamp on my new country.'

B Jenny Orr, Art Director

American Jenny Orr's southern accent seems more at home in the movies than in New Zealand's capital, Wellington. 'I'm from Alabama, but no, we didn't run around barefoot and my father didn't play the banjo!' she jokes, in anticipation of my preconceptions. Having worked in corporate design for ten years in the USA, she was after a change and thought of relocating to New Zealand. It didn't take long for her to land a job with an Auckland design firm, where she was able to gain experience in an unfamiliar but challenging area of design – packaging – and before long, she was headhunted to a direct marketing agency which recently transferred her to Wellington. While she admits she could have the same salary and level of responsibility at home, 'it would probably have been harder to break into this kind of field. I'm not saying I couldn't have done it, but it may have taken longer in the US because of the sheer number of people paying their dues ahead of me.' Ask Jenny how she's contributing to this country's 'brain gain' and she laughs. 'I don't see myself as being more talented or intelligent but opposing views are what make strategies, concepts and designs better and I hope that's what I bring.'

C Sarah Hodgett, Creative Planner

What happens when all your dreams come true? Just ask Sarah Hodgett. Sarah says that she had always dreamed of a career in advertising. 'But I was from the wrong class and went to the wrong university. In the UK, if you're working class you grow up not expecting greatness in your life. You resign yourself to working at the local factory and knowing your place.' New Zealand, on the other hand, allowed her to break free of those shackles. 'It's a land of opportunity. I quickly learned that if you want to do something here, you just go for it, which is an attitude I admire beyond belief.' Within a month of arriving, she'd landed a job in customer servicing with an advertising agency. Then, when an opening in research came up, she jumped at the chance. 'My job is to conduct research with New Zealanders,' she explains. 'So I get to meet people from across the social spectrum which is incredibly rewarding.' Being a foreigner certainly works in her favour, says Sarah. 'Because a lot of my research is quite personal, respondents tend to see me as impartial and open-minded and are therefore more willing to share their lives with me.' She certainly sees New Zealand in a good light. 'I wish New Zealanders could see their country as I do. That's why it saddens me that they don't think they're good enough on the global stage.'

D Lucy Kramer, School Director

Born in Sydney, Australia, Lucy Kramer left for London when she was 23 to further her career as a stockbroker. 'London certainly lived up to my expectations and I had a very exciting, very hectic lifestyle,' Lucy explains. But after four years she felt burnt out and was becoming increasingly disillusioned with her job. 'People at work were far too competitive for my liking,' she says. It was at this time she made two life-changing decisions. 'I signed up for a teacher-training course and shortly after that met my partner, Graeme. He asked me to come back to New Zealand with him and I didn't hesitate.' It wasn't long before she found work in a large Auckland school and, since then, she has rapidly worked her way up to a management position. 'It's fair to say I'm not earning what I used to but my New Zealand colleagues are much more easy-going. A good atmosphere more than makes up for the drop in salary. Another thing that impresses me is that you can leave your stuff on a seat in a café and it'll still be there half an hour later. People are pretty trustworthy here. Sometimes it bothers me that we're so remote – you can feel a bit cut off from what's going on in the rest of the world, but on the whole, I'd say it's one of the best moves I ever made.'

Part 2

For questions **17–22**, choose which of the paragraphs **A–G** on page **51** fit into the numbered gaps in the following magazine article. There is one extra paragraph which does not fit in any of the gaps. In the exam, you will mark your answers on a separate answer sheet.

The story of the lamb-plant

According to a recent survey, 70 per cent of ten-year-olds living in Scotland's big cities think that cotton comes from sheep. It's easy enough to mistake the soft white stuff sold in fluffy balls in plastic bags at the local chemist's shop or supermarket with the curly stuff on a sheep's back, especially when the only sheep you've seen are in books or on the TV.

17	

Rumours had first begun to circulate way back in the Middle Ages. The *borametz*, also known as the 'lamb-plant', was said to exist in Tartary, a far-away land stretching across Eastern Europe and Asia. None of those who told the various tales had actually seen it, but they'd always met men who had.

18	

The man responsible for spreading the story in Britain was John Mandeville, a knight of England who left home in 1322, and for the next 34 years travelled about the world to many diverse countries. His account of what he saw was the medieval equivalent of a bestseller, and was translated in every European language. He wrote that he too had seen a type of fruit that when opened, proved to contain a small white creature that looked in every way to be a lamb.

19	

This was apparently proof enough for Mandeville and those who passed on the story. With each telling, the story gained new details and greater credibility. But in the 16th and 17th centuries, people learned more about the world and its inhabitants. As doubts crept in, more sceptical travellers set out in search of the mysterious lamb of Tartary.

20	

And so it went on. As soon as anyone voiced doubts, someone else popped up with new 'evidence' of the lamb's existence. In 1605, Frenchman Claude Duret devoted a whole chapter of a book on plants to the borametz. But then, 80 years later, the great traveller Engelbrecht Kaempfer went east looking for it. He found nothing but ordinary sheep. The number of believers was dwindling, and in London the renowned scientific academy, the Royal Society, decided it was time to 'kill off' the borametz for good.

21	

This, the Society reckoned, was what had started the ancient rumours. They proclaimed it to be a 'specimen' of a borametz, in fact. Hans Sloane, founder of the British Museum, described the specimen in a contemporary publication: it was made from the root of a tree fern, had four legs and a head and seemed to be shaped by nature to imitate a lamb. The four-footed fake also had 'wool' of a dark golden yellow. Despite this discrepancy in the colour of its fleece, the Royal Society considered the case closed.

22	

The answer was there all along in the writings of ancient travellers. While researching his book *Sea Monsters Unmasked*, the observant Henry Lee kept coming across detailed descriptions of plants that sounded far more like the prototype borametz. The Royal Society, Lee decided, had failed to spot the obvious connection and had settled for something so unlikely it had to be wrong. What so many had imagined to be a mythical animal in fact turned out to be ordinary cotton.

A　And so it was, more or less, for 180 years. Then a little known naturalist pointed out that their so-called 'original' lamb-plant was a false clue. There was, however, a plant that had almost certainly given rise to the notion of the borametz.

B　There's certainly doubt as to whether this was based on first-hand experience, but the contemporary guidebooks were certainly available. A few years earlier, a monk who came from a monastery near Padua, wrote that 'there grow fruits, which when they are ripe and open, display a little beast much like a young lamb'. He claimed he had heard this from reliable sources.

C　The best way, it felt, was by showing people how the idea had begun. It was then lucky enough to suddenly receive a curious object from China, a sort of toy animal made from a plant with a few extra bits stuck on to give it a proper number of limbs.

D　In some versions the 'vegetable lambs' were the fruits of a tree that grew from a round seed. When the fruits ripened, they burst open to reveal tiny lambs with soft white fleeces that the natives used to make their cloth. In others, the seed gave rise to a white lamb that grew on a stalk rooted in the ground, and lived by grazing on any plants it could reach.

E　There's less excuse for the generations of explorers, scholars and philosophers who were perhaps even more naïve. They were all happy to accept the story that the soft fibres from which eastern people wove fine white cloth came, in fact, from a creature that was half-plant, half-animal.

F　Distorted descriptions of the cotton plants seen in India preceded the actual plants by many years. In the meantime, traders bought samples of cotton 'wool' along trade routes that passed through Tartar lands. To those who had never seen raw cotton, this fine 'Tartar wool' looked like something that might come from the fleece of a lamb.

G　Still it eluded them, yet most came home convinced that it existed. One of these was a powerful baron who represented the Holy Roman Empire at the Russian court. The baron had dismissed the sheep-on-a-stalk as fable until he heard the creature described by a 'person in high authority' whose father had once been an envoy to the King of Tartary. The story was enough to convince the baron.

Before you check your answers, go to page 52.
Before you check your answers, go to page 52.

WHAT'S TESTED

Gapped-text task

Part 2 of the Reading Paper tests your ability to recognise the way a text is structured. You are required to read a gapped text on one page and then choose which extracts on the second page fit each gap. There is only one possible answer for each gap.

TIPS

• Read the gapped text first to understand the general idea of the content, meaning and structure.
• If the text is a narrative, look for tenses, words or phrases that indicate time (e.g. *shortly after this, from my previous experience, it was the first time I had...*) and linkers that show cause and effect (*and it was for that reason, in order not to repeat that mistake, it was largely due to that advice that...*).
• If the text presents an argument or discussion, you can look for cause and effect, phrases or linkers that show agreement or contrast (*Many people would go along with that / However, scientists discovered that this was not the case / Nevertheless, researchers continued to maintain...*).
• It is also useful to look for repeated names, dates and pronouns:
  *At last one of the **archaeologists** found what seemed to be **a clue**. It was **this** (clue) that gave **them** (the archaeologists) hope.*
• Don't just read the first and last line of each extract. Often the clues or connecting ideas are in the middle of the extract.

A DETAILED STUDY

The questions below will help you to make sure that you have chosen the correct options for questions **17–22**.

17   The text above 17 says that it is easy for children to confuse the product sold in supermarkets and chemists (manufactured cotton wool) with real wool from sheep. Which option A–G suggests that other people should have been able to recognise whether they were looking at real wool or not?

18   The text under 18 says he wrote that *'he too had seen a type of fruit that when opened, proved to contain ... a lamb'*. The *'too'* suggests that the option must contain a similar description. Which option seems similar? In the text above 18, notice the words *'various tales'*, and under 18, *'the story'*. In the option you use, which words refer to *'tales* and *stories'*?

19   In the text below 19, notice the words, *'This was ... proof enough for Mandeville'*. Which option gives an example of something that John Mandeville would believe he could trust?

20   The text above 20 finishes with *'more ... travellers set out in search of the...lamb'*. Which option starts with a reference to *'travellers'* (plural) and *'lamb'* (singular)? What word in the first line of that option means 'to avoid being found'? The text under 20 starts with *'And so it went on'*. What does *'it'* refer to in the option and in the following sentence?

21   In the text under 21, the text starts with *'This ... was what ... had started the ... rumours. It was a 'specimen''*. Which option contains a 'singular' reference?

22   In the text above 22, it finishes with *'the case* (this particular situation was) *closed'*. Which option begins with a reference to *'the case'*? The text under 22 also mentions *'Henry Lee'*. How has he been introduced in the option?

Now check your answers to Part 2 of the test.

Part 3

Read the following magazine article and then answer questions **23–28** on page **54**. Indicate the letter **A**, **B**, **C** or **D** against the number of each question **23–28**. Give only one answer to each question. In the exam, you will mark your answers on a separate answer sheet.

Virtuous Nature

Chimps show signs of embarrassment, whales and ravens fall in love.
But can animals really have a sense of right and wrong? Marc Bekoff thinks they do.

If you think that we are the only creatures on Earth with a moral sense, then you're in good company. Most experts in behaviour believe that morality is a uniquely human trait, without which our complex social life would never have emerged – yet I'm convinced that many animals can distinguish right from wrong. Decades spent watching wild and captive animals have persuaded me that species living in groups often have a sense of fair play built on moral codes of conduct that help cement their social relationships. The notion of Nature being naturally ruthlessly and selfishly competitive doesn't hold true for those of us who have observed and analysed animal relationships.

That's not all. I suspect that herein lies the origin of our own virtue. Biologists have had real problems trying to explain why people are frequently inexplicably nice to each other. It just doesn't make sense in evolutionary terms, unless there are ulterior motives behind our seemingly altruistic actions. Perhaps we expect a payback somewhere down the line, or maybe our good deeds are directed only towards kin, with whom we share a biological heritage. Nobody has really considered the possibility that being considerate to your neighbours might sometimes be the best way to survive. But I'm starting to find evidence that a well-developed sense of fair play helps non-human animals live longer, more successful lives. I'm particularly interested in social play amongst youngsters because it has its own special rules of engagement, allowing participants to reinterpret acts that might otherwise seem aggressive. My studies of infant dogs, wolves and coyotes reveal that they use a special signal to prevent misinterpretation of playful actions. They perform a 'bow'– which entails crouching on the forelimbs while keeping the rear upright – when initiating play, or in association with aggressive actions such as biting, to modify their meaning. And role reversal is common, so that during play a dominant animal will often allow a subordinate to have the upper hand. Such behaviours reduce inequalities in size, strength and dominance between playmates, fostering the co-operation and reciprocity that are essential for play to occur. Indeed, on the rare occasions when an animal says 'Let's play' and then beats up an unsuspecting animal, the culprit usually finds itself ostracised by its former playmates.

My belief is that a sense of fairness is common to many animals, because there could be no social play without it, and without social play individual animals and entire groups would be at a disadvantage. If I'm right, morality evolved because it is adaptive. It helps many animals, including humans, to survive and flourish in their particular social environment. This may sound like a radical idea, particularly if you view morality as uniquely human and a sort of mystical quality that sets us apart from other animals. But if you accept my argument that play and fairness are inextricably linked, you're halfway there. The challenge then is to show that individual animals benefit from these behaviours. It's hardly radical to suggest that play is essential food for the brain – it hones an individual's cognitive skills, including logical reasoning and behavioural adaptability. The more we learn about how play affects the brain, the more apparent it becomes that the activity is far from idle time-wasting.

Here I am not putting the case forward for a specific gene for fair or moral behaviour. As with any behavioural trait, the underlying genetics is bound to be complex, and environmental influences may be large. No matter. Provided there is variation in levels of morality among individuals, and provided virtue is rewarded by a greater number of offspring, then any genes associated with good behaviour are bound to accumulate in subsequent generations. And the observation that play is rarely unfair or uncooperative is surely an indication that natural selection acts to weed out those who don't play by the rules.

What does this tell us about human morality? First, we didn't invent virtue – its origins are much more ancient than our own. Secondly, we should stop seeing ourselves as morally superior to other animals. True, our big brains endow us with a highly sophisticated sense of what's right and wrong, but they also give us much greater scope for manipulating others – to deceive and try to benefit from immoral behaviour. In that sense, animal morality might be 'purer' than our own. We should accept our moral responsibility towards other animals, and that means developing and enforcing more restrictive regulations governing animal use. While animal minds may vary from one species to another, they are not so different from our own, and only when we accept this can we truly be moral in our relations with nature as a whole.

23   In paragraph 1, what does the writer state about morality?

   A   Humans are the only creatures that demonstrate true emotional behaviour.

   B   A well-developed moral code is not the main reason for civilisation.

   C   Humans and animals share the same selfish instincts for survival.

   D   There is a common misconception that animals are not moral.

24   In paragraph 2, the writer believes that people who

   A   are generous to one another are not always sure why.

   B   don't have good social skills achieve less in life.

   C   behave considerately have selfish reasons for doing so.

   D   treat acquaintances better than relatives are unusual.

25   What has the writer deduced about social play from his observation of animals?

   A   It provides an opportunity for physically weaker animals to develop their survival skills.

   B   It allows animals to prove who is dominant in the group without using real aggression.

   C   It requires animals to abide by the rules or they will be excluded from the rest of the group.

   D   It demonstrates that certain animals possess the same range of emotions as humans do.

26   What does the writer say may be difficult for his readers to accept?

   A   Individual animals benefit from social play.

   B   Humans with moral responsibility are able to succeed.

   C   Spirituality and morality are inseparable.

   D   Moral codes depend on specific circumstances.

27   What does the writer state about the evolution of morality?

   A   There may be a particular gene responsible for morality.

   B   Moral development depends on physical hardships.

   C   There is little point seeking the origin of moral behaviour.

   D   Animals that behave fairly are more likely to breed.

28   In the final paragraph, the writer concludes that people

   A   must treat animals on equal terms with humans.

   B   should be less arrogant in their view of themselves.

   C   are more advanced as they use immorality to their advantage.

   D   should discriminate between which animals display morality and those that don't.

Part 4

Answer questions **29–43**, by referring to the article on pages **56–57** about changing attitudes towards dance in Britain. In the exam, you will mark your answers on a separate answer sheet.

For questions **29–43**, answer by choosing from the different sections on dance (**A–H**). Some of the choices may be required more than once.

In which section of the article are the following mentioned?

evidence for the growing interest in traditional forms of dancing	**29** ....
people also appreciating traditional dance for its amusing aspects	**30** ....
dancing being a fundamental part of human behaviour	**31** ....
a reason why people may not appreciate traditional dance	**32** ....
the fact that modern forms of dance block communication between people	**33** ....
travel allowing people to become more exposed to foreign dance	**34** ....
dance allowing interaction between people who would otherwise be unlikely to meet	**35** ....
contempt for dance as a group activity	**36** ....
some people being frustrated with dance venues today due to their anti-social nature	**37** ....
dance being irresistible to everyone at some point	**38** ....
the health benefits that dance can bring	**39** ....
a psychological advantage of learning to dance	**40** ....
the British having never been acclaimed as good dancers	**41** ....
a particular individual being responsible for social dancing's decreasing popularity	**42** ....
dance being a spontaneous form as well as a rehearsed one	**43** ....

Before you check your answers, go to page 58.

Let's Dance

We do it when we feel good and we feel good when we do it.
Rupert Mellor and friends learn tango, salsa, swing and ballroom.

A

Who really doesn't like dancing? Can even the most bad-tempered dance-floor-avoider last an entire lifetime without a shameless display at a wedding, a triumphant jig after the birth of a child – or a particularly good goal – or refrain from a secret shuffle around the privacy of their living room? Dance can take many forms: whether it comes as an impulsive release of energy and emotion, or within a skilful display of practised artistry, alone or in company, to dance is as fundamental to humans as breathing. The great dancer Martha Graham wasn't overstating it when she said, 'Dance is the hidden language of the soul, of the body.' The first human art form, dancing is an instinctive celebration of physical existence, a language that can be spoken by anyone and understood by everyone. Beyond speech, learnt behaviour, or even conscious thought, we do it when we feel good, and we feel good when we do it.

B

It's a little sad, then, that as a nation, our reputation as dancers has historically earned us no points and no recognition. Always ever-so-slightly embarrassed by fun, Britain has failed to give dancing the status and support it deserves. But times, and dance-floors, are changing. More and more of us are returning home but with glowing memories of cultures in which dance is a vital part of life, and musical cross-pollination has accustomed our ears to exotic dance rhythms from all over the world.

C

Cinema too is having an effect. *Evita*, *The Tango Lesson* and *Strictly Ballroom* all celebrate traditional dance artistry, and expect the profile of the incredible Argentine style to skyrocket after several new releases. For many years, the pop music played in night clubs consigned ballroom, Latin and rock'n'roll to the laughably middle-class scrapheap. And while the faithful kept old-fashioned floorcraft alive in schools and competitions, within 20 years social dancing, that is dancing with a partner or partners, was broadly perceived in Britain as a slightly bizarre cultural quirk practised by people in shiny, spangly outfits.

D

Lyndon Wainwright, of the British Dance Council, lays the decline of social dancing squarely at the fast feet of the actor John Travolta, who as disco dancer 'Tony Manero' in *Saturday Night Fever* struck an iconic, swaggering solitary figure up on stage. But now dancing in all its different styles has made a revival. Behind its rebirth lies a confluence of factors: the global village, delight in the accessories – the glittery hair and the extravagant costumes, and boredom with the loud unfriendliness of modern dance clubs.

E

On an average week in London, the entertainment guide *Time Out* usually lists around 50 Latin dance nights, many of them offering tuition. Meanwhile, traditional dance schools too have started to report significant attendance rises. 'Just across traditional ballroom and Latin styles, we know that 240,000 amateur tests were taken last year,' Wainwright says. 'The schools tell me business is booming, with salsa and Argentine tango especially on the rise.' For those unconvinced, he points to the following: 'An evening's dancing is as good for you as a three-hour hike. It pumps blood up your legs, so it's good for your heart, and it helps posture and breathing, too. And you don't get that kind of fun on an exercise bike.'

F

Dance is also good therapy too, busting stress, promoting relaxation and, with the mastery of a new skill, brings self-confidence and a sense of achievement. 'There is nothing more notable about the Greek philosopher Socrates than that he found time, when he was an old man, to learn music and dancing, and thought it well spent,' the French philosopher Michel de Montaigne once mused. Professor Cary Cooper, of UMIST, says that dancing allows people to have physical contact in a safe, sanctioned environment, that it literally puts people in touch. All humans need tactile contact. The touch of another person affirms that we are real, that we are alive.

G

Whether you're in it purely for the social contact or the romance, there's no denying that social dancing offers unparalleled opportunities to encounter a range of partners, in a forum where ability and enthusiasm transcend age, gender and class. 'We live extremely insecure, isolated lives,' Cooper says. 'More and more of us leave our native communities, work long hours, sacrifice our relationships, neglect our social lives. Clubbing, with its deafening music, solo dancing and heavy competitiveness, provides less and less social contact, and becomes an avoidance activity. Now people are embracing the old forms again. Social dancing is a ritualistic reaching out. People want to reconnect with others.'

H

However, one step forward, another back; not all are happy with recent developments. One venue in Suffolk has banned line-dancing at its Country and Western nights. The DJ Vic Stamp, 77, fumed: 'I'm not against line-dancing but I resent them gate-crashing and taking up all the dance floor. There is nothing worse than dancing round the floor and bumping into people doing a line dance. It stops your rhythm.' Oh dear. Perhaps he should follow the advice offered by the Indian sage, Krishnamurti: 'You must understand the whole of life, not just one little part of it. That is why you must … sing, and dance … for all that is life.'

A DETAILED STUDY

Before you check your answers, do the following vocabulary exercise. All the words are taken from the text or questions.

Look at the words in *italics* in the sentences below and choose the correct meaning, a or b.

1   There is *evidence* that social dancing is becoming more popular.
   a   It's my opinion that more people like dancing.
   b   I have seen several new dance clubs open in my area.

2   I *appreciate* dance for the way it helps me relax.
   a   I understand how dance works.
   b   I recognise the good qualities of dance.

3   He told us a very *amusing* story.
   a   funny and enjoyable
   b   interesting and complicated

4   The use of gestures is a *fundamental* part of communication.
   a   We cannot communicate without gestures.
   b   Gestures are an additional part of communication.

5   When he went to university, he was *exposed to* different ideas.
   a   He was able to hear about and experience new ideas.
   b   He was alarmed by different ideas.

6   Although James is intelligent, he shows *contempt* for anyone he feels is uneducated.
   a   James shows sympathy to uneducated people.
   b   James has no respect for uneducated people.

7   I was *frustrated* by my lack of progress when I tried to learn Italian.
   a   surprised and disappointed
   b   annoyed and impatient

8   There are certain flowers that bees find *irresistible*.
   a   Bees avoid certain flowers.
   b   Bees cannot stay away from certain flowers.

9   What is the reason for the *decline* in the number of children who regularly read books?
   a   rise
   b   fall

10   Many people *refrain from* smoking while having a meal with non-smokers.
   a   They don't smoke although they want to.
   b   They limit the number of cigarettes they smoke.

11   Cats have an *instinctive* dislike of dogs.
   a   Cats have learned to dislike dogs.
   b   Cats have a natural dislike of dogs.

12 I eventually got *accustomed to* the foggy weather in San Francisco.

   a   The weather became familiar and normal.

   b   The weather finally became enjoyable.

13 He is *laughably* supposed to be a good mechanic.

   a   It's ridiculous that people say he's a good mechanic.

   b   It's amusing that he became a mechanic.

14 Sarah takes great *delight in* her grandchildren.

   a   Sarah makes all her grandchildren happy.

   b   Sarah gets pleasure from her grandchildren.

15 There has been a significant *boom* in house prices.

   a   House prices have risen dramatically.

   b   House prices have fallen dramatically.

16 I *resent* the fact that Julie got the promotion before I did.

   a   I am disappointed that Julie was promoted.

   b   I think it's unfair that Julie was promoted.

Now check your answers to Part 4 of the test.

PAPER 2 WRITING 2 hours

Part 1

You **must** answer this question.

1   You are the social secretary of your local outdoor sports club. Some weeks ago you made a booking at a hotel for your members and a guest speaker. However, you now need to make some changes to the booking.

Read the fax below from the guest speaker, Martin Svennson, and part of the confirmation of the original hotel booking, on which you have made some notes. Then, **using the information appropriately**, write:

a)   a **letter** to the manager of the Highbanks Hotel, mentioning any changes and requesting further information;

b)   a **brief reply** to Martin Svennson.

No. pages: 1
Re: conference on Saturday 8/Sunday 9 May   *suggest plan for Friday evening*

I can't get an early flight for Saturday a.m. so I'll be arriving Friday afternoon instead. Could you sort out a room at the same hotel for me and also arrange a pick-up from the airport? (I guess I'll be in the arrivals hall at about 4.30 p.m.)

Carlton Taxis booked – but need flight details

Many thanks,
Martin Svennson

THE HIGHBANKS HOTEL

<u>Accommodation</u>
<u>Saturday 8th May</u>
12 shared twin rooms
5 double rooms
1 single room ←— *also Friday night possible?*

<u>Conference Rooms</u>
Conference Room A has been reserved for you from Saturday 10am – Saturday 5.30pm. We are also able to provide a range of equipment to aid in presentations.

                                  for example?

<u>Catering</u>
Saturday: Dinner: Full menu available
Sunday: Breakfast: Continental

                going hiking – sandwiches
Lunch: Buffet ←— *possible instead?*

Now write your **letter** to the manager of the hotel (about 200 words), and your **reply** to Martin Svensson (about 50 words) as outlined above. You should use your own words as far as possible.

Part 2

Choose **one** of the following writing tasks. Your answer should follow exactly the instructions given. Write approximately 250 words.

2   Your college magazine is requesting reviews of English-language magazines or newspapers (these can also be on-line publications). Choose **either** a magazine **or** a newspaper summarising its content and describing its style, and say why you think others might benefit from reading it.

        Write your **review**.

3   You see the following competition in an English-language magazine and decide to enter it.

        Write your **competition entry**.

        Before you write your answer, go to page 62.

4   You have been asked to write an article for GLOBAL ISSUES, an international magazine which publishes features on current affairs stories around the world. The article must be about the influence of tourism on your country so far, and what future developments you believe will occur.

        Write your **article**.

5   The company you work for has asked you to write a section of a guide about company policy for new English-speaking employees. Your section should describe two or more of the following aspects: dress code, flexitime, holidays, training, claiming expenses, bonuses.

        Write your **guide**.

WHAT'S TESTED

The tasks for Part 2 of the Writing Paper are the same as those for Part 1. However, Question 5 is always a **work-oriented** question. You should only answer this question if you have experience of working for a company because you will need this experience to provide ideas for your answer.

A DETAILED STUDY

Question 3: An entry

Before you read the sample entry below, consider the following questions.

Content
What does Question 3 on page 61 specifically ask you to write about?

Effect on the target reader
What is the purpose of this entry? To advertise something/to entertain the reader/to explain something, etc?

Register
What register should the entry/article have? Serious, humorous, etc?

Format
What is important about the format of an entry or article?

A sample answer
Now read the sample entry below and answer the questions that follow.

You can't escape the net!

Over the last few years, the use of the Internet has increased dramatically in French schools, offices and homes and this trend continues to grow up. Who could have imagined, even in the last decade, that we would be able to contact with our friends, colleagues and clients around the world simply through the click of a mouse and a modem? There's no doubt, like any invention, that the Internet can be used for good or bad but it's here to stay and has revolutionised the way we communicate.

In the world of business, no corporation can be competitive unless it has the access to the Internet. It's become essential to advertise your product and service in this way and an increasing number of companies are using this opportunity for reach a greater number of potential consumers. Indeed, the bigger the web site, the more professional the company seems to be.

Similarly in education, the opportunities that the Internet can provide us are vast. More and more students are relying on the Internet for their researches; for instance, a physics undergraduate in Paris can download information from a university library in the States in minutes. From the latest research in scientific and linguistic fields to new theories in psychology and history; all this may be published on the world-wide web.

What will be the future for the Internet in France? It's been estimated that 60% of homes and 50% of businesses will have access to the Internet within five years. Children, students and professionals will be able to log on and explore the world as they have never done before!

Organisation and cohesion
What different points are made in each paragraph?
What 'linking' or cohesive structures have been used in this article? Underline them.

Range of vocabulary and structure
What adjectives and adverbs have been used to make the article more interesting?
What tenses have been used? Can you find any examples of the passive?

Accuracy
Are there any mistakes in the use of vocabulary or grammar? Correct any that you find.

PAPER 3 ENGLISH IN USE 1 hour 30 minutes

Part 1

For questions **1–15**, read the text below and then decide which word on page **65** best fits each space. The exercise begins with an example **(0)**. In the exam you will put the letter for each question on a separate answer sheet.

Example: | **0** | *D* |

Smart Dog!

Dogs are probably much cleverer than most people think, scientists say. They are **(0)** ...*convinced*... that

dogs can count and that the animals try to **(1)** .... different messages through the pitch and pace of

their barks. Animal behaviourists used to think their bark was simply a way of **(2)** .... attention. Now

a new study suggests that individual dogs have **(3)** .... barks with a range of meanings. For

example, dogs usually use high-pitched single barks when they are **(4)** .... from their owners and a

lower, harsher superbark when strangers **(5)** .... towards them or the doorbell rings.

Dogs also know when they are receiving fewer treats because they have a basic mathematical ability

that **(6)** .... them to tell when one pile of objects is bigger than another. But to count, an animal has

to recognise that each object in a set **(7)** .... to a single number and that the last number in a

(8) .... represents the total number of objects.

The theory has been tested on eleven dogs. They were first **(9)** .... treats before a screen was

lowered so that the treats were out of **(10)** .... The treats were left as they were or some were

added or taken away. If a treat was added or taken away, the dogs looked at them much longer than

they did when the treats were not disturbed, **(11)** .... because they had done their sums and the

numbers did not meet their **(12)** ....

Dogs are **(13)** .... from wolves, which not only have a large neo-cortex – the brain's centre of

reasoning – but live in large social groups. This mathematical ability could have been used to

(14) .... how many enemies and **(15)** .... they had in a pack.

0	A	converted	B	persuaded	C	determined	D	convinced
1	A	transfer	B	convey	C	bear	D	suggest
2	A	paying	B	attracting	C	causing	D	devoting
3	A	specific	B	exact	C	detailed	D	specialised
4	A	split	B	detached	C	separated	D	divided
5	A	approach	B	appear	C	draw	D	move
6	A	assists	B	facilitates	C	enables	D	informs
7	A	corresponds	B	ties	C	fits	D	complements
8	A	sequence	B	system	C	progression	D	succession
9	A	tempted	B	demonstrated	C	shown	D	presented
10	A	view	B	notice	C	perception	D	sight
11	A	likely	B	presumably	C	surely	D	predictably
12	A	estimates	B	calculations	C	suspicions	D	expectations
13	A	descended	B	related	C	connected	D	evolved
14	A	take in	B	work out	C	think over	D	look into
15	A	helpers	B	defenders	C	allies	D	partners

Before you check your answers, go to page 66.

WHAT'S TESTED

Part 1 of the English in Use Paper is primarily a test of vocabulary. Questions typically focus on fixed phrases, collocations, linkers, idioms, and phrasal verbs.

TIPS

- Read the whole text through carefully before choosing the correct option for each space.
- Look at the choice of four words and choose the one that best fits both in terms of meaning and grammar.

A DETAILED STUDY

In the exercise below, choose the correct word in the box to fill the gap in each sentence. Each question relates to the question with the same number in the test.

0 | *converted*   *persuaded*   *determined*   *convinced* |

   a   Sue is .... that she can sing, but everyone else thinks she's terrible!

   b   The government say they are .... to improve the education system.

   c   I used to eat anything from the supermarket but recently I .... to organic foods.

   d   Jim .... his mother to lend him the car for the weekend.

1 | *transfer*   *convey*   *bear*   *suggest* |

   a   If you're bored, I .... you go to the cinema.

   b   The colour red can often .... a sense of energy and strength to people.

   c   I wouldn't like to be senior manager. You have to .... a lot of responsibility.

   d   When he retires, he'll .... his power to his son.

2 | *paying*   *attracting*   *causing*   *devoting* |

   a   By .... attention to themselves, they were rescued from the island.

   b   He laughed in a very strange way, ... everyone to turn round and look.

   c   She won the award for .... her whole life to looking after the poor.

   d   By .... attention to the directions, she arrived quicker than anyone else.

3 | *specific*   *exact*   *detailed*   *specialised* |

   a   'Does someone have the .... time, please?'

   b   You need to be highly trained and have .... skills to work in engineering.

   c   She wrote a .... account of the time she spent travelling across Africa.

   d   I gave him .... instructions about what to say during the meeting.

4 | split   detached   separated   divided |

    a There were ten of us for dinner, so the food was .... up carefully.

    b The log was .... into two halves.

    c They live in a large .... house on the edge of London.

    d The child cried when he became .... from his mother in the crowd.

5 | approach   appear   draw   move |

    a Jane tends to .... on my doorstep whenever I'm about to go out.

    b We watched his train .... into the station.

    c There was a long queue for the sales, but eventually we began to .... towards the shop entrance.

    d The trainer told us to .... the horse slowly and quietly.

6 | assists   facilitates   enables   informs |

    a Richard is great. He .... people whenever he can.

    b Your assistant .... me that the delivery will be here today.

    c The money I inherited .... me to do a lot more things.

    d The new system .... a faster service.

7 | corresponds   ties   fits   complements |

    a Are you sure that a British plug .... a continental socket?

    b This strange weather .... in with global warming.

    c I don't think this remote control .... to this particular model of TV.

    d People who know about wines will choose one that .... their meal.

8 | sequence   system   progression   succession |

    a We had a .... of temporary teachers before the school hired a permanent one.

    b To open a bank safe, you need to remember the exact .... of numbers.

    c How does the .... work if I want to order some new stationery?

    d There are many opportunities for career .... if you work for that company.

9 | tempted   demonstrated   shown   presented |

    a Jane was .... with a beautiful crystal vase when she left her department.

    b I was .... to book the holiday immediately, but I thought I should check with my wife.

    c The surgeon .... how the operation should be performed.

    d We were .... our rooms by the owner of the hotel.

10 | *view   notice   perception   sight* |

   a   If we build that hotel there, the ocean will be hidden from ....

   b   The kite rose into the sky until it was out of ....

   c   Don't take any .... of Chris – he's always rude to everyone.

   d   He showed great .... of the situation – he could see exactly what was really happening.

11 | *likely   presumably   surely   predictably* |

   a $200 for that chair? .... it's got to be a mistake!

   b   .... you'll be coming to the meeting next week since you prepared the documents?

   c   It's .... to rain for the next few weeks.

   d   Paul was .... behind schedule and missed his plane.

12 | *estimates   calculations   suspicions   expectations* |

   a   Unfortunately, the holiday did not meet our ....

   b   The man's strange behaviour aroused the .... of the police officer.

   c   According to my .... , we should have enough money for the rest of the month.

   d   We were given three very different .... for the cost of repairs to our car.

13 | *descended .   related   connected   evolved* |

   a   We share the same surname but we're not .... to one another.

   b   I don't think the problem with this software is .... to a virus.

   c   He said he was .... from a French king!

   d   The idea .... from a brainstorming session with the team.

14 | *take in   work out   think over   look into* |

   a   The company have to .... ways of reducing costs.

   b   I can't .... how the burglar got into the house!

   c   I'll tell you my decision tomorrow. I need some time to .... it ....

   d   It's hard to .... all that complicated information at once!

15 | *helpers   defenders   allies   partners* |

   a   They're equal .... in that company.

   b   They are close friends and .... to the Prime Minister.

   c   Harry and Jane are passionate .... of human rights.

   d   The police asked for .... when they were looking for the lost child.

Now check your answers to Part 1 of the test.

Part 2

For questions **16–30**, read the following text and think of the word which best fits each space. **Use only one word in each space.** The exercise begins with an example **(0)**. In the exam you will mark your answers on a separate answer sheet.

Example: | **0** | *past* |

Bananas are best!

Britain has gone mad for bananas. Over the **(0)** ..*past*.. 12 months Britons have consumed an

unprecedented 3.5bn pieces of the tropical fruit, forcing the native apple **(16)** .... second place.

The nation's banana boom is one of the most remarkable nutritional trends of recent years, a guide

not **(17)** .... to the growing health consciousness of the British people but also to the country's

economic health. **(18)** .... is amazing is that bananas were virtually unheard of during the 19th

century and even up **(19)** .... the end of the 1920s **(20)** .... anyone in Britain had tasted or

even seen **(21)** ....

Early attempts to introduce them to northern countries had met **(22)** .... failure because, by the

time they had been shipped to Britain, they had rotted beyond recognition. **(23)** .... , thanks to

the development of refrigerated shipping, all **(24)** .... changed. Refrigerated shipping meant

that then, as **(25)** .... , bunches of imported bananas could arrive in good condition at ripening

houses in dockyards where they **(26)** .... stored. The first commercial refrigerated shipment

arrived 100 years ago, triggering an enthusiasm from **(27)** .... Britons have never looked back.

'The banana has everything going for it,' says Jeanette Scott of the *Banana Group* marketing

organisation. 'It's easy to open, it is packed **(28)** .... energy and vitamins and is low in calories.

It is also a first-class cure for upset stomachs and it stabilises blood pressure **(29)** .... , its

popularity should **(30)** .... be seen as that surprising.'

Part 3

In **most** lines of the following text, there is either a spelling error or a punctuation error. For each numbered line **31–46**, write the correctly spelt word or show the correct punctuation. Some lines are correct. Indicate these with a tick (✓). The exercise begins with three examples **(0)**, **(00)** and **(000)**. In the exam you will write your answers on a separate answer sheet.

0	*some, for*
00	*necessary*
000	✓

Examples:

Summer in Madrid

0   Although it may seem trivial to some, for me it is a miracle that I

00   managed to park outside my home today! It wasn't neccessary to

000 drive around the block and it did not take me half an hour. Almost a

31   year has passed since this last happened, a sure sign that August, the

32   month Madrid shuts down, is just around the corner. Over the past

33   week, my neighbours have been packing there cars and disappearing to

34   apartements by the beach or villages in the countryside. A curious

35   silence reigns over the buildings. 'See you in four weeks time,'

36   say signs pasted to bar and restaurant doors. Fresh bread and break's

37   for coffee recquire longer walks to the few places left functioning.

38   Visitors to the city may be disappointed because they expect a busy

39   midsummer, but are met by silence; foreign backpackers and scalding

40   heat. Those of us who live here however, are delighted since to us

41   Madrid becomes a secret paradise in August. An unwriten agreement

42   has been signed by all of us: usual rules of behaviour no longer apply.

43   Dress codes are the first to go, shaving is optional and work becomes a

44   liesurely affair. Much of what you want to do cannot be done, because

45   everyone else is away. There's no one here to take your call, Please

46   call back in September,' comes the reply from the answering machine.

Part 4

For questions **47–61**, read the two texts on pages **71** and **72**. Use the words in the boxes to the right of the two texts to form **one** word which fits in the same numbered space in the text. The exercise begins with an example **(0)**. In the exam you will write your answers on a separate answer sheet.

Example: | **0** | *subscription* |

ADVERTISEMENT

Have IN FOCUS magazine delivered direct to your door!

By taking out a 12-month **(0)** ...*subscription*.... , you can be

- up-to-date with **(47)** .... issues and current affairs
- the first to know of **(48)** .... reader events.

Please tick the boxes below:

New members: I would like to receive my first copy of IN FOCUS. ☐

Existing members: I would like to **(49)** .... my current **(50)** .... for 1 year. ☐

Gift: Give IN FOCUS to a friend. We will also send a gift card to the **(51)** .... ☐

(52) .... postage required for overseas $70: ☐

Please indicate method of **(53)** .... :

Cheque ☐   Postal order ☐   Bank Card ☐

0	SUBSCRIBE
47	GLOBE
48	COME
49	NEW
50	MEMBER
51	RECEIVE
52	ADD
53	PAY

ARTICLE

Save our languages!

The linguistic **(54)** .... of an ecological disaster is looming, according to researchers from the University of Manchester who say there is considerable **(55)** .... that many world languages will disappear by 2050. Academics from the linguistics department staged an **(56)** ' .... Languages' day last month where they spoke of their **(57)** .... research. Professor Stephen Perry explained: 'British Romani is an example of a language now almost at the level of **(58)** .... There is no **(59)** .... of languages – at the last count there were about 6,000 – but 4% of them are spoken by 96% of the people. No one needs to worry about them. But the little-spoken languages with a chance of **(60)** .... need help. People know which species are being **(61)** .... but they don't realise that we are leaving languages to die out. A language can only survive if it is transmitted from parents to their children.'

54	EQUAL
55	LIKELY
56	DANGER
57	EXTEND
58	EXTINCT
59	SHORT
60	SURVIVE
61	THREAT

Part 5

For questions **62–74**, read the following note. Use the information in this text to complete the numbered gaps in the formal notice to employees which follows. The words you need **do not** occur in the note. **Use no more than two words for each gap.** The exercise begins with an example **(0)**. In the exam you will write your answers on a separate answer sheet.

Example: | **0** | *banned* |

NOTE

Simon,

Can you draft a notice to give to all department heads? Staff performance is pretty good as usual but we need to remind them of a few things, such as –

– we don't allow smoking in the offices.
– staff need to wear the right kind of clothes to work (dark colour suits, etc.) and tell them it doesn't matter what the occasion is – it isn't possible to wear casual clothes!
– ask them to get to work at 9.00 at the latest! And to get back on time from breaks.
– if anyone's ill, they should phone their head of department and let them know. This would be best before 8.30 am.
– if they're away from work for 3 or more days, they have to get a letter from their doctor.
– if they see anything they think might be dangerous or harmful, they should tell their head of department as soon as possible.

Finally – just thank the staff for doing all this. It makes them feel appreciated!

NOTICE TO EMPLOYEES

We would like to remind staff of the following points:

Smoking:
Smoking has been **(0)** ...*banned*... from all offices.

Dress code:
All staff should be **(62)** .... in either dark blue, grey or black suits.
No member of staff will **(63)** .... to wear casual clothes under any **(64)** ....

Punctuality:
Staff are **(65)** .... to arrive at work no **(66)** .... 9.00 am. We would also like to remind staff that they need to return **(67)** .... from coffee and lunch breaks.

Sickness:
Should any employee be ill, they must call the office **(68)** .... their head of department, **(69)** .... before 8.30am. For **(70)** .... of three days or more, a letter from the doctor must be **(71)** ....

Health and safety:
If any employee becomes **(72)** .... a health risk, please bring it to the **(73)** .... of the head of department.

We appreciate your **(74)** .... in all these matters.

Part 6

For questions **75–80**, read the following text and then choose from the list **A–J** given below the best phrase to fill each of the spaces. Each correct phrase may only be used once. **Some of the suggested answers do not fit at all.** The exercise begins with an example **(0)**. In the exam you will write your answers on a separate answer sheet.

Example: | 0 | J |

Rubbish!

Last Monday our rubbish bin was so full that most of our refuse bags ended up on the pavement. I'm

not proud of the fact that in one week my family managed **(0)** ....J...... . And those bags with all that

refuse – all of it produced by just two adults, two children and one cat – didn't include the stuff we keep

aside **(75)** .... So much waste is a shameful thing but it's quite another thing to have to pay £500 a

year **(76)** .... For that is what we were threatened with last week in a proposal **(77)** .... But

what is too much? Well, anything over two bags per week per household says the government

research team. Oh dear. My family, along with millions of other people, are going **(78)** .... So how

do we reduce the amount of rubbish we create? The obvious answer is **(79)** .... But assuming

that people need everything that comes into their homes, we must consider what can be done

(80) .... Recycling is one possibility but at the moment only half of Britain's households are

offered any kind of recycling service. It's not really good enough, is it?

A   to reduce such a quantity even further
B   to charge for the removal of excess amounts of rubbish
C   to minimise the amount that ends up in rubbish sites
D   to acquire less stuff in the first place
E   to have all this stuff removed
F   to avoid purchasing this type of product
G   to encourage people to do this
H   to have to change our ways
I   to put in our recycling box

J   to accumulate no fewer than 11 bags of rubbish

Before you check your answers, go to page 75.

WHAT'S TESTED

Part 6 of the English in Use Paper tests your ability to recognise coherence (the relationship and connection between ideas and arguments) and cohesion (use of cohesive devices such as *however, despite this,* etc.). You are required to choose six correct phrases or short sentences to complete a text.

TIPS

- Read the text first to gain an idea of the general theme. The answer you choose needs to fit both in terms of meaning and grammatical structure. It may be possible that a couple of answers fit the gap *grammatically* but only one will be suitable for meaning.
- Look carefully at the text before and after each gap for language 'clues' that will help you choose the correct answer, e.g. pronouns, tenses, vocabulary and linkers that show cause and effect.

A DETAILED STUDY

The questions below will help you to make sure that you have chosen the correct options for questions **75–80**.

Question 0
The writer says that he *'isn't proud of the fact that...'* This suggests that the following sentence refers to a 'bad' action or situation that the writer is responsible for. The example answer is 'J'. The writer feels guilty that he and his family are responsible for producing 11 bags of rubbish.

Question 75
The writer is saying that they have produced a surprising total of 11 bags of rubbish but even these bags don't contain *'the stuff we keep aside'* (the rubbish we save). Which option suggests where this 'extra' rubbish could be placed?

Question 76
The writer is saying that he is ashamed of producing so much rubbish, but he is also annoyed that he has to pay the local council to take it away. Which option suggests that the writer is not responsible for the collection of the rubbish himself, but receives this service?

Question 77
Before this question, the writer says *'we were threatened with a proposal'.* The verb *'threatened'* suggests that the writer felt 'attacked' or 'anxious' about something. The text following question 77 says *'But what is too much?'* This suggests that a number, quantity or amount has been mentioned. Which option mentions something which might be 'threatening' and a number/quantity or amount?

Question 78
The writer has already said he produces 11 bags of rubbish a week. Now he mentions that the local government want people to produce two bags a week. Which option refers to the fact that the writer and his family will need to adapt to this policy?

Question 79
The writer starts this sentence by saying *'The obvious answer is ...'.* The sentence should be finished by something positive or a good idea or solution. Several of the options seem to be positive, so it is important that your chosen option also corresponds to the previous sentence, *'So how do we reduce the amount of rubbish we create?'* Which option matches both of these requirements?

Question 80
The text before this question suggests that people need many of the products that produce rubbish. It also says *'we must consider what can be done'.* This implies that the following text will mention a solution or suggestion. Which option states that we should think about reducing the amount of rubbish that we throw away?

Now check your answers to Part 6 of the test.

PAPER 4 LISTENING approximately 45 minutes

Part 1

You will hear a talk about an archaeological discovery. For questions **1–10**, complete the notes using no more than three words.

You will hear the recording **twice**.

Important fossils: The 'Toumai' skull

Age of 'Toumai' skull: [*7 million* | 1] years.

Found by Michel Brunet after spending [*entire...* | 2] searching in Chad.

Region: Chad – close to Sahara – was v. green but surrounded by [*sand dunes* | 3]

The conditions have kept the skull and other fossils [*perfectly...* | 4]

'Toumai' means [| 5] .

Toumai is [| 6] the age of the next oldest skull.

Skull's characteristics: both [| 7] and

[| 8]

Face: [| 9]

Teeth: small and [*human-like* | 10]

Part 2

You will hear part of a radio broadcast about travel in Europe. For questions **11–18**, complete the notes the speaker is using.

Listen very carefully as you will hear the recording ONCE only.

Travel in Europe

Trains: faster, [11] , more

comfortable, and they have [12]

Europass: £300 – 5 days / £500 – up to

[13] days.

Inter-Rail pass: (for under 26s)

for fast trains and [14]

– you may have to pay [15]

Good idea to [16] if travelling at very

busy times of the year.

Accommodation: [17] or

campgrounds.

Lyon/France: underground maze used to

[18]

Part 3

You will hear part of a radio programme in which a new book is being reviewed. For questions **19–24**, choose the correct answer **A**, **B**, **C** or **D**.

You will hear the recording **twice**.

19 The main reason that Isabella was unlikely to become a travel writer was that she

    A believed travel at that time was very dangerous.

    B was under an illusion about her health.

    C had never displayed much imagination.

    D had regarded travel as a man's occupation.

20 Isabella went to Australia in order to

    A begin her writing career.

    B experience the scenery.

    C recover her health.

    D meet different people.

21 Sarah thinks Isabella's trips were surprising because she had previously

    A preferred an inactive lifestyle.

    B been frightened of animals.

    C never experienced extreme climates.

    D spent most of her time socialising.

22 According to Sarah, Isabella's letters

    A should have been published earlier.

    B were based on newspaper articles.

    C may have exaggerated what she saw.

    D failed to provide enough detail at times.

23 In Sarah's opinion, Isabella's personality was unusual because she

    A had rebelled against her father.

    B was at her best in challenging situations.

    C only pretended to be courageous.

    D travelled despite her illnesses.

24 According to Sarah, the book in its current form

    A does not make it clear how the letters have been edited.

    B ought to contain all of the letters Isabella wrote to Henrietta.

    C fails to include examples of Isabella's bad experiences.

    D should be adapted so the style is familiar to readers today.

Before you check your answers, go to page 79.

WHAT'S TESTED?

For Part 3 of the Listening Paper, you will hear a conversation for about four minutes. This conversation will be an interview or a discussion between two or three speakers. You will either have to answer multiple-choice questions or complete a series of sentences.

TIPS

- For both task types, use the pause before each piece is heard to predict the kind of information that is required.
- Questions follow the order of the recording.
- See page 37 for tips on sentence completion.

A DETAILED STUDY

Listen to the recording, fill in the gaps and then answer the questions.

Question 19
Sarah says:

1 *This was .... for a woman. It was usually men going off on expeditions ...*

2 *... out into the unknown and ....*

3 *The irony of it all is that she was a complete hypochondriac – I mean she always had this idea there was something ....*

4 *So anyway, what with all her supposed suffering, it was probably .... she'd ever imagined for herself.*

The question asks for the **main** reason why Isabella was unlikely to become a travel writer. Which two sentences from 1–4 above contain the main reason?

Question 20
Sarah says:

5 *... she'd gone there, apparently – on the advice of a friend who thought the climate would ....*
   ....

6 *... she found she loathed Australia – she thought there was nothing .... and no ....*
   ....

7 *... it was at this point that this 40-year-old woman was on the brink of a ....*

The question asks what Isabella's purpose was in going to Australia. Which sentence from 5–7 shows this purpose?

Question 21
Sarah says:

8 *Imagine – someone who could scarcely .... from the sofa at home in Scotland ...*

9 *... would then be climbing up Mauna Loa in the Pacific, surviving being .... on a ranch in Colorado.*

10 *... and riding a .... through the Malayan jungle and even, at the age of 70, to cross the Atlas mountains alone, on a fierce ....*

11 *It was definitely unusual for someone of her ....*

The question asks why Isabella's trips were surprising. Which sentence from 8–11 suggests a reason and also matches one of the options for question 21?

Question 22

Sarah says:

12 *... the book, you see, contains these diary letters that she wrote to her sister – most of which have until now ....*

13 *She used those letters – or .... – to provide much of the raw material for her other work.*

14 *She goes into particular detail – I mean .... – especially when describing dramatic landscapes.*

15 *... she writes – 'companioned only by stars' beside 'a black lake from which rise fountains of fire' and so on. She certainly can't be accused of ....*

The question asks about Sarah's opinion of Isabella's letters. Which sentence 12–15 fits one of the options for question 22?

Question 23

Sarah says:

16 *Her father was a preacher – he was strict and frowned upon 'fun' and you can see she's .... that aspect.*

17 *... but when under pressure, all her imagined illnesses magically vanish and she just positively .... and ....*

18 *She boasts about her riding about in Colorado – saying that others are describing her as the .... they've seen.*

19 *This image isn't really .... with the poor woman suffering from those ghastly headaches!*

The question asks why Isabella's personality is unusual. Which sentence 16–19 fits one of the options for question 23?

Question 24

20 *Well, Isabella herself .... or heavily edited many letters...*

21 *What you're left with is .... who's edited what – what did Isabella write or cut, and how much .... has the editor had?*

22 *A lot of travel writing comes across as quite ....*

23 *In 'Letters to Henrietta', you're getting a real glimpse of what it was like to be travelling at a time when there was still a sense of .... and ....*

The question asks about Sarah's opinion of the book in its current form. Which sentence 20–23 fits one of the options for question 24?

Now check your answers to Part 3 of the test.

Part 4

You will hear five short extracts in which various people are talking about other people who have had an influence on them. While you listen, you must complete **both** tasks.

You will hear the recording **twice**.

TASK ONE

For questions **25–29**, match the extracts as you hear them with the people, listed **A–H**.

A   a scientist

B   a parent

C   a soldier

D   a politician

E   a teacher

F   a novelist

G   a journalist

H   an athlete

	25
	26
	27
	28
	29

TASK TWO

For questions **30–34**, match the extracts as you hear them with the people being described as influential, listed **A–H**.

A   a writer

B   a pop star

C   a policeman

D   a TV star

E   a parent

F   a coach

G   a teacher

H   a childhood friend

	30
	31
	32
	33
	34

In the exam you will have 10 minutes at the end of the test to copy your answers onto a separate answer sheet.

PAPER 5 SPEAKING

Part 2 (4 minutes)

1 The five senses

For both candidates

Look at the photographs on page 148. They each show people who use one or more of the five senses for their work.

Candidate A: Compare and contrast two of these photographs, saying which senses you think these people rely on and how they use these senses to achieve success in their work. (*1 minute*)

Candidate B: Say how the person in the other photograph uses their senses in their work. (*20 seconds*)

2 Relaxation

For both candidates

Look at the pictures on page 149. They show things which help some people relax.

Candidate B: Compare and contrast two of these pictures, saying what kind of people you think find these things relaxing and in what different ways. (*1 minute*)

Candidate A: Say which of these activities you find the most relaxing. (*20 seconds*)

Part 3 (4 minutes) Responsibility

For both candidates

Look below at the list of different people who have a responsible role in society. Talk to each other and discuss what kind of responsibility each person has and who or what they are responsible for. Then decide who you think has the greatest responsibility.

a teacher   a parent   a police officer   a doctor   a scientist   a journalist

Part 4 (4 minutes) Further discussion

- What other people do you think have a very important role to play in society?
- Who do you think are the role models for young people today?
- In what ways do you think young people today suffer from peer pressure?
- What responsibilities do you feel that you have?
- How far do you agree with the statement 'Everybody has a responsibility to improve their society.'

For Further Practice and Guidance, see page 83.

WHAT'S TESTED

Problem-solving activity

In Part 3 of the Speaking Paper, you are asked to discuss a problem-solving task with your partner(s) based on a set of visual or written prompts. The task may require you to discuss, evaluate, select or hypothesize. There is no right or wrong answer to these problem-solving tasks, but you will be expected to reach a conclusion. However, it does not matter if you and your partner disagree.

This part of the Speaking Paper tests your ability to interact with your partner. This means you need to ask questions as well as respond to them and carry out the task in a way that reflects a normal conversation. It is possible to use natural conversation fillers such as 'Well, let me think...' or 'That's a good point. I hadn't thought about that,' etc.

It is important that candidates allow each other equal participation in the discussion and both make the effort to keep the conversation going.

Using the phrases in the box below, practise Part 3 on page 82 with your partner.

Conversation Fillers	Stating your opinion	Asking your partner	Responding to your partner
• *Well, let me think...* • *Let me see...* • *That's a good/ interesting/ difficult question...* • *Well, I haven't really thought about this before but...*	• *Personally, ...* • *In my opinion, ...* • *If you ask me, ...* • *The way I see it, ...* • *I think/feel/reckon/ guess/believe/would say that...*	• *In your opinion, what would you say is...?* • *What do you think/reckon/feel about..?* • *Do you think that...?* • *Would you agree?*	• *On the whole, I agree with you but...* • *I see what you mean but...* • *That's true but...* • *I'm not sure I agree with you on that.* • *Yes, I think you're right about that and ..* • *Good point/True and what about...?*

Part 4

In Part 4, the interlocutor will ask the students a series of questions which relate to the topic(s) in Part 3. These questions tend to become more general and more abstract as the discussion develops. This part is testing your ability to further express your opinion by using a range of structures and vocabulary. Don't worry about having different ideas to the examiners – they are only interested in listening to your English. For this reason, try to develop the conversation as much as possible. If you only give short answers, you are not demonstrating your ability.

TEST THREE

PAPER 1 READING 1 hour 15 minutes

Part 1

Answer questions **1–17** by referring to the book reviews on page **85**. In the exam, you will mark your answers on a separate answer sheet.

For questions **1–17** answer by choosing from the list (**A–D**) on the right below. Some of the choices may be required more than once.

Of which book is the following stated?

It is both informative and highly amusing.	1 ....
It has been heavily edited by the author.	2 ....
Its minor characters come across as real people rather than stereotypes.	3 ....
The overall excellence of the book makes up for a disappointing ending.	4 ....
It makes no clear reference to the time in which the story is set.	5 ....
The reader will not find the style of writing confusing.	6 ....
There is little order to how the reader is introduced to the characters.	7 ....
Its quality of writing is irregular throughout the book.	8 ....
It contains well-known themes but has an unusual way of dealing with them.	9 ....
Its style makes it difficult to read without regular interruption.	10 ....
It assumes that the reader will be able to understand its subject matter.	11 ....
It takes a while for the reader to discover what the main idea is.	12 ....
One of its characters has a way of speaking which affects the pace of the book.	13 ....
It contains ideas that could easily be separated into different books.	14 ....
It is eventually a satisfying read, despite requiring an effort on the reader's part at first.	15 ....
Its authorship remains a matter of uncertainty.	16 ....
It may come across as trying too hard to make the central characters convincing.	17 ....

A Crow Lake

B By the Lake

C Everything is Illuminated

D The Bondwoman's Narrative

On the shelves this month

A
Crow Lake
by Mary Lawson

These are stories familiar to all of us; 'orphaned children determined to stay together' and 'inspiring teacher aids exceptional student, allowing escape from a limited life'. What distinguishes Mary Lawson's *Crow Lake* is that she combines these plots with a twist. The brilliant teacher is a brother, Luke, who never gets himself an education, having chosen instead to raise his brothers and sisters. The narrator, Kate, is the little sister he inspires, who – though she becomes a university professor – can neither accept nor escape the sacrifice that was made for her. *Crow Lake* is in its structure, its major characters and its effect, a quite traditional novel; and in its earnest determination to make Kate and Luke and their choices credible, it is perhaps a young one. The constant hinting at what is to come can be a bit heavy-handed and the necessary solemnity of the heroine-narrator is a somewhat stifling influence. But the assurance with which Mary Lawson handles both reflection and violence makes her a writer to read and to watch. Peripheral portraits are skilfully drawn; the young child Bo with her minimal vocabulary of mostly shouted words, speaks to the heart without a scrap of sentimentality and Kate's in-laws, also professors, unusually for fictional academics are funny without being ridiculous.

B
By the Lake
by John McGahern

One cannot truly appreciate *By the Lake* unless one realises that for every published page, there are six that John McGahern discarded. Eager as one is, it is a difficult novel to get into since one cannot immediately locate the centre of the narrative. It opens on an uneventful Sunday. 'The morning was clear. There was no wind on the lake. They had the entire world to themselves.' A man enters a house by the lake. He calls out. After a moment, someone answers. A novel follows. The place itself is what this initially demanding but ultimately rewarding novel is about. It follows a year in an unnamed village where a couple, Joe and Kate, return to live. We randomly assemble a picture of others in the community: Jamesie is the most likeable, Bill, the strangest, Johnny, the one disappointed in love. We are never quite sure when the novel's events take place and McGahern has indicated that the novel's dating is deliberately vague. Seasonal time is something else. The novel is teasingly precise about the turning moments of the year and is punctuated with lush descriptions of the countryside. The biggest event of the year is the arrival of a telephone pole. The outside world has come closer. But the lake will not change.

C
Everything is Illuminated
by Jonathan Safran Foer

It's hard to get through this book's first chapters. You keep laughing out loud, losing your place, starting again, then stopping because you're tempted to call your friends and read them long sections of Foer's assured, hilarious prose. The narrator, Alexander, is enchanted by everything American. He speaks English like someone who has taught himself by painstakingly translating a really abysmal novel aided by a badly outdated dictionary. Nevertheless, he is fluent enough to work as a translator for a travel agency that organises trips for rich foreigners. Any attempt to explain the complex narrative strategy of this book – who is saying what and when – makes it sound more complicated than it is. Actually, it's not hard to follow, since the structure reveals itself in stages, and each one of these revelations is a source of surprise and pleasure. Indeed, one of the book's attractions is its writer's high degree of faith in the reader's intelligence. In fact Foer has got his sights on higher things than mere laughs, on a whole series of themes so weighty that any one of them would be enough for an ordinary novel. The combination of serious theme and comic description is so appealing that you hardly care when big chunks of the book start to crumble in the last 50 pages. By then, the novel has provided so much enjoyment that such lapses barely matter.

D
The Bondwoman's Narrative
by Hannah Crafts

Who was Hannah Crafts? The author of *The Bondwoman's Narrative*, an autobiographical novel written in the 1850s, describes herself as a 'fugitive slave' making her text a remarkable discovery. Published from a manuscript bought at auction by Henry Louis Gates, it is quite probably the first novel written by a female slave. This claim, of course, hinges on the authenticity of Crafts' manuscript, a subject all but laid to rest in Gates' long introduction to the book. Although Gates never manages to identify Hannah Crafts, who probably wrote under a pseudonym, he presents a formidable array of evidence authenticating her story. But the book need not be read for its historical importance alone. It is also an immensely entertaining and illuminating novel. Always interesting, if only intermittently well written, it uses a combination of literary styles to heighten the drama. Then it goes over the top as Hannah's adventures multiply improbably. She faces not only the evils of slavery but ghosts and great gusts of the ominous weather so typical of 19th century fiction. Nevertheless, Crafts transcends the melodrama of her fictional styles to address the complexities of the slave experience.

Part 2

For questions **18–24**, choose which of the paragraphs **A–H** on page **87** fit into the numbered gaps in the following magazine article. There is one extra paragraph which does not fit in any of the gaps. In the exam, you will mark your answers on a separate answer sheet.

Mountain Challenge

When the Army asked him to go on a climbing mission, Alex Wade said 'Yes, sir!'

I was managing the mountain climb fairly well until we got to the crevasse – a two-metre wide crack in the ice. 'What do I do with my ice axe?' I yelled. 'Don't worry about it,' the leader of the expedition, Mark Smyth, shouted back at me. 'Just jump.' I obeyed but with the knowledge that a tumble on the other, lower, side would result in an express ride to the perilous glacier below. I just about made it. For an average climber like myself, this seemed more like a military operation!

| 18 | |

I had met Mark a year previously on a climb in Russia. He had dropped me a line: 'I'm climbing Mont Blanc in June. Interested?' I'd had a rough time there on a previous attempt, failing to reach the summit because of altitude sickness. Here was a chance to try again with a serious mountaineer. But still, this was a full military expedition, so, technically, I wouldn't be his responsibility. If I climbed with them, would I be OK? 'Put it this way, I'm not going to let you fall off,' he said.

| 19 | |

As Mark put it, 'Climbing Mont Blanc from this approach is not technically difficult but is never to be underestimated. The weather can change in minutes, and freezing temperatures and 120kph winds are common. At over 5,000 metres, these extreme conditions test the endurance limit of all but the hardiest of mountaineers.'

| 20 | |

Looks can be deceptive. After a few days' walking to acclimatize to the altitude I was exhausted. Come the climb itself, we camped on the Col du Midi (3,542 metres), having hiked down the exposed ridge from the cable car station. Everyone was coping fine with the altitude, and the warm sunlight made Mont Blanc seem harmless. Around 3am the next morning

we began the long slog up Tacul. From the shoulder of Tacul we had a perfect view of the route across the Col du Mont Maudit. It was on the Col that I had turned back two years ago.

| 21 | |

Even digging snow pits for the tents was a real struggle. Teams of two or three dug holes, got their tents up and got warm. On my own, I was the first to start digging and the last to finish. No one said much, too exhausted to waste energy on speech.

| 22 | |

I couldn't have been more wrong. The descent made everything that had gone before seem easy. After eventually negotiating the crevasses, we staggered down to just above the glacier – all that lay between us and safety. The ice on the glacier would be unstable, but there was a chance we would make it. Then a lump of ice the size of a house crashed to pieces right on our prospective path.

| 23 | |

Sure enough, as I forced my legs to go down the agonizingly steep slope, I slipped. Though I managed to slam my axe into the ice, I committed the worst crime of failing to secure my feet before I stood up. I slid further down, ice axe stuck in the snow above me, into the next man on the rope. Fortunately neither of us slid any further.

| 24 | |

We had done it. We had climbed Mont Blanc the hard way. Some of the soldiers were muttering that the glacier was the scariest they'd ever experienced. No one looked keen to take up mountaineering on a regular basis. For Mark, though, this was routine. 'The aim of the expedition was achieved,' he said. 'Now they know what it's like to be on a mountain.'

A   This time it seemed I was having better luck and the climb went well save for the near-vertical ice wall which stood before our next brief stop on the Col de la Brenva. We laboured up the wall and I could scarcely stand by the time we came to camp. By this stage, though, everyone was suffering and slowing down.

B   It looked like the decision had been made for us. There was no choice but to trudge back up the mountain and spend the night at the Grands Mulets refuge. Next morning we headed off to re-attempt our glacier crossing. But it only takes a moment to make a mistake, and they usually happen when you're tired.

C   I wasn't the only one! Our destination seemed no nearer although we'd been on the move for hours, and so far, we'd all managed to maintain a reasonable pace. But at this point, we could hardly turn around and head back. And more than this, I didn't want to let Mark down.

D   Despite that welcome reassurance, I wondered whether I could keep up with the other, very fit expedition members. I didn't feel too optimistic when I learned of the route – 'The Grand Traverse' – which takes in two other mountains, Mont Blanc du Tacul and Mont Maudit, and is often done in a day starting from the Aiguille de Midi cable car station. We would be carrying full rucksacks with food and equipment for three days.

E   After another early start in temperatures of around –20, we finally made it to the summit. The wind was now roaring and I could barely see the peaks of the mountains around us. It was a long way to come for such a poor view but at least the worst was over.

F   To add to my apprehension, it was this same route that had beaten me the last time around. But after two months of frantic aerobic training since Mark's invitation, there I was, with the army in Chamonix. They seemed a decent bunch, and didn't appear too fit.

G   Despite my humiliation and exhaustion, I went on with the rest and I found some extra energy to move quickly when I felt the ice shudder beneath us. Eventually, thanks to superb route-finding by Mark and despite many further stumbles, we made it over the ice to the cable car.

H   But that, however, was exactly what it was. I was the 13th man on an army expedition to climb Mont Blanc. As Mark said, 'The aim is to put the soldiers into a challenging environment in order to develop the qualities of team spirit and self-confidence.' A good aim, yes, but the difference between them and me is that I was the sole civilian.

Before you check your answers, go to page 88.

A DETAILED STUDY

Below you can see extracts from the paragraphs **A–H**. Read the extracts and answer the questions.

A

1   *'This time it seemed I was having better luck and the climb went well…'*

This part of the sentence suggests the writer has already mentioned

a   a bad experience.
b   a reasonable experience.
c   a good experience.

2   *'We laboured up the wall… I could scarcely stand by the time we came to camp.'*

This part of the sentence suggests the writer

a   improved his climbing technique.
b   needed to stop and have a rest.
c   wanted to continue the climb.

3   *'By this stage, though, everyone was suffering and slowing down.'*

What would you expect to follow this sentence?

a   An example of how well some of the soldiers were doing.
b   An example of what the soldiers managed to do with difficulty.
c   An example of how the writer was coping better than the soldiers.

B

4   *'It looked like the decision had been made for us. There was no choice but to trudge back…'*

This means that

a   everyone decided to return.
b   Mark (the leader) wanted everyone to return.
c   something else forced everyone to return.

5   *'…we headed off to re-attempt our glacier crossing.'*

This suggests that

a   they had already tried to cross the glacier.
b   it was the first time they tried to cross the glacier.
c   they had tried to cross a different glacier before.

6   *'But it only takes a moment to make a mistake.'*

What is the purpose of this sentence?

a   To warn the reader about the dangers of mountain climbing.
b   To introduce an example of a mistake.
c   To suggest that everyone on the team did very well.

C

7   *'Our destination seemed no nearer although we'd been on the move for hours.'*

What does this sentence mean?

a   We were close to our destination and we had only been travelling a short time.
b   We were far away from our destination because we had only been travelling for a short time.
c   We were far away from our destination and we had been travelling for a long time.

8   *'we'd all managed to maintain a reasonable pace.'*

This means that

a   the team had made a lot of progress on the climb.
b   the team had done fairly well on the climb.
c   the team had moved quite slowly on the climb.

9   *'we could hardly turn round and head back.'*

What is the writer suggesting?

a   He thinks they should return to the starting point.
b   He thinks it will be a challenge to find the same route home.
c   He thinks that they must continue in the same direction.

D
10   *'Despite that welcome reassurance…'*

This suggests that someone has said something to the writer to make him feel more

a   nervous.
b   confident.
c   enthusiastic.

E
11   *'…we finally made it to the summit.'*

What does this tell you about the team's progress?

a   They reached the lower slopes.
b   They reached a flat area.
c   They reached the highest point.

12   *'…but at least the worst was over.'*

The writer believes

a   the climb will get easier.
b   he is experiencing the most difficult part of the climb.
c   the worst part of the climb is coming next.

F
13   *'To add to my apprehension…'*

This suggests that the writer has just heard something that

a   worries him.
b   makes him feel safe.
c   interests him.

14   *'They* (the soldiers) *didn't appear too fit.'*

The writer believes the physical condition of the soldiers is

a   excellent.
b   quite good.
c   not as good as it should be.

G
15   *'Despite my humiliation…'*

This suggests that the writer has just experienced something which made him feel

a   proud.
b   satisfied.
c   ashamed.

16   *'…despite many further stumbles…'*

What is a synonym for *'a stumble'*?

a   a climb
b   a rest
c   a slip

H
17   *'But that, however, was exactly what it was.'*

This sentence means that the writer has

a   correctly identified something.
b   incorrectly identified something.

Now check your answers to Part 2 of the test.

Part 3

Read the following newspaper article and then answer questions **25–30** on page **91**. Indicate the letter **A**, **B**, **C** or **D** against the number of each question **25–30**. Give only one answer to each question. In the exam, you will mark your answers on a separate answer sheet.

A career in comedy? It's no laughing matter!

At one time the notion of a career on stage may have been frowned upon, but nowadays parents would be well advised to actually push their offspring into the safe and lucrative world of comedy. If the number of awards, the profusion of clubs and the amount of lucrative broadcasting work available are anything to go by, comedy is the new accountancy. Where once a stand-up comedian would have to endure years on the circuit of small-time venues and get paid in free drinks and curled-up sandwiches, comedians can now work in several media and even be paid a regular salary for writing jokes for TV and media. The live comedy circuit has mushroomed and the general public seem to have an insatiable appetite for comedic talent both in front of and behind the camera.

'The advent of multi-channel TV is behind this comedy revolution,' says William Burdett-Coutts, artistic director of one of the top venues for comedy during the famous Edinburgh Festival Fringe. 'I put it down to when television programmers at Channel 4 created a new interest in comedy. That's what sparked it off, and now with so many channels there are hours of airtime to be filled. There is a fairly constant demand for new talent.' The festival sees the culmination of five comedy awards that are regarded in the industry as one long audition for lucrative TV work. 'The eventual winners will possibly get guaranteed runs at the prestigious Montreal and Melbourne comedy festivals but the ultimate lure for many, though, is the thought of being snapped up by a top agent,' he says.

Edinburgh is only one of the many comedy festivals in Britain where comedians can ply their trade. Several other British cities have festivals but Burdett-Coutts cautions that it's not all milk and honey for those seeking fame and fortune. 'Manchester struggles to keep its venues going, Newcastle has closed them all, and London is a hard one to crack as there is so much going on there all the time. There are many, many comedians who have been around for years without a breakthrough.' Nevertheless, he still maintains that there's room for another comedy festival in a seemingly overcrowded market and points out that October sees the launch of the Brighton Comedy Festival.

Despite the risk of obscurity, the openings for talented funny people are many and varied – and it's not necessarily performers that TV wants to lure. As Lisa Thomas, director of an agency which handles several top comics, says, 'Not so long ago, TV producers would want to see someone up there performing live, and audience reaction was the bottom line. What you have these days is a concern with the comic's creative potential. They may think someone doesn't quite have it on stage, but has a talent that could be put to better use coming up with ideas for sketches in established TV shows or even for editing scripts.'

While Thomas welcomes the extra money and audience interest that awards attract, she believes they are hardly an automatic guarantee of well-paid comedy life, but rather they act as an industry 'shop window'. 'They are definitely the foot in the door,' she says. 'The awards do secure work for newcomers and a lot of them feel they have to pay their dues and do live performance for a couple of years before they can call themselves a comedian. It certainly helps in terms of knowing whether a joke is "sayable" or if the timing's right when they go into writing or production.'

One comedian who made the deviation from delivering the jokes himself to writing for others is Phil Whelans. Although he does the occasional live performance and voiceover work for commercials, he now considers himself a writer and made the career change in the late 1990s after his comedy act with a partner broke up. 'I couldn't face starting over, doing try-out sessions,' says Whelans. 'The scene is so diluted now – there are hundreds of competent, blandish, slightly uninteresting stand-ups who I would be up against and my heart sank at the thought.' And the money? 'The rates vary wildly,' says Whelans, who is currently devising an improvised sitcom for TV. 'I've seen writers turn ashen with jealousy when they hear what others can earn, but believe me, it's a very decent living for most.'

25   What does the writer state about a career in comedy in the past?

    A   Comedians used to expect a reasonable salary.

    B   There was a range of awards comedians could aim for.

    C   A career in comedy tended to last longer than today.

    D   There was disapproval of people giving public performances.

26   According to William Burdett-Coutts, comedians often take part in the Edinburgh Festival

    A   to challenge current notions of comedy.

    B   to demonstrate their comic ability.

    C   to appear to as wide an audience as possible.

    D   to compete with each other for money.

27   What does Burdett-Coutts state about the current opportunities for comedians?

    A   A career in comedy may not always be rewarding.

    B   Comedians should avoid venues in large cities.

    C   There are many inadequate comedians seeking work.

    D   The launch of another festival is fairly pointless.

28   According to Lisa Thomas, TV producers are looking for comedians who

    A   are capable of producing material for others.

    B   come across as confident in live performance.

    C   enjoy a good rapport with their audiences.

    D   are realistic about their chances of success.

29   What does Lisa Thomas say about comedy awards?

    A   They ensure comedians gain experience before entering comedy festivals.

    B   They usually mean that comedians will enjoy a successful career.

    C   They lead to opportunities where comedians can experiment with material.

    D   They help comedians decide which branch of comedy they are suited to.

30   Why did Phil Whelans choose to become a comedy writer?

    A   He felt he was no longer at competition standard.

    B   He believed he would earn a regular salary as a writer.

    C   He had found it difficult to work as part of a team.

    D   He did not have the enthusiasm to develop a new act.

Part 4

Answer questions **31–52** by referring to the magazine article on pages **93–94**, in which five men are interviewed about their jobs. In the exam, you will mark your answers on a separate answer sheet.

For questions **31–52** answer by choosing from the list of men (**A–E**). Some of the choices may be required more than once.

Note: When more than one answer is required, these may be given **in any order.**

He appreciates the fact that his work has received professional recognition.	**31**		
His job requires a constant high level of concentration.	**32**		
He does not consider himself to be a full-time professional.	**33**		
He has more of a managerial role than he used to.	**34**		
His current career is the result of a desire to work from a permanent location.	**35**		
He is prepared to take limited risks.	**36**	**37**	
He admits that he does not perform one of his duties particularly well.	**38**		**A** John Hughes
He would appreciate greater freedom in one aspect of his work.	**39**		**B** Mick Beasley
He appreciates the ability of the people he is responsible for.	**40**		**C** Johnny Kitts
He gets a sense of satisfaction from knowing people rely on him.	**41**	**42**	**D** Chris Macrae
He appreciates the comments that other people have made about his skills.	**43**		**E** Jarrod Scott
He likes the fact that he is exposed to constant change in his job.	**44**		
He resents the bureaucracy that is part of his job.	**45**		
His training did not require any academic component.	**46**	**47**	
He dislikes the poor conditions that he sometimes has to face.	**48**	**49**	
He accepts the fact that there is a negative aspect to his work.	**50**	**51**	
He likes to see the moods and reactions of each person he is responsible for.	**52**		

Take a step outside!

Do you ever feel 'stuck in the office'? We spoke to five men with outdoor jobs and asked them about the reality of working outside.

A Name: John Hughes   Occupation: Academic Leader for Adventure Recreation

I've been working in the outdoor sports and activities industry since I was 22, but whereas I used to go climbing myself, I've got more of an academic position now I'm at the polytechnic. I work with students and focus my skills on demonstrating how mountaineering groups should be run and organised. The best aspect is the quality of the students but this is the course's first year and we still have to see how it works out. But so far, so good. I've always got a lot out of my work but a day that jumps to mind was when I was working with the Wild South film crew in Antarctica. We had to climb down into the crater of Erebus and the volcano was semi-active that day, but it was the only day the cameras could go down. The volcano was throwing bits and pieces at us, so it was pretty amazing being inside while it was partly erupting. That kind of thing appeals to me. I can't think of anything that is particularly frustrating, other than that sometimes on a lovely day you have to work inside and on a horrible day you're outside. Unfortunately, there isn't currently a way around having enough flexibility in the programme to accommodate that. What does bother me are the endless meetings and things to do within the polytechnic system, which don't always seem relevant to how you might actually improve the programme for students.

B Name: Mick Beasley   Occupation: Mountain Guide

For years I was going back and forth between the USA and New Zealand teaching skiing – 25 winters in a row. Eventually, I just wanted to settle down and find a base. That meant I needed a summer job so I started learning about summer mountain guiding. Now I have a great affection for this season and the advantage of working in a small company is that I'm hardly ever indoors. I prefer trips which aren't technical, but difficult, and where without a guide it would be beyond most people's ability, and it's rewarding to know they appreciate that fact. I only deal with groups of 4–5 people as it's hard to find wilderness when you travel in large numbers. I'm at an age when I resent doing things that I don't enjoy so I offer places to the clients that I want to go to anyway. Dealing with some of the older dilapidated shelters is not always pleasant, especially having to clean up after irresponsible previous occupants. Working with people is not difficult in the mountains; they are so far out of their element that they tend to have faith in you implicitly and are easy to get along with. To do a job like mine I think it's essential that you attend the best courses, although it's not a legal requirement. To go through this training and have other people look at your work and get their input is invaluable.

C Name: Johnny Kitts   Occupation: Jet-boat driver

I've been driving commercially for 18 years on various rivers and every day is a highlight. Probably on a day-to-day basis, it's just the varying nature of the area we operate in. What isn't so pleasant is picking hikers up on dangerous parts of the river. We do get a lot of hikers wanting to cross the river and we try our best to get people in and out of those areas no matter what the conditions are like. There are cut-off points that we believe are not safe to operate above, but mostly we try our hardest to get the trekkers out by boat. There's probably not a dull part with any jet-boat job, especially on commercial trips. You've got to be aware of what is happening all the time, you can't switch off about anything on the trip. That's when the boat ends up stuck in the shallows. I am now more involved in scheduling other drivers, so I don't spend as much time on the river as I did, which is a bit of a downpoint at times. For commercial driving it's learning as you go – time on the river with checks done by the local harbour master. You get a good idea of a driver's ability after about 25 hours. Some people have trouble reading shallow water and if you're colour blind this is a major problem as you can't pick out colouration in the water. It's experience of the river and conditions that counts and that continues for as long as you jet-boat.

D **Name: Chris Macrae   Occupation: Snow photographer**

All my training for this career has been completely hands-on. I've been skiing since I was a kid and was lucky enough to get sponsorship which allowed me to get up to serious competition level. But I'd also been into photography since I was twelve and my camera always went with me to the slopes. This year I was invited to take part in the biggest ski photography competition in the world. There were twelve of the world's best skiers who teamed up with their selected photographer and we had to create the world's most startling ski shots. It was overwhelming just to be asked along to the competition and then I was over the moon to actually win something! I've been skiing in Alaska for seven years now and every time it's unique. Basically my whole life is just waiting for that period to come around. In the meantime, waiting on payment from people you work with is a frustration you have to put up with. It's difficult because sometimes you might spend $400 or $500 on film and then there's the travel costs, and you might not get paid for months while you wait for magazines to run the shots. And filing photos is not my strong point. It's the most tedious and most important part of the job.

E **Name: Jarrod Scott   Occupation: Black-water rafting guide**

The village where we operate is pretty small but it's got great atmosphere and the caves we raft through really are astonishing – a totally different world. One of the best things is meeting people from different backgrounds and you get to see them at their highs and lows. Occasionally some people get scared stiff and I get a lot out of helping someone overcome that. I could do without the freezing cold in the middle of winter when getting into a wetsuit can be a bit of a torture, and I've had a few incidents where clients have completely ignored me because I'm still quite young. I used to get really offended, but now I'm resigned to it. When I started out I had no caving experience so I was 'tagged' for 10 trips. That means you join in like a normal client on a guided trip. During that time the other guides assess you: the idea is that they train you in the technical skills but you won't make a guide if you don't have what it takes regarding personality. Once you're accepted, it's full on into training, like water safety and risk management. It's a good place to work; while the guides are really safety-focused, the atmosphere is pretty laid-back. Having said all this, I love caving but I wouldn't class myself as a caver. In my spare time I prefer aboveground activities like training in different martial arts.

PAPER 2 WRITING 2 hours

Part 1

You **must** answer this question.

1 You work at a health club where there has recently been a fall in the number of members. Your manager has asked you to prepare a report on customer satisfaction.

Read the results of a questionnaire that was given to members on which you have made some notes. Then, **using the information appropriately**, write the **report** for your manager, including recommendations for improvements.

Questionnaire Results:
(125 completed Questionnaires)

	Overall response from customers	Comments	
Showers	Poor	– dirty – poor condition	*fair comment – new ones necessary*
Changing rooms	Poor	– dark + depressing	*Say how we could improve them*
Facilities	Satisfactory	– gym equipment OK, but poor music facilities	*get screens for TV music channels?*
Staff	Good	– helpful – friendly	

Other comments:

• Limited opening hours   *offer earlier opening?*

• Not many health treatments available   *make some suggestions*

Now write your **report** for your manager as outlined above (about 250 words). You should use your own words as far as possible.

Before you write your report, go to page 96.

A DETAILED STUDY

Read the following sample answer to Question 1 on page **95.** When you have read it, answer the questions which follow.

Report on customer satisfaction with the health club

This report is based on a total of 125 questionnaires that members returned to us.

I am happy to say that members are happy with staff and the service they provide. However, there is considerable dissatisfaction with a number of other areas.

Firstly, the condition of the showers and changing rooms was felt to be poor. I realise that the showers were renovated only three years ago but I would strongly recommend that we have them done again. Perhaps the changing rooms could be decorated with lighter colours to create a brighter atmosphere?

Secondly, it might be an idea to install several screens in the gym. Most sports centres now offer this facility as members often like to watch music channels while they work out. It would increase their motivation as many people find exercising very repetitive.

Another possibility might be to increase our range of treatments. I recommend that we employ a physiotherapist to treat our members' sports injuries and a nutritionist to advise people on their diets.

Finally, based on the feedback forms from our members, I suggest that we consider extending our opening hours. More and more people are going to their local gym before work and therefore I feel we should be open from 7am. We could do this for a trial period, of say, two months, and see what effect on membership it has.

I appreciate that all the suggestions above would involve considerable expenditure but I feel that the cost would be worth it in the long term.

---

1   Are all the content points included? Underline the five key points.
2   Who is the writer? Who is the target audience? What effect does the writer want to achieve and what register does he use to do this?
3   In what ways has the writer expanded on the five content points?
4   How has the writer organised the report? How does he make the report clear to read?

FURTHER PRACTICE

A question regarding 'suggestions, advice and recommendations' may require you to be diplomatic and polite when you are writing to a senior person, or someone you need to make a good impression on. As always, the effect on the target reader is vital and for this type of question you will have to choose your language very carefully to achieve the right effect. It is very easy to sound tactless and rude instead of tactful and reassuring if the wrong words and expressions are used.

Look at the pairs of sentences below and choose the sentence which sounds the most polite.

1 a   I **was wondering** if we might hold the conference elsewhere.
    b   I **wonder** if the conference might be held elsewhere.

2 a   I **was hoping** that the office could be redecorated.
    b   I **hope** that the office can be redecorated.

3 a   I **think** that our advertising might need some changes.
    b   I **was thinking** that our advertising might need some changes.

4 a   **Could we** go to a different venue?
    b   **Would it be possible to** go to a different venue?

5 a   **Perhaps** we could encourage younger people to join our group.
    b   **Maybe** we could encourage younger people to join our group.

6 a   I suggest **you should reduce the prices** if possible.
    b   I suggest **that the prices should be reduced** if possible.

7 a   I **feel** that our employees' morale **would** improve if we **gave** them a bonus.
    b   I **think** that our employees' morale **will** improve if we **give** them a bonus.

8 a   If we **offer** our visitors a range, I feel certain that there **will** be far fewer complaints.
    b   If we **offered** our visitors a range, I feel certain that there **would** be far fewer complaints.

Part 2

Choose **one** of the following writing tasks. Your answer should follow exactly the instructions given. Write approximately 250 words.

2   You have received a letter from a friend in England whose son is at school. Read the following extract from your friend's letter.

> Simon's doing a project on 'eating habits around the world'. It would be great if you could send him a description of eating habits in your country – something about usual meal times, traditional meals and any changes to eating habits you have noticed in recent years.

Write your **letter** to Simon.

3   A television company is looking for locations to include in a documentary about your country. You have been asked to choose a location and submit a proposal, explaining:

– why you feel this location would be an important part of the documentary
– what local features you would include and why
– what different groups of people you would interview and why.

Write your **proposal**.

4   Your local English language newspaper has asked you to contribute a section on how to prevent minor crimes in your area, explaining what kind of minor crimes are occurring and giving advice on how to prevent them.

Write your **contribution**.

5   Your company has recently sent you on two different courses and is considering which course other employees should attend. You have been asked to write a memo describing the content of each course and giving reasons why one is more suitable for employees in your department than the other.

Write your **memo**.

PAPER 3 ENGLISH IN USE 1 hour 30 minutes

Part 1

For questions **1–15**, read the text below and then decide which word on page **100** best fits each space. The exercise begins with an example **(0)**. In the exam you will put the letter for each question on a separate answer sheet.

Example: | 0 | D |

VENICE UNDER WATER

A team of experts has arrived in Venice to save it from increasing **(0)** ..*incidences*.... of flooding. A controversial plan to construct a barrier with 79 gates, each weighing 300 tonnes, has been given permission to **(1)** .... ahead. Once constructed, this will be **(2)** .... whenever a high tide **(3)** .... to cover the city.

Everyone has known for centuries that Venice is **(4)** .... further into the mud, but floods are becoming a regular nuisance. Rising sea levels have gradually **(5)** .... the salt marshes and mud-banks that **(6)** .... between the city and the Adriatic. Winter storms cause higher waves, which are **(7)** .... the walls of the old palaces.

But there are fears about how the **(8)** .... of such a barrier might affect the Venice lagoon, particularly the possibility that it could further **(9)** .... the flushing of the city's waterways by the tide, making the famous foul-smelling canals even more **(10)** ....

To avoid making a bad situation worse, the experts have been **(11)** .... to analyse tidal flows, marine plants and sediment deposits, and then suggest ways to prevent the city becoming the first high-profile **(12)** .... of global warming and rising sea levels.

But with global warming **(13)** .... to add at least another half metre to the sea level this century, the situation is bound to **(14)** .... A spokesman for the team said, 'We cannot hope to stop Venice submerging eventually, but we can slow the whole **(15)** .... down and so enjoy the city for a while longer.'

0	**A**	situations	**B**	circumstances	**C**	occasions	**D**	incidences
1	**A**	be	**B**	proceed	**C**	go	**D**	advance
2	**A**	erected	**B**	raised	**C**	lifted	**D**	installed
3	**A**	threatens	**B**	endangers	**C**	risks	**D**	jeopardizes
4	**A**	decaying	**B**	sinking	**C**	collapsing	**D**	falling
5	**A**	eroded	**B**	worn	**C**	corrupted	**D**	broken
6	**A**	faced	**B**	occurred	**C**	featured	**D**	stood
7	**A**	offending	**B**	crashing	**C**	assaulting	**D**	opposing
8	**A**	building	**B**	theory	**C**	intention	**D**	result
9	**A**	delay	**B**	direct	**C**	restrict	**D**	impose
10	**A**	motionless	**B**	stationary	**C**	inactive	**D**	stagnant
11	**A**	asked over	**B**	brought in	**C**	called up	**D**	taken on
12	**A**	victim	**B**	target	**C**	sufferer	**D**	subject
13	**A**	believed	**B**	imagined	**C**	expected	**D**	supposed
14	**A**	destabilise	**B**	deflate	**C**	detract	**D**	deteriorate
15	**A**	damage	**B**	process	**C**	water	**D**	event

Part 2

For questions **16–30**, read the text below and think of the word which best fits each space. **Use only one word in each space**. The exercise begins with an example **(0)**. In the exam you will mark your answers on a separate answer sheet.

Example: | **0** | *would* |

Too late to learn?

After I had fallen over for the eighth time in 25 minutes, I realized I **(0)** ...*would*... not be able to teach

myself to ski. I had fallen forwards, backwards and to both sides. I had landed on my wrists, arms,

knees, thighs and shoulders and it seemed **(16)** .... were no new ways left, **(17)** .... I was

going to **(18)** .... knocked down by someone else. I asked a friend **(19)** .... I could do to

improve my technique. 'Stop crashing into things,' she said, at **(20)** .... point I gave up. I tucked

my skis under one arm, dropped them, tucked them under the **(21)** .... and stomped home through

the snow in my very uncomfortable snow boots. **(22)** .... my anger, I booked a lesson

with an instructor called Jane who was surprised that a 37-year-old could live life **(23)** .... no

co-ordination. It was **(24)** .... disability that meant my first lesson was wildly unsuccessful.

The difference **(25)** .... skiing and sliding out of control down a steep hill is **(26)** .... ability

to 'snowplough', meaning that you have to position the skis in an open V-shape with the apex parallel

to your nose. If you **(27)** .... make a snowplough, you simply aren't going to stop. I found

(28) .... impossible to turn my feet to the correct angle, and when I finally **(29)** .... make a

V-shape, it was **(30)** .... wide I could not move out of it! Jane was unimpressed.

Part 3

In **most** lines of the following text, there is **one** unnecessary word. It is either grammatically incorrect or does not fit in with the sense of the text. For each numbered line **31–46**, find this word. Some lines are correct. Indicate these with a tick (✓). The exercise begins with two examples **(0)** and **(00)**. In the exam you will write your answers on a separate answer sheet.

Examples:

0	*its*
00	✓

Book reviews on-line

0   Although the act of writing a book is by its necessity a solitary process,

00   it's often after publication that the sense of isolation is strongest. Many

31   writers long for their critical feedback, but have little access to the average

32   reader's opinion. While it may not be true that good reviews in newspapers

33   and magazines can be gratifying, they're of little help in establishing what

34   do ordinary people think of your work. So, well done to those websites

35   where anyone with access to the internet can post an own opinion about

36   any book. Having said this, these customer reviews are not without risk.

37   Most of writers can expect some glowing praise from family or friends

38   but these reviews are easy to recognize since they tend to be sent in there

39   anonymously. On the other hand, visits to these websites can also result

40   in great anxiety. It might well be the case that you receive such an unkind

41   review and there is no kind editor to shield you feelings. You can expect

42   most reviewers to be brief but there are those who too write long, strangely

43   formal essays, which usually containing references to classical literature,

44   presumably in an attempt to impress on others with their literary knowledge.

45   If you are a sensitive author, I suggest you to think twice before you go off

46   searching for reviews on-line rather than in the safer, traditional places.

Before you check your answers, go to page 103.

WHAT'S TESTED?

Part 3 of the English in Use Paper is a correction exercise of which there are two types. In the first, you have to identify extra words which have been included in the text; in the second you have to identify spelling and punctuation errors.

TIPS

- Don't just look at the numbered line when deciding if there is a mistake. Always read the complete sentence, which may involve looking at the preceding and following lines.
- Make sure that if you are copying (correct) words from the paper, you do not misspell the word. You will lose a mark if you do.

A DETAILED STUDY

Before you check your answers, study the following pairs of sentences. (The numbers match the line numbers in the text.)

31   Jill was tired and longed for her bed. (*bed* = countable noun)

Jill longed for feedback on her work. (*feedback* = uncountable noun)

32   A: I think the four of us should hire a car. It's cheaper than going by train.

B: While that may be true, if we travel by train we will get to the coast faster. (= Although that is true)

B: That may not be true because there's a special offer on train fares at the moment.

34   An English-Japanese dictionary is not much help in finding out what colloquial words mean.

What do you think of my new dictionary?

35   My partner and I don't always agree. She has her own opinion about certain things.

My partner has an opinion about eating meat that I just don't agree with.

37   Most of the museums I've visited in London have been quite interesting.

Most museums are quite interesting.

38   I sent in my application form yesterday.

John went to Paris last week. He was sent there to improve his French.

40   She asked him to carry such a heavy suitcase that he couldn't lift it.

She asked him to carry a heavy suitcase but he couldn't lift it.

41   Sunglasses shield your eyes from the sun.

When the lion approached the young zebra, its mother shielded it.

42   I am scared of spiders and there are other people who too have this phobia.

I think the car you want to buy is too expensive.

43   He hates flying, which usually means we have a holiday at home.

He hates flying, meaning we usually have a holiday at home.

44   They tried to impress on their children the importance of a good education.

They tried to impress me with their brand new sports car.

45   I advise you to think carefully before you accept that job.

I suggest you take traveler's cheques with you, not cash.

Now check your answers to Part 3 of the test.

Part 4

For questions **47–61**, read the two texts on pages **104** and **105**. Use the words in the boxes to the right of the two texts to form **one** word which fits in the same numbered space in the text. The exercise begins with an example **(0)**. In the exam you will write your answers on a separate answer sheet.

Example: | 0 | *fluency* |

ADVERTISEMENT

Bilingual Graduates Required for Sunworld Travel

Sunworld Travel is currently looking for recent graduates who are interested in a career in tourism.

If you

- have a high degree of **(0)** ...*fluency*... in two or more languages

- are **(47)** .... and hard-working

- are ambitious and would like to **(48)** .... in the travel industry

then come along to our **(49)** .... day to be held on 16th

March, at the Queen's Hotel, South Malden. We have

(50) .... in various departments, but **(51)** .... will be

given to **(52)** .... who are willing to travel abroad or be

willing to **(53)** .... in the UK.

0	**FLUENT**
47	RELY
48	SUCCESS
49	RECRUIT
50	VACANT
51	PREFER
52	APPLY
53	LOCATION

ARTICLE

It's noisy in space!

Inside the International Space Station, it is so noisy that the astronauts cannot hear one another. As a result, United States and Russian engineers have launched a **(54)** .... repair programme which they hope will lead to the **(55)** .... of the station's 72-decibel roar: the equivalent of standing beside a busy motorway. 'It is not a **(56)** .... situation,' said Mike Engle, a **(57)** .... for the engineering team. 'Apart from astronauts losing sleep, there is a danger one of them will **(58)** .... a colleague's instruction and press an incorrect button!' Ironically, most of the noise comes from the equipment needed to keep them alive. 'The coolers are the worst,' Mr Engles explained. 'But without them, the station would become **(59)** .... hot! When we put together the station we faced a choice. We could either spend extra years **(60)** .... that the station would be totally quiet, or we could get on and build the thing. Now it's assembled, we are doing our best to **(61)** .... it down.'

54	PRIOR
55	REDUCE
56	HEALTH
57	SPEAK
58	HEAR
59	BEAR
60	SURE
61	QUIET

Part 5

For questions **62–74**, read the following informal note about the opening of a new children's park.
Use the information in the note to complete the numbered gaps in the formal letter to a local celebrity which
follows. The words you need **do not** occur in the informal note. **Use no more than two words for each
gap.** The exercise begins with an example **(0)**. In the exam you will write your answers on a separate
answer sheet.

Example:

0	*behalf of*

INFORMAL NOTE

MEMORANDUM

John

Good news! You know I wrote and asked Steve Peterson to open the children's park – well, he's agreed! We're
bound to get loads more people coming along now – all wanting his autograph probably. Anyway, can you write
to him and say thanks from all of us? Remind him that we want to make about £3,000 on the day (the money, of
course, is for buying more stuff for the Activities Hut like binoculars for bird-watching, notice boards for the
kids' pictures, etc.). Mention that we have 2 things in mind: first, Katy Marsden has agreed to take photos all
day long and cheaply, too. Then, there's the huge amount of stuff the local businesses have given us for the
prize draw. Maybe you could ask Steve if he'd mind picking out the winning ticket? And tell him how grateful
we are for everything he's doing for us!

Thanks

Lizzie

FORMAL LETTER

THE GREEN PROJECT
Stapleton Grange ● Heathfield ● E. Sussex

Dear Mr Peterson,

I am writing to thank you on **(0)** ..*behalf of*.... all the members of THE GREEN PROJECT for agreeing
to open the new children's park next month.

We are certain that your **(62)** .... of our invitation will mean a great number of people will now
attend the event. As I believe our director Lizzie Brent mentioned to you in her previous letter, we are
hoping to **(63)** .... a considerable amount of money on the opening day which will **(64)** .... to
purchase further **(65)** .... for the Activities Hut. Our target is £3,000 and we **(66)** .... two events
which we hope will enable us **(67)** .... it.

Firstly, we have **(68)** .... for a photographer from the local newspaper to spend the day taking
professional portrait shots of families for a **(69)** .... Secondly, we are asking local businesses to
(70) .... for a prize draw and so far, the response has been **(71)** .... We were **(72)** ....
whether you would also **(73)** .... enough to draw the winning ticket for us.

Once again, I would like to **(74)** .... appreciation for your support and encouragement.

Yours sincerely
John Carter   (Social Secretary)

Before you check your answers, go to page 107.

WHAT'S TESTED?

Part 5 of the English in Use Paper tests your ability to transfer the content of one text to another, but using a different register. This means that you may be given an informal text to read (a note, a memo, a set of instructions or directions, a friendly letter) and you have to rewrite or re-organise the information in a more formal way (a formal letter, a job advertisement, a report, etc.). Or, you may be given something formal to read and have to write it in a more informal way. You are **not** tested on acronyms or short forms (a.s.a.p = as soon as possible / etc. = et cetera), and you are **not** allowed to use the words or a form of the word that the original text contains.

A DETAILED STUDY

Read the informal letter and memo in 1 and 2 below. Then use the underlined information to complete the formal letters by choosing a word or phrase from the box.

	whether	however	convenient	large	currently
contact	advance	(re)confirm	further	grateful	considerable
require	enquire	vacancy	would like	should	in advance

1   INFORMAL LETTER

Dear Jonathon,

I read your advertisement the other day and I just (1) <u>wanted</u> to (2) <u>ask</u> (3) <u>if</u> there was (4) <u>any chance of a job</u> (5) <u>Right now</u> I'm working as a receptionist in a (6) <u>big</u> hotel in London and before that in a hotel in Brighton so I've got (7) <u>lots</u> of experience.

(8) <u>It'd be great</u> if you could send me the application form,
Yours,

Kara Clarke

FORMAL LETTER

Dear Mr Vargas,

I read your advertisement in this month's issue of 'Hotel and Catering' and I
(1) .... to (2) .... (3) .... you still have a
(4) .... for the position of receptionist.

I am (5) .... working as a receptionist for a (6) ....hotel in London and prior to this, I was employed by the 'Royal Brighton' for five years. I therefore feel that I have (7) .... experience in this kind of work.

I would be (8) .... if you could send me an application form.

Yours sincerely,

Kara Clarke

2 MEMO

> Things to do: Answer Mr King's letter about his class's visit to our company:
> – (1) <u>yes – it is possible</u> for them to come in July.
> – (2) <u>but</u> – on July 3, not the 13th. – (3) <u>tell us</u> if this isn't (4) <u>OK</u>.
> – he should (5) <u>let us know</u> two weeks (6) <u>before</u> the visit if he's still coming.
> – (7) <u>if</u> he (8) <u>needs</u> any (9) <u>more</u> information, he can ring me at work.

FORMAL LETTER

Dear Mr King,

With reference to your letter concerning a class visit to our company, I am happy to (1) .... that this would be possible in July.

(2) ...., we would prefer it if the visit were conducted on July 3rd instead of the 13th. Please would you (3) .... me if this time is not (4) .... , so we can make an alternative arrangement.

We would be grateful if you could (5) .... this booking two weeks (6) ....

(7) .... you (8) .... any (9) .... information, please do not hesitate to contact me.

Yours sincerely,

Sharon Samuels

Now check your answers to Part 5 of the test.

Part 6

For questions **75–80**, read the following text and then choose from the list **A–J** given below the best phrase to fill each of the spaces. Each correct phrase may only be used once. **Some of the suggested answers do not fit at all.** The exercise begins with an example **(0)**. In the exam you will write your answers on a separate answer sheet.

Example: | 0 | J |

What made the mysterious patterns in the wheat fields?

The first picture of a strange pattern in a British wheat field appeared on television in the late 1970s **(0)** ....*J*..... . However, by the early 1980s, the patterns were getting larger and sometimes there were groups of six or more **(75)** .... The media took notice and the resulting publicity attracted hoards of mystics and scientists. While the mystics claimed the patterns were caused by UFOs or by cosmic energy, the scientists put it down to unusual weather conditions, **(76)** .... The patterns couldn't have been created by humans working under cover of darkness **(77)** .... As the patterns in the fields grew more elaborate, they became tourist attractions **(78)** .... As the mystery deepened, the patterns were discussed in Parliament, debated on TV and written about by the press.

Then in 1991, two elderly men told a British newspaper that they were responsible for the patterns. They claimed they'd made the first one as a joke one Friday night in 1978 **(79)** .... They proudly admitted to creating around 1,000 patterns, and to prove it, they created one while a reporter watched. In the article that followed, the reporter expressed his amazement at how simple the process was, which involved string, a pole and some wooden planks, **(80)** .... While they accepted that the men had been responsible for some of the patterns, this didn't explain the 9,000 others.

A   but many people still thought there was more to it
B   because there would never be time enough
C   and that this had continued over 13 years
D   which would appear in the same field overnight
E   but there was one matter both agreed on
F   because these were unlikely to be considered
G   which in turn offered a financial opportunity to farmers
H   and nobody would have noticed for those reasons
I   which seemed to be the most convincing so far

J   but at this point nobody paid much attention

PAPER 4 LISTENING approximately 45 minutes

Part 1

You will hear a radio presenter talking about an extreme-sports event that takes place in Britain. For questions **1–9**, fill in the missing information.

You will hear the recording **twice**.

New event called: *The National Adventure Sports Show*

It takes place from Friday to [_____ **1**]

Expect to see lots of high-speed thrills and [_____ **2**]

Up to [_____ **3**] people could be there.

On sale – lots of sports wear and [_____ **4**]

Apart from competitions, there's also a [_____ **5**]

Fans says the festival has a [_____ **6**]

The organisers want people to see [_____ **7**] from other countries.

Weather this weekend: sunny and [_____ **8**]

The festival is being broadcast by [_____ **9**]

Part 2

You will hear part of a radio programme in which the presenter is talking about a report on current eating habits in Britain. For questions **10–18**, complete the notes the presenter is using.

Listen very carefully as you will hear the recording ONCE only.

Report: UK Food trends

Chinese food has replaced [_____ **10**] as the nation's favourite.

Total no. of restaurant meals eaten last year:
[_____ **11**]

5,410 [_____ **12**] restaurants vs. 5,200 Indian restaurants.

Italian restaurants more popular than [_____ **13**] restaurants.

'Fusion cuisine': a combination of food from [_____ **14**]

40% of restaurants are part of [_____ **15**]

The survey doesn't include takeaways and [_____ **16**]

Most people eat out every [_____ **17**]

30% of restaurants said they made a [_____ **18**] last year.

Part 3

You will hear a radio interview with a researcher for an advertising agency. For questions **19–28**, complete the notes.

You will hear the recording **twice**.

When people reach the age of 35, their spending habits [_____ 19]

Billions of pounds are wasted on advertisements aimed at the [_____ 20]

Married couples are unlikely to be [_____ 21] by new trends.

A quarter of the British advertising budget is spent on [_____ 22]

Older people are important to advertisers because they are the [_____ 23]
of the market.

The UK, France and the United States have a [_____ 24] of young people.

Darren says older people no longer worry about being [_____ 25]

Older people prefer to feel [_____ 26]

Future advertising aimed at older consumers will concentrate on quality and
[_____ 27]

According to Darren, there is a big gap between teenage consumers and the people who
[_____ 28]

Part 4

You will hear five short extracts in which various people are talking about an aspect of tourism. While you listen, you must complete **both** tasks.

You will hear the recording **twice**.

TASK ONE

For questions **29–33**, match the extracts as you hear them with the people, listed **A–H**.

A   pilot

B   restaurant owner | 29 |

C   tour guide | 30 |

D   coach driver | 31 |

E   flight attendant | 32 |

F   tourist

G   hotel receptionist | 33 |

H   travel agent

TASK TWO

For questions **34–38**, match the extracts as you hear them with the words that best describe each speaker's attitude, listed **A–H**.

A   irritated

B   unenthusiastic | 34 |

C   worried | 35 |

D   curious | 36 |

E   accepting | 37 |

F   afraid | 38 |

G   disappointed

H   angry

In the exam you will have 10 minutes at the end of the test to copy your answers onto a separate answer sheet.

Before you check your answers, go to page 114.

A DETAILED STUDY

Listen again to Part 4 of the test on page **113** and answer the following questions by either writing **T** (true) or **F** (false) in the box provided. You may wish to change your answers to this part of the test after you have done this.

Speaker 1 says:

1   she has a job she always wanted. ☐

2   she stays in hotels. ☐

3   she enjoys a good social life. ☐

4   she travels long distances by plane. ☐

5   her work is repetitive. ☐

6   she has to deal with complaints. ☐

7   the job is what she expected it to be. ☐

Speaker 2 says:

8   she works at an airport. ☐

9   she is affected by plane delays. ☐

10   she has to wait for tourists to arrive. ☐

11   she doesn't mind working overtime. ☐

12   she is often told she has to stay at work at short notice. ☐

Speaker 3 says:

13   he helps customers find what they're looking for. ☐

14   some customers take a long time to make decisions. ☐

15   his customers have to pay a lot of money. ☐

16   he finds his customers' behaviour irritating. ☐

Speaker 4 says:

17   he has enjoyed holidays in St Lucia and Antigua. ☐

18   he knows a lot about Greek history. ☐

19   he is interested in learning about Greek customs. ☐

20   he is anxious about making mistakes. ☐

Speaker 5 says:

21   he was willing to go to an art gallery. ☐

22   he is responsible for a group of people. ☐

23   he would prefer to relax than go sightseeing. ☐

24   he believes that every statue he sees is unique. ☐

Now check your answers to Part 4 of the test.

PAPER 5 SPEAKING

Part 2 (4 minutes)

1 Protective clothing

For both candidates
Look at the pictures on page 150. They each show people who require protective clothing and equipment in their work.

Candidate A: Describe two of these pictures, saying what protective clothing and equipment the people require and how it protects them. (*1 minute*)

Candidate B: Say what protective clothing and equipment the person in the other picture requires and how it protects them. (*20 seconds*)

2 Emotions

For both candidates
Look at the photographs on page 150. They show people experiencing different emotions.

Candidate B: Say what you think the relationship is between the people in the photographs, what emotions they might each be feeling and what could have happened to make them feel this way. (*1 minute*)

Candidate A: Say what you think the people in the picture might be saying to one another. (*20 seconds*)

For Further Practice and Guidance, go to page 116.

Part 3 (4 minutes) Happiness

For both candidates
Look at the pictures on page 151. Talk to each other and discuss how these different things might contribute to people's happiness, and how people might sometimes find them disappointing. Then say which three things you think would offer the most satisfaction in the long term.

Part 4 (4 minutes) Further discussion

For both candidates
- What other aspects of life make people happy?
- Are the things that make people happy today different to what made people happy in the past?
- How far do you agree with the statement 'Money can't buy happiness'?
- What role do you think advertising plays in people's ideas of how to achieve happiness?
- What would you to like to achieve in your life that would give you a sense of satisfaction?

PAPER 5

WHAT'S TESTED

In Part 2 of the Speaking Paper, you may be asked to hypothesize and speculate about a set of pictures. This means that you need to guess what the situation in the picture is, or what people are feeling, or what they have just done etc. You should avoid saying, e.g. 'He is a businessman on a business trip' or 'This little girl has got lost – that's why she looks upset.'

A DETAILED STUDY

Using the examples of speculative language below, take turns with your partner to be the interlocutor and the student and do the task on 'Emotions'.

* *It looks to me as if/as though…*

* *It seems/appears that…*

* *The impression I get is that…*

* *It could/might be that…*

* *She/he/they could/might be/have, etc.*

* *She/he/they could/might have been/seen, etc.*

* *She/he/they could be/might be + -ing*

* *Judging by…*

* *I imagine that…*

* *I'd guess that…*

TEST FOUR

PAPER 1 READING 1 hour 15 minutes

Part 1

Answer questions **1–18** by referring to the book reviews on page **118**. In the exam, you will mark your answers on a separate answer sheet.

For questions **1–18**, answer by choosing from the list (**A–D**) on the right below. Some of the choices may be required more than once.

Of which book is the following stated?

Its particular ideas make it stand out from books with the same broad theme.	**1**	
The progress of the storyline sometimes takes second place to character development.	**2**	
It can be read slowly or quickly with equal enjoyment.	**3**	
It shows great insight into the way people think.	**4**	
It brings to mind a variety of moods.	**5**	
It has received other good reviews.	**6**	
It is difficult to remember who all the characters are.	**7**	**A** Halfway to Africa
Character development is dealt with briefly but effectively.	**8**	
The characters all suffer from the same kind of problem.	**9**	**B** The Devil's Larder
Its amusing style holds the reader's attention.	**10**	**C** Life of Pi
The reader is deliberately made to keep guessing what will happen next.	**11**	**D** The Emperor of Ocean Park
There is hardly any detail about where the action takes place.	**12**	
It contains conversation which seems realistic.	**13**	
It is likely to cause conflicting reactions in readers.	**14**	
One of the characters does not come across as convincing.	**15**	
The complicated storyline requires concentration from the reader.	**16**	
It deals with themes that are both deep and ordinary.	**17**	
Its title may mislead readers about the content.	**18**	

This season's new books

A   Halfway to Africa by Bronwyn Tate

If the words *Halfway to Africa* conjure up visions of the exotic, forget it. It's a metaphor for where most of us are in our lives – halfway to somewhere more interesting than the place in which we seem stuck, but this is not a gloomy novel either. The characters are ordinary people and Tate has the knack of articulating the awkwardness of social intercourse when difficult decisions are made or when conversation fails. There are dissatisfactions, though. The key characters are two sisters who are friends rather than rivals during their childhood. Tate's portrayal of Monica struck me as inconsistent. She has a university degree and, after her marriage and the birth of her two sons, spends the evening in a darkroom working on her photography. During the day she cleans other people's houses – for the satisfaction of restoring order out of chaos, rather than for economic necessity. Structurally, this novel has its challenges. We're expected to keep track of a plethora of characters and their relationships to one another as well as the time frame within which a particular chapter operates. This stems partly from the desire to maintain suspense but that's less of a problem if you can read the book in large chunks.

B   *The Devil's Larder* by Jim Crace

As this is a collection of brief short stories connected only by the theme of food and not by characters or plot, the *Devil's Larder* should not come close to satisfying. I suspect it's only because Jim Crace enjoys an auspicious shake of the talent dice that they do. Such a varied plate of ideas and situations can be partaken of at leisure, but it is delivered with enough pace, momentum and invention that it can be consumed in one go without a touch of indigestion. The tales are rich with the intimate links between eating, ritual and relationships: the piece of dough left on the window for the angels; the masterful letter to a longtime lunch friend; the eating of stolen deer. The backstory of the characters in these tales is revealed in just a few words. Little is wasted on precise geographic location, but sparse descriptions are still evocative. We are not sure either if the narrator is male or female. There are spooky and wry tales, sad and bleak, while the cute and touching ones should meanwhile remind you of what fun he must have had while working on the book. All of them have been written with great style and tone and all are imbued with a loving tenderness.

C   *Life of Pi* by Yann Martel

This ingenious and gently philosophical novel by Martel has enjoyed great critical acclaim, and it is easy to see why. The witty narrative engages from the start, making probing digressions into matters of faith and commonly held belief, and involves an Indian boy, Pi, adrift on a lifeboat with a Bengal tiger. During his peculiar isolation on the lifeboat, the young Pi questions the nature of existence. Here Martel offers witty and insightful comments with Pi as his mouthpiece. But Pi/Martel also questions more mundane precepts. It is almost an accepted fact that zoos are anathema to right-thinking people but his witty and eloquent defence of them – how animals in the wild are far from free but live in constant terror – makes for amusing and politically incorrect reading. There is a great tradition of isolation literature and there are multiple isolations here, emotional and intellectual as much as physical, but it is what Pi reflects upon which is uniquely engrossing. Readers will no doubt find *Life of Pi* to be a highly readable and a pleasingly troublesome book – especially in the hallucinatory ending – that irritates as often as it brings a smile.

D   *The Emperor of Ocean Park* by Stephen L. Carter

Since a publisher broke records by bidding $4.2 million for it, this book was a legend before it rolled off the press. A sprawling legal thriller set amid the affluent, east-coast African-American community, this is a big book – 650 pages – and takes its own time to get through. The pages teem with characters and subplots and you can't afford to ignore any of them. And beneath the crowded stage, the common ground between all the players, is the undeniable chasm of loneliness – of being alone in a crowd – that indeed seems to underlie American society and often its literature. Our hero, a law professor at a top-notch university, reflects matter-of-factly at one point on 'how friendless an existence I have managed to create.' Carter's skill lies not just in his superb management of the complex plot, which has as its motif a particularly complicated chess manoeuvre, but in his ability to sketch a state of mind, or a dilemma. For a thriller, the pacing is frustratingly slow at times as Carter indulges his delight in character construction. If you have time on your hands, you could probably relax into this discursive style and simply enjoy the slow escalation of tension and danger.

Part 2

For questions **19–24**, choose which of the paragraphs **A–G** on page **120** fit into the numbered gaps in the following newspaper article. There is one extra paragraph which does not fit into any of the gaps. In the exam, you will mark your answers on a separate answer sheet.

Baby Talk

All those gasps and gurgles that babies make may mean something after all, researchers have found.

There is no basis to this strange feeling that your infant is smiling at you, and smiling because he knows you're his mother. He might look as wise as the ages when he gazes into your eyes – but face up to the facts. There's nothing in there, unless we count the blank slate. And don't read too much into his babbling either. He's just learning how to use his face muscles. That's what my doctor told me when I took my baby for his check-ups. I doubted this, but I knew science was on her side so I kept my opinion to myself.

19	

This is not just hopeful theorising. Thanks to new technology that allows scientists to study living brains, the bank of evidence is growing fast. Another great advance was made last week with the publication of research by neuroscientist Laura Ann Petitto of Dartmouth College. The aim of the study was to challenge the traditional understanding of early language development, which holds that babies must develop motor skills before they can begin to connect sounds to meanings.

20	

They looked at the way babies moved their mouths when babbling (making sounds with a consonant-vowel repetition) and contrasted this with the movements when they smiled or made non-babbling noises. They studied five English infants, five French infants and five Spanish to be sure they weren't studying mouth movements specific to one language.

21	

'The mouth is being carved out depending on the function of what's coming out,' Petitto explains. 'And this function could only occur if different parts of the brain are participating in the control of different functions.' Her researchers deduced that 'the right side of the face – used for smiling – is controlled by the left hemisphere of the brain, where the emotional control centres are located.' But babbling 'is a left-side mouth function and controlled by the right side of the brain – the centre for speech.'

22	

And that is not all it can do. According to other researchers in the field, babies can 'distinguish human faces and voices from other sights and sounds and prefer them'. Although they are born short-sighted, they can see people and items clearly at a distance of about 30 cms. Their preference for stripes and other patterns shows they are imposing order on their perceptions in early infancy. Long before they can crawl, they can tell the difference between happy features and sad features.

23	

They can grasp simple arithmetic by using the same capacity, according to Petitto. 'It is well established that infants look longer at things that are unexpected or surprising to them. In a recent study, the researchers built up the expectation that a puppet would jump, say two times.' When the infants lost interest, they continued to show one group of infants what they had already been watching. Another group was shown a puppet that jumped three times. Petitto explains, 'The infants looked longer at the puppet when it jumped three times, showing they had detected the change in number.'

24	

But this is not the end of the story, as the nature side of the nature/nurture divide has claimed for so long. Despite this standard capacity, babies depend on their vast reserves of innate knowledge in the way you and I depend on the programs we put into our computers. What matters most is what we do with these programs, and it's the same with babies. They're born with powerful learning tools that allow them to explore and learn about the world around them. And what they learn goes on to determine the way their brains are wired, and how they think.

A   'What this tells us', says Petitto, 'is that 'language processing starts far earlier than we ever thought and without much language experience. As young as five months, the brain is already discriminating between a purely physical response and an oral one.'

B   But they depend on more than innate knowledge and learning abilities. People instinctively want to help babies learn. A lot of this tuition is, they claim, unconscious and unwilled. The typical example would be the stern businessman who, if left holding the baby, lapses into baby talk.

C   The results showed uniformity in all cases. When the babies smiled, they opened the left sides of their mouths, using more muscles on the left side of the face. When they were making 'non-babbling' noises they used the middle of the mouth, and when they babbled they pulled down on the right side of the mouth, using more right-side muscles.

D   Now at last it is science that is having second thoughts. It turns out that babies know a lot more than our best minds previously suspected. If they smile, it may well be because they recognise your voice. When they babble, they are probably not speaking nonsense but practising speech.

E   This is borne out by the fact that they can imitate these same expressions, and by the time they're old enough to pick up a phone they can mimic what they've seen others doing with it. This means they can learn how to use things just by watching people.

F   So much for the blank slate then. Much of this research would seem to disprove many of our oldest and fondest assumptions, not just about speech but about how people are like us and how we are like other people. It appears that our brains all start out with the same approach to learning and development.

G   Petitto and her team take a different view. 'When a child babbles, it's not just trying to get control over its facial muscles,' she says. Babies are 'literally trying to say the sounds' they hear, and trying to make sense of 'the patterns of sounds in the world around them.'

Part 3

Read the following newspaper article and then answer questions **25–30** on page **122**. Indicate the letter **A**, **B**, **C** or **D** against the number of each question **25–30**. Give only one answer to each question. In the exam, you will mark your answers on a separate answer sheet.

Are you a tourist or a traveller?

Less than 40 years ago, tourism was encouraged as an unquestionable good. With the arrival of package holidays and charter flights, tourism could at last be enjoyed by the masses. Yet one day, it seems feasible that there will be no more tourists. There will be 'adventurers', 'fieldwork assistants', 'volunteers' and, of course, 'travellers'. But the term 'tourist' will be extinct. There might be those who quietly slip away to foreign lands for nothing other than pure pleasure, but it will be a secretive and frowned upon activity. No one will want to own up to being *one* of *those*. In fact, there are already a few countries prohibiting tourists from entering certain areas where the adverse effects of tourism have already struck. Tourists have been charged with bringing nothing with them but their money and wreaking havoc with the local environment.

It won't be easy to wipe out this massive, ever growing tribe. Today there are more than 700 million 'tourist arrivals' each year. The World Tourism Organisation forecasts that by 2020, there will be 1.56 billion tourists travelling at any one time. The challenge to forcibly curtail more than a billion tourists from going where they want is immense. It is so immense as to be futile. You cannot make so many economically empowered people stop doing something they want to do unless you argue that it is of extreme damage to the welfare of the world that only the truly malicious, utterly selfish and totally irresponsible would ever even consider doing it. This is clearly absurd. Whatever benefits or otherwise accrue from tourism, it is not, despite what a tiny minority say, evil. It can cause harm. It can be morally neutral. And it can, occasionally, be a force for great good.

So tourism is being attacked by more subtle methods, by being re-branded in the hope we won't recognise it as the unattractive entity it once was. The word 'tourist' is being removed from anything that was once called a holiday in the pamphlet that was once called a holiday brochure. Adventurers, fieldwork assistants and volunteers don't go on holidays. 'Un-tourists' (as I will call them) go on things called 'cultural experiences', 'expeditions', 'projects' and most tellingly, 'missions'. The word 'mission' is, perhaps unintentionally, fitting. While this re-branding is supposed to present a progressive approach to travel, it is firmly rooted in the viewpoint of the Victorian era. Like nineteenth-century Victorian travellers, the modern day un-tourist insists that the main motive behind their adventure is to help others. Whereas the mass tourist and the area they visit are condemned as anti-ethical and at loggerheads, the ethos of the un-tourist and the needs of the area they wander into are presumed to be in tune with each other.

The re-packaging of tourism as meaningful, self-sacrificing travel is liberating. It allows you to go to all sorts of places that would be ethically out of bounds to a regular tourist under the guise of mission. Indeed, the theory behind un-tourism relies upon exclusivity; it is all about preventing other people travelling in order that you might legitimise your own travels. Mass tourists are, by definition, excluded from partaking of this new kind of un-tourism. Pretending you are not doing something that you actually are – i.e. going on holiday – is at the heart of the un-tourist endeavour. Every aspect of the experience has to be disguised. So, gone are the glossy brochures. Instead the expeditions, projects and adventures are advertised in publications more likely to resemble magazines with a concern in ecological or cultural issues. The price is usually well hidden as if there is a reluctance to admit that this is, in essence, a commercial transaction. There is something disturbing in having to pay to do good.

Meaningful contact with and respect for local culture also concerns the un-tourist. In the third world, respect for local culture is based on a presumed innate inability within that culture to understand that there are other ways of living to their own. They are portrayed, in effect, as being perplexed by our newness, and their culture is presented as so vulnerable that a handful of western tourists poses a huge threat. This is despite the fact that many of these cultures are more rooted, ancient and have survived far longer than any culture in the first world. None of this ought to matter as un-tourism makes up less than 4% of the total tourism industry. But un-tourists have been so successfully re-branded that they have come to define what it means to be a good tourist.

All tourism should be responsible towards and respectful of environmental and human resources. Some tourist developments, as well as, inevitably, individual tourists, have not been so and should be challenged. But instead, a divide is being driven between those few privileged, high-paying tourists and the masses. There is no difference between them – they are just being packaged as something different. Our concern should not be with this small number but with the majority of travellers. But why should we bother? We who concern ourselves with this debate are potentially or probably un-tourists. We aren't interested in saving leisure time abroad for the majority of people: we're interested in making ourselves feel good. That's why we've succumbed to the re-branding of our enjoyment, and refuse to take up a term we believe to be tainted. How many times have *you* owned up to being a tourist?

25   The writer suggests that in the future,

   A   there will be a limited choice of destinations available to tourists.

   B   tourists will be required to pay more for any holidays they take.

   C   holidays will not exist in the same form as we know them now.

   D   people going on holiday to relax will feel obliged to feel ashamed.

26   What does the writer say about stopping tourism?

   A   The expansion of the tourism industry will continue.

   B   Countries economically dependent on tourism would suffer from any restrictions.

   C   The industry will not be able to cope once tourist numbers reach a certain limit.

   D   Tourists must be persuaded that having a holiday is ethically wrong.

27   According to the writer, the aim of re-branding tourism is to

   A   ensure the skills of travellers match the needs of the area they go to.

   B   deceive travellers about the purpose of their trip to foreign countries.

   C   make travellers aware of the harmful effects of traditional tourism.

   D   offer types of holidays that bring benefits to poor communities.

28   In paragraph four, the writer suggests that 'un-tourists' are

   A   more concerned with environmental issues than other tourists.

   B   unwilling to pay for the experience of helping people.

   C   able to take holidays without a sense of guilt.

   D   pressing for the introduction of laws to ban mass tourism.

29   The writer states that third world cultures

   A   are unlikely to be disturbed by the presence of foreigners.

   B   cannot always comprehend other cultural traditions.

   C   risk losing their identity by exposure to tourism.

   D   can only be encountered through careful integration.

30   According to the writer, the belief that mass tourism is bad has resulted in

   A   more tourists deciding to take holidays in their own country instead.

   B   the increasing construction of environmentally friendly tourist resorts.

   C   certain people being hypocritical about their reasons for travelling.

   D   the possibility of charging different prices for identical holidays.

Part 4

Answer questions **31–49** by referring to the newspaper article on pages **124–125**, in which four editors are interviewed about their jobs. In the exam, you will mark your answers on a separate answer sheet.

For questions **31–49**, answer by choosing from the list of editors (**A–D**). Some of the choices may be required more than once.

Of which editor is the following true?

She mentions the fact that writers need discipline to work to time constraints.   **31** ....

She did not believe she would reach the level of editor.   **32** ....

Her current position at work is a temporary one.   **33** ....

She prefers to hire people who have experience of working for other magazines.   **34** ....

She rejects a certain stereotype about women's magazines.   **35** ....

She compares a serious side of journalism to a more enjoyable one.   **36** ....

She is exceptionally positive about the editorial position she now holds.   **37** ....

A	Jayne West

She likes her work now as much as she did at the beginning of her career.   **38** ....

She is not impressed by inexperienced people who are overconfident.   **39** ....

B	Celia Howard

She had no definite ambition when she began her career.   **40** ....

She was discouraged from attempting a career in journalism.   **41** ....

C	Karen Goss

She appreciates people who have put considerable effort into becoming a journalist.   **42** ....

She managed to become a writer by initially working in a different role.   **43** ....

D	Gillian Rolland

She advises new writers to work on establishing a reputation.   **44** ....

She believes that only certain people are suitable for one area of journalism.   **45** ....

She states that only new writers with exceptional talent are likely to get work.   **46** ....

Her skills as a writer were acquired through experience rather than study.   **47** ....

She says her first experience of journalism was not in the field she intended to stay in.   **48** ....

She believes that self-confidence is an important quality.   **49** ....

The Dream Career?

Many people dream of a career in journalism, but what's it really like? Four editors who have made it to the top tell us how they got there.

A
Jayne West

When she decided that magazines would be the career for her, Jayne West applied to do a journalism course in London. She was told at the interview by both the lecturers present that she didn't have what it takes. That was the late eighties. But as current editor of *Venus* magazine, she is living proof that persistence, and a willingness to 'get in by the back door if necessary' can pay off. 'Only in my wildest dreams did I think I would end up as an editor,' she says. 'I just hoped I'd be a features writer. My first aim after my degree was to get a foothold. I learned to type – no one should underestimate the importance of this skill – and that enabled me to get work temping.' After landing a job as a PA in the editor's office at *City* magazine, Jayne, 35, took on other roles including feature writing. 'I had such brilliant training,' she says, 'but most of it was on the job. It absolutely pays to get as much experience as possible. If someone is starting out, work experience is the best way to get a foot in the door. I can always tell who will do well. It's the young woman or man willing to do anything – not those who think they should be writing a feature on the first day.'

B
Celia Howard

Celia Howard, 35, has been editor of monthly magazine, *Mode*, for two years. Her career in women's magazines spans seven years but before this she worked on a variety of small trade publications across a range of editorial roles. Her enthusiasm for her current job and the team of people working with her is overwhelming. 'People must have a real passion for the job and for the magazine they are working on,' she says. 'They don't always realise what hard work it's going to be.' She started her career at 'ground level,' she says, but had no idea of what her ultimate aim was. 'I just knew I wanted to work in publishing. In my experience, so long as someone believes in themselves and is tenacious enough, they can go for whatever they want. It depends on the magazine and type of work someone wants to do,' she adds. 'With fashion, for example, you can't teach someone about it. I think people are probably born with it. But lots of people aspire to be feature writers or interviewers. Celebrity interviewing is a very popular choice.' She says the perception of women's magazines being competitive environments is unfounded. 'In my experience they are a very open place to work. People come in from all sorts of backgrounds, and I have always worked with great teams of talented people.'

C

Karen Goss

After 20 years in the women's magazine business in various editorial roles, Karen Goss, 46, says her love for the job has not diminished. 'It is a supportive and caring environment, but it is also intensely professional.' Junior positions are few and far between among her 36 staff, she says, but if someone stands out, as one applicant did recently, they can get in. 'While a postgraduate qualification is important, there's also the fact that people move around a lot in this industry and I am more likely to look for people who have done this. At the lower end it is not very well paid but at the top level, salaries can be extremely good.' This, she emphasises, is limited to a handful of people. The people she admires are those who take risks later in life and have re-trained in an attempt to enter the industry. 'The sheer hard work it takes to re-train is a serious undertaking,' she says. 'But people with a specialist knowledge have a better chance than someone wanting to be a general journalist. Some people might come into magazines thinking they will be able to have flexible working hours further down the line. But to have any chance of this, they need to remember that it takes time to make a name for yourself.'

D

Gillian Rolland

While the editor of *International* is on maternity leave, Gillian Rolland, 35, the deputy editor, has stepped into her shoes and has taken on what she calls a 'caretaking role.' ' I trained as a newspaper journalist but always aspired to work on a glossy magazine. I started out at *Charm* magazine but also did a spell in newspapers before moving into glossies. They are different from newspapers – and a big difference is the number of women. It is true that there are a few perks to the job – free stuff we get given us. The features team will have to go out to parties and have fun as part of their job, but likewise they can end up at fundraisers for charities we are working with. On a magazine as big as *International* you quite simply have to work very hard. Deadlines are not as fast paced as newspapers of course, but to stay at our standard we have to work for it. It's often heads down and getting on with it.' Gillian says the 30-strong editorial team is made up of 'all sorts' of people. 'They are all talented,' she says. 'The work is full time and full on. Writers' positions are very sought after. The last time we advertised, over 500 people responded.'

PAPER 2 WRITING 2 hours

Part 1

You **must** answer this question.

1   You have recently seen an advertisement about summer work in American children's camps and you have decided to apply for one of the positions.

Read the advertisement below on which you have made some notes. Then, **using the information appropriately**, write a **letter** to American Summer Camps, applying for a position.

American Summer Camps

**Are you free for a period of six weeks between
June 15th – August 30th?**   *yes – mention when*
**Do you want the chance to meet lots of new
people and travel round the USA?**

American Summer Camps offers people from all over the world the chance to come to the USA and take part in one of our summer camp programs located in many states.   *work in California possible?*

We are now recruiting staff to look after and be responsible for American children between the ages of 9–15.

We are looking for people who can offer either of the following: *mention relevant experience*
• general experience of working with children
• experience in teaching or an interest in sport and outdoor activities.

It is also important that you
• have the right personal skills   *give details*
• have a good command of English.

* Our flight, accommodation and camp food will be provided free.
*You will receive a basic salary.
* **Your visa will allow you to travel in the US for up to six weeks after camp finishes.**

If you are interested, apply to us in writing, telling us what you can offer and why you are suitable.

American Summer Camps PO Box 1088 Albany NY 981767 7392   USA

Now write your **letter** to American Summer Camps as outlined above (about 250 words). You should use your own words as far as possible.

Before you write your letter, go to page 127.

A DETAILED GUIDE

Letters of application

Choose the right word or phrase in the sentences below. All the sentences could be used in formal or polite letters.

1 I am used to **deal/dealing** with the public.

2 I **am/have been** at Peugeot for three years.

3 I am writing to apply **for/to** the **job/position** of interpreter, which was advertised in last Thursday's Guardian.

4 I **know/feel** I am **the right person/a suitable candidate** for the following reasons.

5 From 1989 to 1993, I **had worked/worked** for Crédit Suisse in Zurich in the Customer Relations Department.

6 I am familiar **to/with** all the major software systems.

7 I graduated **from/at** the Korean University in Seoul in 1991.

8 I have a pleasant telephone **behaviour/manner.**

9 I feel that my **diplomas/qualifications** and **experience/experiences** would be extremely **relevant/suitable** to the post.

10 My responsibilities **involve/consist** managing a team of five people, **discussing/liaising** with our offices abroad, and **making/setting** up meetings with clients.

Part 2

Choose **one** of the following writing tasks. Your answer should follow exactly the instructions given. Write approximately 250 words.

2   As part of a college project on problems facing the environment, you've been asked to contribute to the student magazine. Your feature should refer to environmental problems in your country and the steps that have been taken to improve the situation.

Write your **article**.

3   You were recently unable to attend an event that a friend had organised. Write to your friend, explaining why you didn't attend, asking for details about the event and suggesting an event that both of you could attend in the future.

Write your **letter**.

4   A friend of yours has recently opened a café in your local area. He has asked you to prepare a leaflet in order to attract English-speaking customers, mentioning what kind of food the café serves, where it is located and anything else you think would attract new customers.

Draft your **leaflet**.

Before you write your answer, go to page 129.

5   The company you work for has asked you to design an information sheet to be given to potential English-speaking customers. The sheet should contain a brief section about the background of your company and describe in more detail the product(s) or service(s) that your company offers. You may add any other information that you think will help with the publicity.

Write your **information sheet**.

A DETAILED STUDY

Part 2 A leaflet

Read through this sample answer for Question 4 and answer the questions on page **130**.

---

* Do you appriciate a good cup of coffee and a chat?
* Do you want the chance to meet interesting people from all over the world?
* Are you looking for a warm atmosphere and friendly service?

Then why not come along to:

The Language Exchange Coffee Shop

convienently located near Kolonaki Square in the heart of Athens
open 9am to 12pm Mon-Sat / 11am to 8pm Sun

What's on offer?

* A wide range of delicous sandwiches, continental snacks and hot meals
* Really exellent coffee from many South American and European countries
* We have English-speaking staff so don't be afraid to ask what they reccommend!
* All refreshments are at reasonible prices.

Fed up with the daily routine?

If you're feeling like a break from work, come inside and choose from our extensive selection of reading material. You can:

* plan your next holiday as you browse through one of our fascinating travell guides
* find out what's going in the world in one of the foreign newspapers
* improve a foreign language as you enjoy a classic or modern novel

Fancy travelling round the world during your lunch hour?

We have five terminals where you can acess the Internet and speak to new friends around the globe! It's certainly quicker than a postcard and definitly much more fun! Our staff will be happy to give you a hand if you're a 'first-time' surfer.

Of course, the best way to improve your fluency in another language is by practicing – so don't be shy – smile at the customer at the next table!

Find us at: 125 Saint Anna Street, Kolonaki, Athens Tel. 6467 456

Content
Does the sample answer refer to what kind of food the café serves and the location?
What else does it mention that might attract new customers?

Effect on the target reader
Do you feel that someone reading this leaflet would be interested in going to the café?
In what ways is this leaflet a successful advertisement?

Range of vocabulary and structure
What adjective-noun collocations can you find in this leaflet?

Format
What makes this leaflet eye-catching?

Register
How does the punctuation help make this a successful advertisement?

Accuracy
What spelling mistakes can you find?

Paper 2 GENERAL IMPRESSION MARK SCHEME

Note: This mark scheme should be interpreted at CAE level. It should be used in conjunction with a task-specific mark scheme for each question.

Band 5
Minimal errors: resourceful, controlled and natural use of language, showing good range of vocabulary and structure. Task fully completed, with good use of cohesive devices, consistently appropriate register. No relevant omissions. N.B. Not necessarily a flawless performance. Very positive effect on target reader.

Band 4
Sufficiently natural, errors only when more complex language attempted. Some evidence of range of vocabulary and structure. Good realisation of task, only minor omissions. Attention paid to organisation and cohesion; register usually appropriate. Positive effect on target reader achieved.

Band 3
Either (a) task reasonably achieved, accuracy of language satisfactory and adequate range of vocabulary and range of structures or (b) an ambitious attempt at the task, causing a number of non-impeding errors, but a good range of vocabulary and structure demonstrated. There may be minor omissions, but content clearly organised. Would achieve the required effect on target reader.

Band 2
Some attempt at task but lack of expansion and/or notable omissions/irrelevancies. Noticeable lifting of language from the input, often inappropriately. Errors sometimes obscure communication and/or language is too elementary for this level. Content not clearly organised. Would have a negative on target reader.

Band 1
Serious lack of control and/or frequent basic errors. Narrow range of language. Inadequate attempt at task. Very negative effect on target reader.

Band 0
	(a) Fewer than 50 words per question.
or	(b) Totally illegible work.
or	(c) Total irrelevance (often a previously prepared answer to a different question).

Please note: Correct at the time of going to print. Contact UCLES for detailed, up-to-date information.

PAPER 3 ENGLISH IN USE 1 hour 30 minutes

Part 1

For questions **1–15**, read the text below and then decide which word on page **133** best fits each space. The exercise begins with an example **(0)**. In the exam you will put the letter for each question on a separate answer sheet.

Example: | 0 | B |

What does every top corporate boss need? Lego

The success of many **(0)** ...*leading*... companies depends on an effective management team and they

are always **(1)** .... ways to encourage those managers to **(2)** .... along with each other. In

previous years, those ways have **(3)** .... from weekends where managers went camping together

to white-water rafting. Now the latest corporate team-building technique that is becoming increasingly

popular in the management **(4)** .... is sitting for hours round a table making shapes out of Lego, the

well-known building bricks that so many children have **(5)** .... up with. But don't be **(6)** .... by

those familiar green and yellow plastic blocks – this is Lego for adults, and among senior executives it

is the hottest management **(7)** .... since the go-everywhere laptop. Companies are now **(8)** ....

to send senior staff along to learn what Lego can do for their corporate ethos, and management

consultants are even **(9)** .... themselves to running Lego sessions to **(10)** .... the demand.

They claim that the multicoloured bricks can **(11)** .... free managers from a limited imagination.

What does this mean in **(12)** .... ? For a start, staff **(13)** .... a session are encouraged to

'unlock their creative potential' while they build models to understand how their businesses work. By

(14) .... their firms as three-dimensional structures, they can build models which are metaphors for

the issues that often occur at **(15)** .... , such as what makes an ideal employee or whether the

sales force is larger than necessary.

0	A	foremost	B	leading	C	primary	D	chief
1	A	searching	B	enquiring	C	requesting	D	seeking
2	A	go	B	come	C	get	D	work
3	A	covered	B	included	C	ranged	D	consisted
4	A	circle	B	world	C	level	D	area
5	A	grown	B	brought	C	come	D	taken
6	A	attracted	B	concerned	C	directed	D	fooled
7	A	tool	B	equipment	C	instrument	D	gadget
8	A	enthusiastic	B	agreeable	C	eager	D	excited
9	A	specialising	B	focusing	C	concentrating	D	dedicating
10	A	fill	B	recognise	C	meet	D	supply
11	A	assist	B	help	C	aid	D	support
12	A	theory	B	truth	C	practice	D	reality
13	A	joining	B	following	C	participating	D	entering
14	A	symbolising	B	demonstrating	C	illustrating	D	representing
15	A	times	B	last	C	once	D	work

Part 2

For questions **16–30**, read the text below and think of the word which best fits each space. **Use only one word in each space**. The exercise begins with an example **(0)**. In the exam you will mark your answers on a separate answer sheet.

Example: | 0 | *with* |

Models wanted

If you are a student, unemployed or retired **(0)** ...*with*... time on your hands and fancy doing something you have always wanted to do **(16)** .... never had the confidence, a bit of modelling, perhaps, or appearing in your favourite soap opera, **(17)** .... could be the right time. **(18)** .... glamour nor good looks are necessary to give it a go. Modelling agencies aren't just looking for beauty; they also need normal models to appear **(19)** .... TV ads, while similar candidates **(20)** .... wanted by casting agencies as extras for film and TV. **(21)** .... you are exceptionally lucky, you won't earn a huge amount, but it can provide the extra you need to get by on. Nor, **(22)** .... some may hope, is it likely to lead to a new career as an actor. But most people, **(23)** .... , do find it enjoyable and appreciate the chance to meet people.

(24) .... you don't need experience or training, anyone has the potential to become an extra as **(25)** .... as you are reliable, available **(26)** .... short notice and are prepared to do any work that comes **(27)** .... way. If you think modelling is **(28)** .... your style, then your best bet is to approach one of the big model agencies that have real-looking people in their books. You'll be surprised at **(29)** .... much demand there is **(30)** .... 'the average person' from the advertising world.

Part 3

In **most** lines of the following text, there is either a spelling error or a punctuation error. For each numbered line **31–46,** write the correctly spelt word or show the correct punctuation. Some lines are correct. Indicate these with a tick (✓). The exercise begins with three examples **(0), (00)** and **(000)**. In the exam you will write your answers on a separate answer sheet.

0	✓
00	*destruction*
000	*Diggers*

Examples:

0	A medieval wooden ship dubbed the Welsh Mary Rose has
00	been saved from distruction, just days before building work
000	would have buried it under tons of concrete for ever. Digger's
31	excavating the ship have so far found pottery, textilles and parts
32	of sales. The 25-metre ship, unique in Britain, was found in mud
33	during construction of an orchestra pit at a new arts centre in
34	Newport, south Wales. Unlike the original Mary Rose, the ship
35	preserved in Portsmouth, the Newport ship cannot be lifted in
36	one piece because several steal rods have already been driven
37	into some of the timbers. Following a campaigne to save the ship,
38	the government has provided £3.5m to disassemble; record and
39	protect the timbers, which have been dated to the winter of 1465.
40	The ambitous rescue scheme will involve building a new basement
41	below the arts centre where visiters will be able to view the ship
42	threw a glass floor. 'I'm happy that the old lady of the sea has
43	been saved and will now be conserved.' said Charles Ferris, a
44	spokesman for Save our Ship. 'The fact that the ship is going back
45	into the arts centre basement is better then it going in the bin. But
46	speaking personally, what a pity that its going to be hidden away.'

Part 4

For questions **47–61**, read the two texts on pages **136** and **137**. Use the words in the boxes to the right of the two texts to form one word which fits in the same numbered space in the text. The exercise begins with an example **(0)**. In the exam you will write your answers on a separate answer sheet.

Example:

0	*exhibition*

ADVERTISEMENT

Wrexham Village: 50 Years of Photographs	
Next week sees the opening of an **(0)** ..*exhibition*.... of photographs by local **(47)** .... and professional photographer, John Taylor. In the fifty years that John has been taking photographs, he has amassed an incredible **(48)** .... record of village life. The show is **(49)** .... *History Through the Lens* and contains black and white portraits of local people and dream-like images of the **(50)** .... countryside which almost have a **(51)** .... effect on the viewer. There is also a section on **(52)** .... important events which is equally fascinating. The **(53)** .... charge for adults is £4.50 and it is free for children and pensioners.	**0** **EXHIBIT** **47** RESIDE *RESIDENTS* **48** VISION *VISIONARY* **49** TITLE *TITLED* **50** NEAR *NEAREST* **51** HYPNOTISE *HYPNOTISING* **52** HISTORY *HISTORICAL* **53** ADMIT *ADMITTANCE*

ARTICLE

Jewellery stolen

Police have reported that a burglary took place at the home of Mrs Jean Dunn, in Bakersfield Rd yesterday afternoon. They believe that the burglar gained **(54)** .... to the house by climbing over the back wall and breaking the kitchen window. Mrs Dunn was **(55)** .... upset when she said, 'A lot of what the burglar took was **(56)** .... , just cheap jewellery and a faulty TV. But he also took a box of letters that friends have written over the years and those are **(57)** .... '.

A spokesman for the local police force said, 'Unfortunately, **(58)** .... in this area is on the increase and people need to take extra **(59)** .... They need to get an alarm installed and extra locks fitted by a **(60)** .... professional.' Mrs Dunn was unimpressed by this advice. 'What we need is more of a police **(61)** .... on the street,' she said.

54	ENTER
55	UNDERSTAND
56	WORTH
57	REPLACE
58	THIEVE
59	CAUTIOUS
60	RELY
61	PRESENT

Part 5

For questions **62–74**, read the following informal note about a work reference. Use the information in the note to complete the numbered gaps in the reference which follows. The words you need do not occur in the informal note. **Use no more than two words for each gap.** The exercise begins with an example **(0)**. In the exam you will write your answers on a separate answer sheet.

Example: | **0** | *been employed* |

INFORMAL NOTE

> Julie
>
> Could you write a reference for Karen Adams, please? She's applying to the Kingsland Hotel as assistant hotel manager. I can't see why she couldn't do the job – she's got quite a bit of experience now and she's always shown she's very good at whatever she does and she's been a hard worker. I've had a quick look in her file and noted a couple of key points:
>
> October 1998: started work here as junior receptionist
> Duties: checking in guests and taking bookings on the phone
> Comments: she did her job well + had a positive attitude
> January 1999: we asked her to take over as Reception Manager
> Duties: sorting out customer problems and doing the schedule for her team
> Comments: not much experience but did a good job anyway
> January 2001: went away to do course + exam in 'Conference Organisation' and passed it.
> Duties: now helping our conference manager.
>
> You could also mention that she gets on well with everyone she works with and listens to what the other staff tell her.
>
> Thanks,
> Sue

REFERENCE

> **To whom it may concern:**
>
> Karen Adams has **(0)** ...*been employed*... by the Forest Hotel since October 1998 and has **(62)** .... considerable experience in various aspects of working in and running a hotel.
>
> Karen started work as a junior receptionist on the front desk which involved checking guests into the hotel and handling **(63)** .... She carried out her work both efficiently and **(64)** .... and when the reception manager retired, she **(65)** .... to this position. As reception manager, her responsibilities included **(66)** .... with customer complaints and queries and **(67)** .... the work schedule for a team of five people. Despite her **(68)** .... experience, she quickly adapted to this new role and demonstrated excellent interpersonal and organisational skills.
>
> Karen held this position for two years before she took two months' **(69)** .... to retrain as a conference organiser. On the **(70)** .... of her course, she returned to the Forest Hotel where she became **(71)** .... our current conference manager.
>
> During the time Karen has worked at the hotel, she **(72)** .... herself to be a highly capable and hard-working member of staff. Although she is certainly ambitious, she has been prepared to co-operate as part of a team and **(73)** .... the comments and suggestions of her colleagues.
>
> I am confident that Karen would be able to meet the challenge of working as assistant hotel manager and I have **(74)** .... in recommending her for the position she is seeking.

Part 6

For questions **75–80**, read the following text and then choose from the list **A–J** given below the best phrase to fill each of the spaces. Each correct phrase may only be used once. **Some of the suggested answers do not fit at all.** The exercise begins with an example **(0)**. In the exam you will write your answers on a separate answer sheet.

Example: | **0** | *J* |

The World's Largest Tomato Fight

The town of Buñol in Spain is famous for *La Tomatina*, the world's largest vegetable fight. The event takes place during a week-long celebration filled with festivities **(0)** ....*J*..... . *La Tomatina* started during the 1940s, when a number of friends started a tomato fight and passers-by got dragged into it. From that day forward, the fiesta has been celebrated annually **(75)** .... The reason for the fight has never been established **(76)** ....

La Tomatina has blossomed into a huge fiesta that coincides with the festival for the town's patron saint. This is partly in an effort to draw more tourism into Buñol, **(77)** .... The night before *La Tomatina*, the narrow streets are filled with tomatoes, **(78)** .... No one can do battle on an empty stomach so huge pans filled with delicious paella are on offer. Then, early Wednesday morning, shopkeepers set about covering windows and doors in preparation for the mess. Large trucks rumble up the streets to arrive in the square **(79)** .... Men on top of the trucks then begin the attack with soft tomatoes from the four corners of Spain. The victims retaliate against the truckers, each other, **(80)** .... When all the tomatoes have been demolished, everyone heads to the river to clean it all off.

A   and is expected to draw record numbers this time around
B   and be cheered by the 20,000 strong crowd·
C   and anyone else that strays within their range
D   and at the same time many more targets
E   and avoid wearing anything that can't be cleaned
F   and is estimated to be about 90,000 tonnes
G   and it hardly matters since the point is fun
H   and not only for residents, but any passing tourist
I   and in a *much* more appealing form than the next day

J   and with even greater anticipation for the battle ahead

PAPER 4 LISTENING approximately 45 minutes

Part 1

You will hear the organiser of a conference on script-writing talking about the seminars that people can attend. For questions **1–9**, look at the programme of events and fill in the missing information.

You will hear the recording **twice**.

Afternoon Seminar Programme Sunday 4th August		
Speaker	**Title**	**Room**
Eliza Stirling	_____ **1** (for first-time writers)	Room 5/first floor
Elaine Johnson	Three-Dimensional Heroes and Heroines (how to write _____) **2**	_____ **3**
Terry Hunt	_____ **4**	Room 9/second floor
Ian Walters	_____ **5** (surprise endings)	_____ **6** /ground floor

Time: _____ **7**

Don't forget: _____ **8** on booking form

+ also write your _____ **9**

Part 2

You will hear a tour guide talking about the history of a building. For questions **10–18**, complete the notes the speaker is using.

Listen very carefully as you will hear the recording ONCE only.

Tour notes

863 AD: First building was Saxon _____ 10

All that remains today: _____ 11

East + west walls had _____ 12

1258 AD: Landowner added _____ 13 and a moat.

1324 AD: Castle destroyed by _____ 14

1329 AD: Charles Dereham built a _____ 15

Cost in today's money: £ _____ 16

Catherine Dereham responsible for extending
_____ 17 and designing garden.

In chapel ceiling there are beautiful
_____ 18

Part 3

You will hear part of a radio interview in which a careers adviser is giving advice on how to write CVs (curriculum vitae). For questions **19–27**, complete the notes.

You will hear the recording **twice**.

Nowadays, competition for jobs is [19]

Graduates should not lie on their CV or
[20] their experience.

Graduates' CVs often don't contain enough interesting or
[21] information.

Because they have no work experience, graduates need to focus on their
[22] and skills.

This could include being a member of a club or
[23]

CVs shouldn't be too long or written [24]

Your CV gives a potential employer their
[25]

Graduates with general degrees need to show they are
and [26]

Graduates who took a holiday after university must show this time was
[27]

Part 4

You will hear five short extracts in which various people are talking about a problem of living in a city. While you listen, you must complete **both** tasks.

You will hear the recording **twice**.

TASK ONE

For questions **28–32**, match the extracts as you hear them with the people, listed **A–H**.

A   taxi driver

B   commuter   [ ] 28

C   policeman   [ ] 29

D   teacher

                                                      [ ] 30

E   parent

F   politician   [ ] 31

G   homeowner   [ ] 32

H   cyclist

TASK TWO

For questions **33–37**, match the extracts as you hear them with the problem the speaker refers to, listed **A–H**.

A   lack of green spaces

B   longer working hours   [ ] 33

C   heavy traffic   [ ] 34

D   high prices

E   inconsiderate neighbours   [ ] 35

F   crime   [ ] 36

G   pollution   [ ] 37

H   loneliness

In the exam you will have 10 minutes at the end of the test to copy your answers onto a separate answer sheet.

PAPER 5 SPEAKING

Part 2 (4 minutes)

1 Spending money

For both candidates
Look at the photographs on page 152. They each show people who might buy something.

Candidate A: Describe two of these photographs in detail, saying what the people might want to buy and how they might be feeling. (*1 minute*)

Candidate B: Say which photograph has not been described. (*20 seconds*)

2 Chimpanzees

For both candidates
Look at the photographs on page 153 of people and chimpanzees.

Candidate B: Describe two of these photographs in detail, saying what different reasons these people might have for watching the chimpanzees. (*1 minute*)

Candidate A: Say which photograph has not been described. (*20 seconds*)

Part 3 (4 minutes) Human achievement

For both candidates
Look at the list below. Discuss some of the important achievements that have occurred in these areas and how they have influenced the world we live in. Then decide which three achievements have offered the greatest benefit.

sport	transportation	politics	medicine	trade	engineering
	space exploration	buildings	science		

Part 4 (4 minutes) Further discussion

For both candidates
- What other important things has the human race achieved so far?
- What achievements would you like to see in the next 20 years?
- How far do you agree with the saying 'Necessity is the mother of invention'?
- What is more likely to lead to achievement – competition or teamwork?
- What areas of possible achievement do you think deserve more funding or sponsorship?

PAPER 5 SPEAKING

VISUAL MATERIAL

Test 1 Part 2 Ambition

Test 1   Part 2   Holiday destinations

Test 2   Part 2   The five senses

Test 2   Part 2   Relaxation

Test 3   Part 2   Protective clothing

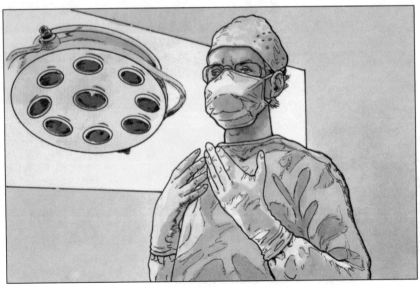

Test 3   Part 2   Emotions

Test 3   Part 3   Happiness

Friendship

Fitness and sport

Food

Work

Holidays

Family

Entertainment

Learning

Test 4   Part 2   Spending money

Test 4   Part 2   Chimpanzees

PAPER 1 READING ANSWER SHEET

UNIVERSITY *of* CAMBRIDGE
ESOL Examinations

Candidate Name
If not already printed, write name
in CAPITALS and complete the
Candidate No. grid (in pencil).

Candidate Signature

Examination Title

Centre

Supervisor:
If the candidate is ABSENT or has WITHDRAWN shade here

Centre No.

Candidate No.

Examination Details

SAMPLE

0	0	0	0
1	1	1	1
2	2	2	2
3	3	3	3
4	4	4	4
5	5	5	5
6	6	6	6
7	7	7	7
8	8	8	8
9	9	9	9

Multiple-choice Answer Sheet

Use a pencil.

Mark ONE letter for each question.

For example, if you think C is the right answer
to the question, mark your answer sheet like this:

0   A B C D E F G H I

Rub out any answer you wish to change with an eraser.

1	A B C D E F G H I		21	A B C D E F G H I		41	A B C D E F G H I
2	A B C D E F G H I		22	A B C D E F G H I		42	A B C D E F G H I
3	A B C D E F G H I		23	A B C D E F G H I		43	A B C D E F G H I
4	A B C D E F G H I		24	A B C D E F G H I		44	A B C D E F G H I
5	A B C D E F G H I		25	A B C D E F G H I		45	A B C D E F G H I
6	A B C D E F G H I		26	A B C D E F G H I		46	A B C D E F G H I
7	A B C D E F G H I		27	A B C D E F G H I		47	A B C D E F G H I
8	A B C D E F G H I		28	A B C D E F G H I		48	A B C D E F G H I
9	A B C D E F G H I		29	A B C D E F G H I		49	A B C D E F G H I
10	A B C D E F G H I		30	A B C D E F G H I		50	A B C D E F G H I
11	A B C D E F G H I		31	A B C D E F G H I		51	A B C D E F G H I
12	A B C D E F G H I		32	A B C D E F G H I		52	A B C D E F G H I
13	A B C D E F G H I		33	A B C D E F G H I		53	A B C D E F G H I
14	A B C D E F G H I		34	A B C D E F G H I		54	A B C D E F G H I
15	A B C D E F G H I		35	A B C D E F G H I		55	A B C D E F G H I
16	A B C D E F G H I		36	A B C D E F G H I		56	A B C D E F G H I
17	A B C D E F G H I		37	A B C D E F G H I		57	A B C D E F G H I
18	A B C D E F G H I		38	A B C D E F G H I		58	A B C D E F G H I
19	A B C D E F G H I		39	A B C D E F G H I		59	A B C D E F G H I
20	A B C D E F G H I		40	A B C D E F G H I		60	A B C D E F G H I

CAE 1

DP306/080

PAPER 4 LISTENING ANSWER SHEET

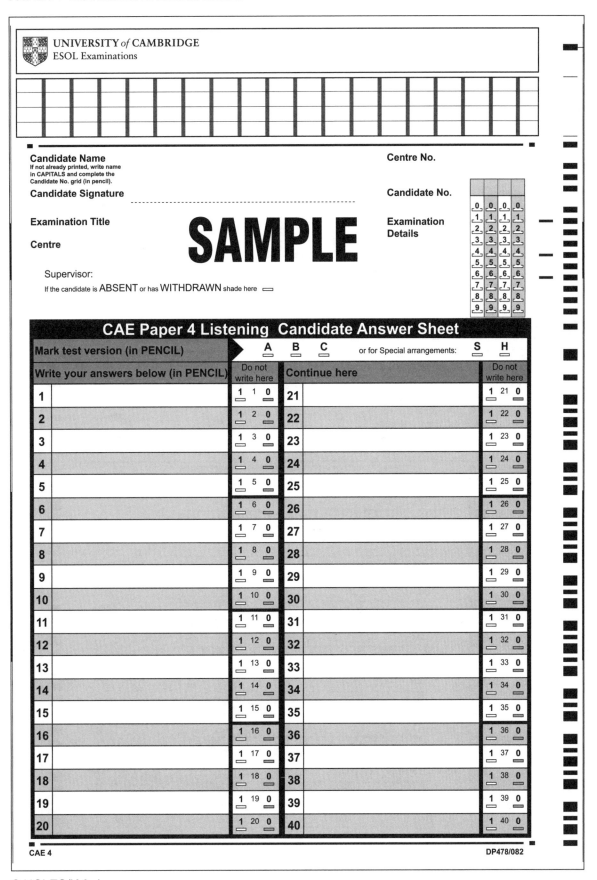

UNIVERSITY *of* CAMBRIDGE
ESOL Examinations

Candidate Name
If not already printed, write name
in CAPITALS and complete the
Candidate No. grid (in pencil).

Candidate Signature

Examination Title

Centre

Supervisor:

If the candidate is ABSENT or has WITHDRAWN shade here ⊂⊐

SAMPLE

Centre No.

Candidate No.

**Examination
Details**

CAE Paper 4 Listening Candidate Answer Sheet

Mark test version (in PENCIL)	▶	A B C	or for Special arrangements:	S H
Write your answers below (in PENCIL)	Do not write here	Continue here		Do not write here

1		1 1 0	21		1 21 0
2		1 2 0	22		1 22 0
3		1 3 0	23		1 23 0
4		1 4 0	24		1 24 0
5		1 5 0	25		1 25 0
6		1 6 0	26		1 26 0
7		1 7 0	27		1 27 0
8		1 8 0	28		1 28 0
9		1 9 0	29		1 29 0
10		1 10 0	30		1 30 0
11		1 11 0	31		1 31 0
12		1 12 0	32		1 32 0
13		1 13 0	33		1 33 0
14		1 14 0	34		1 34 0
15		1 15 0	35		1 35 0
16		1 16 0	36		1 36 0
17		1 17 0	37		1 37 0
18		1 18 0	38		1 38 0
19		1 19 0	39		1 39 0
20		1 20 0	40		1 40 0

CAE 4

DP478/082

© UCLES/K & J

PAPER 3 ENGLISH IN USE ANSWER SHEET

UNIVERSITY *of* CAMBRIDGE
ESOL Examinations

Candidate Name
If not already printed, write name
in CAPITALS and complete the
Candidate No. grid (in pencil).

Candidate Signature

Examination Title

Centre

Supervisor:
If the candidate is ABSENT or has WITHDRAWN shade here ▭

SAMPLE

Centre No.

Candidate No.

Examination Details

Candidate Answer Sheet

Use a PENCIL (B or HB). Rub out any answer you wish to change with an eraser.

For **Parts 1** and **6**:
Mark ONE letter for each question.
For example, if you think **B** is the right answer to
the question, mark your answer sheet like this:

0	A	B	C	D

For **Parts 2, 3, 4** and **5**:
Write your answers in the spaces next to the
numbers like this:

0	example

Part 1

	A	B	C	D
1				
2				
3				
4				
5				
6				
7				
8				
9				
10				
11				
12				
13				
14				
15				

Part 2

		Do not write here
16		1 16 0
17		1 17 0
18		1 18 0
19		1 19 0
20		1 20 0
21		1 21 0
22		1 22 0
23		1 23 0
24		1 24 0
25		1 25 0
26		1 26 0
27		1 27 0
28		1 28 0
29		1 29 0
30		1 30 0

Turn over for Parts 3 - 6 →

CAE 3

DP394/338

Part 3

	Do not write here
31	1 31 0
32	1 32 0
33	1 33 0
34	1 34 0
35	1 35 0
36	1 36 0
37	1 37 0
38	1 38 0
39	1 39 0
40	1 40 0
41	1 41 0
42	1 42 0
43	1 43 0
44	1 44 0
45	1 45 0
46	1 46 0

Part 4

	Do not write here
47	1 47 0
48	1 48 0
49	1 49 0
50	1 50 0
51	1 51 0
52	1 52 0
53	1 53 0
54	1 54 0
55	1 55 0
56	1 56 0
57	1 57 0
58	1 58 0
59	1 59 0
60	1 60 0
61	1 61 0

Part 5

	Do not write here
62	1 62 0
63	1 63 0
64	1 64 0
65	1 65 0
66	1 66 0
67	1 67 0
68	1 68 0
69	1 69 0
70	1 70 0
71	1 71 0
72	1 72 0
73	1 73 0
74	1 74 0

Part 6

	A	B	C	D	E	F	G	H	I
75	A	B	C	D	E	F	G	H	I
76	A	B	C	D	E	F	G	H	I
77	A	B	C	D	E	F	G	H	I
78	A	B	C	D	E	F	G	H	I
79	A	B	C	D	E	F	G	H	I
80	A	B	C	D	E	F	G	H	I

SAMPLE

KEY AND EXPLANATION

TEST ONE

p.6–9 PAPER 1 Part 1

FURTHER PRACTICE AND GUIDANCE (p.8–9)

1 f 2 c 3 a 4 l 5 b 6 j 7 e 8 h 9 g 10 m 11 i
12 d 13 k

p.8–9 PAPER 1 Part 1 (Test)

1 **D**: *it has taken until this, the ensemble's second album, to define its voice.* This suggests that the group has now developed their own style and is now playing the type of music they play best.
A: this new group has only released one album, so it cannot be referred to as the 'current one'.
B: the critic says this group has always been, and still is, theatrical. So, there is no sense of their 'musical identity' changing.
C: The critic suggests that Bobby Previte has always been, and still is, a musician who is influenced by many musical styles. So, there is no sense of his 'musical identity' changing.

2 **C**: *Just Add Water … is … exuberant … and uplifting.* Both these adjectives suggest the listener will feel really happy/joyful when listening to the album.
A: The music on this album is described as *tender* (gentle) and *peculiar* (strange).
B: The last but one line says *you're never sure whether you should be grinning* (smiling) *or flinching* (showing pain).
D: There is no mention here of how a listener may feel.

3 **B**: *Oh, My Dog! … is theatrical … and profound.* These adjectives correspond to 'a sense of drama' and, in this context, *profound* suggests 'deeper meaning'.
D: *Just Add Water* is described as *exuberant* and *thoughtful* but these more closely suggest 'very happy' and 'sensitively written'.

4 **D**: *But of course, it is the end not the means that counts.* The *end* = 'the result'; the *means* = 'the way something has been achieved'; to *count* = 'to be important'.

5 **B**: *their album, Oh, My Dog! will not confound their reputation.* The expression *to live up to* (someone's) *expectations* is used in a positive way. You expect something to be good / interesting / amusing, etc, and you then find out that it is. The positive language the critic uses suggests he appreciates the style of this group; *will not confound their reputation* means 'will not change their image'.
D: *As might be expected from a … jazz group, there is a … broad selection from* (different types of music) *but…* The critic suggests that this broad selection is typical of a modern jazz group, but he does not specifically indicate that this is a positive thing. The *but* in this sentence also suggests that this *broad selection* is not something he appreciates.

6 **A**: *They take a few daring liberties with some of the pieces.* To *take liberties with something* means 'to use something or someone with too much freedom.' The three musicians have adapted famous songs by introducing *a reggae beat* and only letting *fragments of the original melody emerge.*

7 **A**: *Inspiration is a celebratory investigation of the … composers and performers that have made their mark on them.* To *make a mark* on someone means 'to make an impression' or 'influence' someone. The musicians in the trio have chosen songs by earlier musicians such as Duke Ellington and Thelonious Monk, as these were musicians who influenced them.
B: *Musician Ab Baars pays homage to the composer Charles Ives.* This also suggests that Baars has been influenced by an earlier composer but this is only *one* song and *one* earlier musician, not *the music on the album* and *original artists.*

8 **B**: *The opening improvisation … is a little miracle of nine people making a decent noise without getting in each other's way.* The use of the word *miracle* shows that the critic is 'surprised'. In this context, *a decent noise* corresponds to a 'reasonable sound'.
A + B: Both of these groups are praised for their 'rapport' with each other, but the critics do not express surprise at this.

9 **B**: *Michael Moore plays his pieces with a tight delivery that is an excellent counter to Baars' gloomy style.* This suggests that Moore plays in a very precise, controlled way, whereas Baars plays music in a sad, slow style. The word *counter* means 'opposite'; the use of *excellent* suggests that putting these opposite styles together makes them both sound better.

10 **A**: *It's always thrilling when a new star shines … but Lynne Arriale is an exceptional talent.* A *new star* corresponds to *previously unknown* and *an extraordinary performer* goes with *exceptional talent*.
B: The musicians in this group are already known in the jazz world. It isn't clear whether Michael Moore is previously unknown, but the critic doesn't describe him as an extraordinary performer either.
C: Bobby Previte and his long-time associates cannot be described as previously unknown. Steve Swallow is described as *peerless*, which means 'without equal'. This does suggest he is an extraordinary performer but there is no indication that he is unknown.
D: Hakon Kornstad is a *prodigiously gifted young man*, which could correspond to *an extraordinary performer*. However, this is Wibutee's second album and there is no suggestion that Hakon is new to the group.

11 **C**: *Bobby Previte has epitomised that … movement's adventurousness.* In this context, to be the *epitome* of something means to be 'the symbol' or 'typical example of' something. The *musical trend* is the *movement* which searches for *inspiration from diverse music styles.*
B: Han Bennick, Misha Mengelberg and Willem Breuker could possibly be symbols for Dutch-style jazz, but the question states *one musician in particular.*

12 **A**: *she turned to jazz because she wanted 'the challenge of combining performance and composition on the spot'.* The words *turned to jazz* imply that Lynne Arriale made the decision to play jazz instead of classical music. *Performance and composition* correspond to *play* and *invent*. *On the spot* corresponds to *without preparation*.
B + D: Both these groups also like to *improvise* (invent and play music spontaneously) but neither text mentions a *single* musician's *decision* to *take up* (begin to learn/play) jazz.

13 **B**: *you're never sure whether you should be grinning or flinching in alarm.* This critic is the only one to say *you're never sure.* The two reactions, grinning and flinching, also emphasise this uncertainty. To *grin* means 'to smile', suggesting amusement, whereas to *flinch* suggests you are reacting to something painful or shocking.

p.10–11 PAPER 1 Part 2

14 **C**: The last sentence in C states *the kakapo also has a unique breeding system.* This is further explained in the next two sentences of the following text: *Males gather at an arena to compete for females. After mating, the females head off and raise their young alone.* C also describes the unique features of the kakapo: its appearance, the noises it makes and the important fact that it can't fly. In the following paragraph, Don Merton says that these unique features / peculiarities have made the kakapo *vulnerable*, in other words, easy to attack.

15 G: In the paragraph above 15, we read that there used to be millions of kakapo. Their only enemies were birds who found it difficult to find kakapo as their green colour meant they could hide in the forest. G says that when men arrived *it was a different story*. In other words, the situation changed. They brought dogs and rats which killed kakapo. At the end of G, it says that people believed the kakapo was extinct in the 1960s. The text under 15 then shows that this belief was wrong: Merton found one bird that was still alive.

16 A: The text above 16 says that the team thought the kakapo were safe and then discovered they were still being killed in large numbers. The first two sentences in A say that the team then began to carry out a rescue operation by moving the kakapo to islands where there were no cats, stoats or possums. Unfortunately, there were kiore (rats) on the new islands – but in the text under 16, it mentions that the team were trying to catch the kiore with traps.

17 D: The last sentence of the text above 17 mentions that the team successfully moved the birds to Maud and Codfish Island where they were safe. D starts with *persuading the birds to breed was harder*. This contrasts with the easy success of moving the birds. D also mentions the fact that the birds only breed when the rimu trees produce many seeds so that they have plenty to eat. The text under 17 mentions that the team try to find a diet/food that the birds like. The birds become healthier with the extra food, but still don't breed. The text mentions the rimu tree again, saying that the birds seem to be waiting for it to produce a lot of seed.

18 F: The text above 18 indicates that the birds will not breed until the rimu tree produces a lot of seed, so they have to let nature *take its course*. This means that they have to wait for the rimu trees to mast. The last sentence of F states that the team *recognised the fact that it was only the rimu tree that would turn things around* (change the situation). The text under 18 begins with *Armed with this … knowledge. The fact* and *the knowledge* both refer to the understanding that kakapo breed according to good seed production.

19 B: The text above 19 mentions that the team are using electronic monitoring equipment. The last sentence of B says that the birds don't realise they are being watched by *electronic eyes*. B also says that the females look for a *mate* (a breeding partner) – and the text under 19 mentions the result – a large group of kakapo chicks.

p.12–15 PAPER 1 Part 3

FURTHER PRACTICE AND GUIDANCE (p.14–15)

20 A: No, only that they will find the advertisements absorbing. It doesn't necessarily mean they will buy products after having seen them.
B: The grammar is passive. It suggests that someone else, in this case the advertisers, will choose the advertisements for the viewers.
C: In this case, *medium* means a way of communicating a message. The *mediums* mentioned in the text are the fans' T-shirts which will receive and display digitised logos and the increasing use of TV to also display logos.
D: The text only mentions the Superbowl, and as record numbers of people are watching it, we cannot really say it is less popular or appreciated.

21 A: It refers to the way in which viewers are exposed to advertising. If someone is just a *casual observer* – someone who hasn't thought about how or why advertisements appear on the TV – he won't realise they have been specifically chosen for each individual.
B: *To target a group of people* is an advertising term which means 'to choose or focus on a specific group for promotion'. An *omnipresent* thing is 'everywhere' and you cannot avoid something which is *inescapable*. These words relate to the previous sentence as they refer to *the changes that are happening.*

C: The text doesn't mention viewers' reactions, but just mentions the fact that this technology will exist.
D: There is no mention of viewers feeling forced to purchase the disposable products; simply that the products are advertised.

22 A: *To condemn* means 'to express strong disapproval' and is negative. *Nifty* in this case means 'stylish' and is therefore positive.
B: If someone feels *indignant*, they feel that something isn't fair. The writer suggests the viewers will *tend to like advertising better.*
C: If something is *cost-effective*, it saves money. The text states that the advertiser will save money.
D: A tailor makes clothes to exactly fit and suit one person. The expression *tailor to somebody's tastes* means that you design something suitable for one person or company.

23 A: No, it just says these mediums will be *inadequate* (not enough).
B: *The rest of the world* refers to different media: art, entertainment and journalism.
C: It mentions that advertising has increased in music entertainment nowadays, not that it will become more important.
D: A *backlash* means 'a sudden adverse or negative reaction'. It suggests that people once liked having so many outlets, but they will change their minds and really dislike it. *Inevitable* means something will definitely happen.

24 A: Parks are being renamed after corporations; The Boston Garden was renamed the Fleet Centre; a town has now adopted the name of a dotcom company.
B: He says *surely people … are capable of distinguishing between a commercial* (subjective) *message and an editorial* (truthful) *one*.
C: It says that journalists relied on money from *private sources*: rich people who supported their work as patrons. It does not say the journalists were trying to get money from the public.
D: Although he accepts that advertising has found its way into art, he does not see it as a dangerous thing since he believes people can recognise what is advertising and what is pure art.

25 A: *vulnerable* means 'easily attacked'. There is no mention of any specific group which is most likely to be attacked by advertisers.
B: *to dispel* means 'to make something go away'. The writer has said in previous paragraphs that there will be far too much advertising in the future, so he is not trying to tell us that we have nothing to worry about.
C: The answer is in the last line of the final paragraph – *That's when advertising has gone too far: when it's become something we are, rather than something we see.*
D: No, he seems to disapprove of the amount of advertising that many companies use, but he does not say that any specific company is dishonest. He has also already mentioned that people are fully aware of what a commercial is, so there is no need for it to be exposed.

p.12–13 PAPER Part 3 (Test)

20 C   **21** B   **22** D   **23** D   **24** A   **25** C

p.16–18 PAPER 1 Part 4

26 D: The answer comes from *Zirker's explanations are clear and sharp, although don't expect him to lead you by the hand*. This means 'don't expect him to make the explanations easy'.

27 A: The writer says that *I had her* (the author) *filed in a 'sentimental nature-lover …' category … a few years ago, I read my first Kingsolver* (book) *and ditched my ill-founded prejudice.* In other words, the author is saying that she had previously believed Barbara Kingsolver's books were too sentimental but recently she has discovered that this is not true.

28 C: The writer says … *others have often sketched out an answer. But in Zoo, Eric Baratay gives us an unprecedented, in-depth answer.* The writer is saying that other writers have written about zoos before, but Baratay is the first person to write about them in such detail.

29 D: The answer comes from *His story-meets-textbook approach mainly avoids confusing scientific equations.* The writer is saying that the author has chosen to combine a story-telling approach with an academic style which does not become too complicated.

30 C: The book presents *a grim* (depressing) *story.* There is a *wealth of statistics on the death rate in collections.*

31 B: The writer makes several mentions of how the book combines certainty and doubt: *This book gives us … a clear-eyed look at the subject's … uncertainties … The focus on uncertainty paradoxically has the effect of highlighting the areas in which seismologists are confident, which makes it easier to deal with the ambiguities.*

32 A: The writer mentions one of her first memories: *The pleasure of deciphering that first word (C-A-T, of course) remains with me to this day.* She is saying she can remember the first time she managed to read a word.

33 D: The answer comes from *In 'Journey from the Center of the Sun' Jack Zirker goes on a breakneck* (very fast) *trip … explaining as much as possible about our star on the way.*

34 B: The writer compares earthquake predictions with car engines and repairs, suggesting that both provoke a feeling of uncertainty which leads to stress and anxiety: *Anyone who has ever driven an elderly … car knows the feeling: it's going to break down, but who knows when, where and what part of the system will fail? Predicting earthquakes is much the same.*

35 A: The writer says of Barbara Kingsolver: *Possessed of an analytical mind, she's capable of putting it all down with real passion* (enthusiasm): *a rare find.*

36 C: The answer comes from *The text has been translated from the French and in places retains a certain unnatural clunkiness* (the translation sometimes sounds unnatural). The writer also says that the book contains *appalling zoological errors* (factual mistakes about animals). However, the writer also says that these few problems with style and content are *forgivable.*

37 D: The answer comes from *Up, down, in or out. If that's about as much attention as you pay the Sun, you're ignoring something mind-boggling* (amazing). In other words, if you only think of the sun as coming up in the morning/going down at night, etc. you are not thinking about all the other amazing facts about it.

38 C: The writer says that the book *neither apologises for nor criticises the modern zoo.*

39 B: The writer says that *her findings* (conclusions) *do not make easy reading.* This suggests that readers may not get all the answers they hoped to find. There is still a lot of uncertainty about earthquake prediction.

40 D: The writer says that the author *shows how solar research has progressed* (developed) *from inspired speculation* (guessing about the sun) *into a flourishing science.*

41 C: The answer comes from *the authors show that the desire to display our domination over nature has long been a hidden feature of zoos.* The writer is saying that the book shows us that people want to prove their dominance over animals, and that is the real reason we put them in zoos.

42 A: The answer comes from *'Small Wonder' is … a great place to set out from before you tackle her backlist.* The writer is saying that people should read Small Wonder before reading the books that the author has previously written.

p.19–22 PAPER 2 Part 1

FURTHER PRACTICE AND GUIDANCE (p.21–22)

Content
- the time when the free drinks were served
- the fact that the chef is experienced
- the other guests seemed satisfied
- David Vaylet, the owner, visited his guests
- there is room for a party downstairs.

Effect on target reader
The purpose of the letter is to show that Mike Champion's review is unfair/inaccurate. The reader (the editor) might be willing to print the letter if the tone of your letter is polite and if you point out the facts in a clear way.

Sample letter
1 am writing	7 being left
2 published	8 seemed
3 was also dining	9 visited
4 had looked	10 had asked
5 would have seen	11 would have found out
6 were being served	

Organisation and cohesion
The purpose of paragraph 1 is to indicate the reason for the letter – to disagree with Mike Champion's review. Your purpose for writing should always be clear in the first paragraph.
Paragraph 4 contains two points: the fact that customers were satisfied and the fact that the owner of the restaurant spoke to all of his customers. When you write your answer, put similar content points in the same paragraph.
Linkers: *which, also, first of all, in fact, further, finally*

Range
Passive: (*which was*) *published/were being served/tips being left*
Third conditional: *if he had looked … he would have seen/If he had asked … he would have found out*
Past modal: *should have looked*
Reporting verbs: *complains/suggests/states*

Mark: *Band 5*
As Karen has thoroughly responded to all the content points, used a wide range of grammatical structures, vocabulary and cohesive devices, and used the correct register and format, her letter would receive the top mark.

p.24–25 PAPER 3 Part 1

1 D: *expanse* collocates with the adjective *vast*; *expanse* means a wide and open area so it can be used for the sea; *territory* is used for an area which is under control of a country or ruler; we use *distance* to talk about the number of kilometres between two places; a *range* can either mean the same as distance or a selection or number of things, e.g. a range of mountains/suits for sale/magazines.

2 A: *connected* takes the preposition *to* and can be used to say that one piece of land was joined to another; *united* takes *with* and shows an agreement or common aim between people or groups; *integrated* takes *into* and can mean to combine two or more things so that they work together, e.g. *an integrated transport system* would involve trains, buses, taxis, etc.; *coupled* takes *with* and often means 'joined together', e.g. two pieces of equipment or machinery.

3 D: *to nourish/feed the imagination* is a collocation; *to raise* has many collocations: some common ones are *raise a family/a question/your hand/animals*; *to rear* means 'to care for animals or children until they are independent'; *to supply* means 'to provide someone/a group with what they need', e.g. you could *supply a product/food to someone* for instance.

4 **C:** *to assimilate information* is the correct answer as it can mean 'to fully understand information and then use it'; *congregate* means 'to come together as a group', e.g. people meeting in a church / in the main square of a town; *to amass* is wrong because it is a synonym for *gather* in the text; we say *to construct an idea/building*.

5 **D:** You can often *provide information, help* or *ideas*; you *grant someone permission/wishes/someone a loan*; we can say to *confer an award on somebody*; we often say *to contribute to a discussion*.

6 **A:** *to be suspended from* means to be hung from a high point, e.g. *the lamp was suspended from the ceiling*; we say to be *located in, situated in* and *attached to*.

7 **C:** *perspective* means 'view' in this context; the adjective *visionary* would not collocate with *inspection, observation* and *assessment*, which all suggest a formal evaluation.

8 **D:** *gazing* is the only verb of 'seeing' here that can take the preposition *down*.

9 **A:** *familiar* takes the preposition *to*, e.g. *this problem is familiar to us* (we know about this problem). The other adjectives would normally finish without the preposition, e.g. *Mercator's name is famous/memorable/recognizable because…* .

10 **C:** The collocation is *to devise a solution*. You can *invent a story/new technology*, *contrive a plan*, *scheme* (plan) *against somebody*.

11 **C:** *the entire surface* means the 'complete surface'; *sheer* is used to emphasize the size, degree or amount of something, e.g. *the sheer size of the crowd was frightening*; we often use *utter* in expressions such as *to my utter* (complete) *horror/amazement*; we would not use *full* with *surface* as it suggests depth and volume.

12 **A:** *to pioneer something* means to be the first to study and develop a certain area of knowledge; we often say *to initiate a programme* (to make a programme or project begin), *to lead people/a group* (to be in charge of them) and *to prepare something or someone to do something*; *to prepare* is not followed by the gerund.

13 **D:** *to bear in mind* is a fixed expression. A similar expression would be *to take into consideration*.

14 **B:** *common knowledge* is a collocation; the other adjectives cannot be used with *knowledge*.

15 **D:** *altered* means 'changed'; *distorted* sounds too negative as it means that something cannot be seen clearly, e.g. *a distorted image*; *substituted* needs the preposition *for*, e.g. *We substituted one thing for another thing*; *converted* requires the structure *convert one thing into another thing*.

p.26–28 PAPER 3 Part 2

FURTHER PRACTICE AND GUIDANCE (p.28)

1 Despite
2 Although
3 However
4 Whereas / Although / Even though
5 whereas
6 however
7 Despite
8 Nevertheless / However
9 Despite

p.26 PAPER 3 Part 2 (TEST)

0 **just / only / simply:** All have the same meaning in this sentence and context.

16 **few / no:** *We make few/no demands* means 'we ask for little or for nothing' / 'we don't want to be treated differently to right-handed people'.

17 **yet / but / though:** In this sentence, these words are all synonyms. The writer says that he used to make a weak joke about being left-handed, *but* at the same time, he wants to be proud of it.

18 **so:** *so far* means 'until now'.

19 **in:** *in* is the preposition that precedes *circulation*.

20 **to:** *to the contrary* is the standard phrase.

21 **is:** We need *is* to form the present simple passive with *claimed*.

22 **without:** The writer is saying that there is also no proof that Einstein was left-handed.

23 **in:** The phrase *there is no truth* takes the preposition *in* followed by the object.

24 **Despite:** *Despite* means the same as *although* but it is followed by a noun phrase. *Although* is followed by a whole clause.

25 **by:** *mean* ('intend' or 'have in mind') collocates with *by* in this context.

26 **who:** *who* is used to connect the verb *write* back to *those* ('people').

27 **However:** *However* is used to contrast this sentence with the previous one. It always requires a comma immediately afterwards when used as a conjunction.

28 **what:** (not *how*) This word can be used when referring forward, e.g. **What** *you need is a good holiday. He didn't realise* **what** *was going to happen next.*

29 **even:** *even so* means 'despite this', e.g. *He worked really hard; even so, he didn't get the promotion.*

30 **does:** *as does* means the same as 'so does'. Compare *I live in Madrid as does my sister* to *I live in Madrid. So does my sister.*

p.29 PAPER 3 Part 3

0 ✔

00 **these:** *these* is wrong because the text has not mentioned packers before.

31 **stuff:** A simpler sentence would be *In terms of how much they carry, some people believe less is more. Much* is referring to quantity, not frequency, as in *How much/often do you go on holiday?*

32 **more:** *further* is already in the comparative form and so *more* is incorrect.

33 ✔

34 **to:** The verb *to head* can take the preposition *for* with a specific place, e.g. *He was heading for the bank/the beach.* With an adverb, such as *overseas*, there is no preposition.

35 **there:** This sentence is not a question, so *there* cannot go after the auxiliary *are*.

36 ✔

37 **some:** The writer is talking in general about what events might occur. *Some* sounds too specific.

38 **you:** The verb *suggest* can be followed in these ways: *I suggest (that) you visit Paris in the autumn; I suggest visiting Paris in the autumn.* You cannot say *I suggest you that.*

39 **even:** In the previous line, the writer is recommending that people only need one suitcase. By using *even*, it sounds as though he thinks his suggestion is unlikely to be useful. This does not make sense in the sentence.

40 ✔

41 **so:** You cannot use *so* after an *if* clause.

42 **is:** This sentence is not a question so there can be no auxiliary after *whatever*. *I'm going to buy that pair of jeans whatever they cost!* (It doesn't matter what they cost.)

43 **could:** It is OK to say *If you could* in a polite request, but the writer is giving general advice.

44 ✔

45 **not:** The writer is saying that if you think something is probably not necessary, leave it at home. *Not* makes the sentence give the opposite advice, which does not fit in with the sense of the text.

46 ✔

p.30–33 PAPER 3 Part 4

FURTHER PRACTICE AND GUIDANCE (p.32–33)

For the correct parts of speech, see the explanations to the questions in the test.

0 c 47 d 48 d 49 d 50 a 51 c 52 a 53 c

p.30–31 PAPER 3 Part 4 (TEST)

0 **improvements** (n.): things which improve (*We need to make several improvements to the structure of this building.*) **(c)**
improvable (adj.): having the possibility to be improved (*His work is not satisfactory but I think it's improvable.*) **(d)**
improvisation (n.): the performance of a task or act without preparation (*Many comedians rely on improvisation instead of learning jokes by heart.*) **(b)**
improver (n.): a person who improves things (*Kate is a home-improver – she's always buying new furniture or decorating.*) **(a)**

47 **analysis** (n.): the careful study of a subject (*Scientists are carrying out a careful analysis of the bacteria.*) **(d)**
analytical (adj.): capable of analysing (*The Prime Minister has a very analytical mind.*) **(c)**
analyst (n.) / a person who analyses (*Business analysts predict that there will be an economic recovery next year.*) **(a)**
analyticant does not exist.

48 **championships** (n.): the contests held to find the winner (*Each year, the chess championships are being won by younger players.*) **(d)**
The other three words do not exist.

49 **systematic** (adj.): in order and carefully planned (*Simon has a systematic approach to organising his paper work.*) **(b)**
systematically (adv.): in an ordered way (*Simon organises his paper work systematically.*) **(d)**
systemise (v.): arrange in a system (*We need to systemise the way we deal with customer complaints.*) **(c)**
systemate does not exist.

50 **statistical** (adj.): relating to a numerical approach to analysing data (*Statistical analysis suggests that most families in the West are having fewer children.*) **(a)**
statistically (adv.): mathematically (*Statistically speaking, there's a greater chance of being robbed in the city rather than the countryside.*) **(b)**
The other two words do not exist.

51 **existence** (n.): the state of existing (*At one time, people believed in the existence of fairies and witches.*) **(c)**
existent (adj.): to be living / real (*Although rare, this type of parrot is still existent in a few remote islands.*) **(a)**
The other two words do not exist.

52 **miraculous** (adj.): like a miracle (*They had a miraculous escape when their boat turned over.*) **(a)**
miraculously (adv.): in a very surprising way (*The company performed very badly last year but has miraculously recovered in the last few months.*) **(b)**
The other two words do not exist.

53 **exceptionally** (adv.): unusually or outstandingly (*Ann plays the piano exceptionally well.*) **(c)**
exception (n.): something or someone not included in a rule or pattern or group (*We all went to the party, with the exception of Steve.*) **(a)**
exceptionable (adj.): making you feeling angry or offended (*He made an exceptionable comment about her appearance.*) **(b)**
exceptive does not exist.

54 **attraction** (n.): something which attracts (*The Eiffel Tower in Paris is a well-known tourist attraction*)

55 **additional** (adj.): another (*Living at home often saves money and an additional advantage is that you have the support of your family.*)

56 **educational** (adj.): about or providing education (*You should be reading educational books, not comics!*)

57 **ascent** (n.): the act of moving upward (*The climbers found that the ascent up the mountain was exhausting.*)

58 **unmissable** (adj.): too important or good to miss (*That new play is really fantastic – it's absolutely unmissable.*)

59 **unbelievable** (adj.): not seeming to be possible or likely (*She told me a pretty unbelievable story about her last job.*)

60 **achievement** (n.): something that has been accomplished (*Sarah got four As in her exams, which was a remarkable achievement.*)

61 **reasonably** (adv.): moderately (*I did reasonably well in the test.*)

p.34 PAPER 3 Part 5

62 used to
63 look
64 head / take off
65 good reason
66 save
67 long run
68 bargain / good deal
69 decide for
70 turns
71 loads / plenty / lots
72 good / reasonable / fair / better
73 supply
74 dangerous

p.35 PAPER 3 Part 6

0 **J:** In the first sentence, sleep is described as *the dark third* of our lives. The next sentence says that we are *familiar with* sleep (we all know we do it) but we only know a little about what really happens.

75 **E:** The sentence starts with the writer disagreeing with the idea that sleeping is a waste of time. He uses *but* to contrast the idea of *wasting time* with a *positive activity essential to our…well-being.*

76 H: In this sentence the writer is saying that most people need eight hours' sleep and the results (*consequences*) of less than eight hours' sleep over a period of time will be serious. The next sentence suggests what these consequences may be: slower driving reactions, bad memory, etc.

77 C: The writer is saying that those people who claim that they don't dream are wrong. They do have dreams but they forget them.

78 I: The writer describes two types of dreams: rapid-eye movement dreams / proper dreams and dreams where we see confusing images which are called *hypnagogic dreams*.

79 A: The writer is saying that there is some evidence that people are able to control *lucid* dreams – the type of dream where you know you are dreaming.

80 F: The writer is saying that he does not believe people can predict the future through dreams. He says it is unsurprising that some people's dreams seem to come true because millions of people dream every night and so it is likely that some of the things they dream about will happen.

p.36 PAPER 4 Part 1

1	feast	5	lakeside stage
2	ancestral homes	6	sunset / midnight
3	deserted	7	(their) relatives
4	three-hour	8	several layers

p.38 PAPER 4 Part 2

9	church hall	14	lead / main
10	Tuesday	15	third witch
11	costumes, sets	16	4.50
12	lighting (equipment)	17	wintondrama.co.uk
13	fund-raising / suitable		

p.39 PAPER 4 Part 3

18 C: She tried rock-climbing, and then other *new things* and then she *got round to trying* (finally tried) *kayaking*.
A: Amelia says that she was *working in London, stuck in an office*. She does not say any of her colleagues helped her.
B: Amelia's boyfriend introduced her to rockclimbing, but not kayaking.
D: Amelia says that she *needed a change of scene*. This means that she wanted a different lifestyle, not a new place to live.

19 A: She says *I knew I had the fitness*.
B: She mentions that she is always training and kayaking on the river but she does not say that she finds this frustrating or boring.
C: Amelia says *once I'd entered* (the race) *it was simply a question of pulling together a suitable training regime*. She is planning her own training. No other trainer is involved.
D: Amelia says that the race is very prestigious. In other words, the race has a good reputation or image. She makes no reference to her own reputation.

20 B: She says *I can only assume it's because the race is seen* (by women) *as too extreme* (dangerous).
A: Amelia says the male and female competitors have a lot of respect for each other so the men do not discourage the women.
C: Amelia says that sea-kayaking is a popular hobby for both men and women in Britain and she believes this means that they will take part in the Norway race in the future. She does not say that they only want to kayak in Britain.
D: Amelia says that women do *paddle some way behind the men* in the race, but she does not give this as the reason why women do not take part.

21 A: She says that *for long-distance sea-kayaking you need to make sure the muscles you work are the ones you'll actually need … This involves lots of gym work on the upper back.*

B: Amelia says that she trains on a local reservoir every other day, so she is not limiting her training to the sea.
C: Amelia says that the *touring style* will put a strain on the back. She uses *a forward paddling style* instead.
D: Amelia says that for long-distance kayaking, it is important to train the right muscle groups – not all of them.

22 D: She says that *you must be able to read the water … the race coincides with the tides … Crossing an eddy line in the wrong place might mean you are battling against the tide, but getting it right can get the tide behind you and save time.*
A: Amelia mentions that *half the race is on the open sea* but she does not say the kayakers need to concentrate on this fact.
B: Amelia mentions that some of the race is *island-hopping* (sailing between islands) but she does not say that they are used for shelter. She says that there are *black eddies – swirling pools of water which can measure up to two kilometres in diameter* between the islands, so this means that island-hopping is dangerous.
C: It is the race organisers that tell competitors where to go. The competitors do not plan and then memorise a route.

23 C: Amelia mentions that high waves could turn the kayak over during the race. She says that *competitors paddle between islands in swells* (waves) *of over three metres … that's how high the water is above you*. She adds that *competitors who capsize* (whose kayak turns over) *are just allowed help from other paddlers*.
A: Amelia does not say that her physical strength declines – only that it is important to be fit.
B: Amelia says that when the kayaks are close to shore, the water is more dangerous. The water may turn the boat over, but she does not say she is worried that her boat will be pushed onto the shore.
D: Amelia says that she manages to *settle her nerves*. This means that she does not panic and lose control.

24 B: She says *There's usually someone around to load you back into your kayak.*
A: Amelia does not say that any capsized competitor is disqualified. She says that another competitor will help you and *set you on your way* (help them start racing again).
C: Amelia says that the rescue teams are not allowed to help.
D: Amelia says that *anybody* (any competitor) *losing time going to the aid of someone in trouble is automatically awarded the same time as the person finishing first*. So, if the helper gets the top points, it will certainly benefit him / her.

p.40–42 PAPER 4 Part 4

FURTHER PRACTICE AND GUIDANCE (p.41–42)

Speaker 1
1 foreign clients, remember names
2 professional, position
3 Have you met
4 assistant

Speaker 2
5 equipment
6 lens
7 offended, paying money, portrait
8 business, recommendations

Speaker 3
9 self-confidence
10 department
11 looking down on
12 small

Speaker 4
13 terms
14 much to say, contrived
15 gap of 20
16 physics teacher

Speaker 5
17 showing my c.v (curriculum vitae), restaurants
18 catering
19 take me on

p.42 PAPER 4 Part 4 (TEST)

Speaker 1: 25 E 30 C
The first speaker says *when I'm supposed to be showing foreign clients around* – this suggests he is in business. He also says *it* (this inability to remember names) *...does not come across as professional for someone in my position* and mentions that he has an assistant. This suggests he has an important position in his company – in this case a manager. He says that he finds himself saying *Have you met?* which is the way to begin an introduction.

Speaker 2: 26 G 31 B
The second speaker is a photographer who takes pictures of children. She is saying that she is not always able to recognise whether a small baby is male or female so sometimes she says *Have you got a name yet for...?* and doesn't say 'him' or 'her'. She worries that this will offend the parents who will not recommend her to others. She mentions *equipment, the lens* and *portrait* which tell us that she is a photographer. She also says *They* (the parents) *feel offended and they're paying money to have their kid's portrait* (formal photograph) *taken. It's not good for business or personal recommendations*.

Speaker 3: 27 F 32 G
The third speaker is talking about her inability to order from a foreign menu – she is embarrassed about making a mistake with pronunciation when ordering – or not exactly understanding what the dishes are. We can understand that she is an office worker from *we've gone out to eat after work*, and *I'm the new girl in the department*. We know that the other people in her department make her feel inferior from *I don't have much self-confidence in general ... I feel exposed* and *I'm fed up with them looking down on me. It makes me feel small* (inferior).

Speaker 4: 28 H 33 F
The fourth speaker starts by talking about his time at school. He then talks about his old classmate, Peter, who has organised a reunion of all the people in his class 20 years later. He finds the reunion very embarrassing because nobody knows what to say to each other. We can understand that the speaker is talking about school from *a couple of terms ... I was in the same dormitory ... everybody remembered hating the physics teacher*. The idea of an unnatural social situation comes from *nobody had much to say to anybody and the few conversations we had were utterly contrived* (unnaturally created / not genuine).

Speaker 5: 29 D 34 H
The fifth speaker is talking about a trip to Greece. He practised some Greek phrases on a restaurant owner but the owner laughed at him. He says that he wants to improve his Greek so that when he returns to Greece, other restaurant owners will be more impressed and more likely to give him a job. We know he is a chef from *my catering skills are alright*. We know he is trying to impress potential employers from *I thought it might make more of an impact if I could show I knew a bit of the language...showing my CV to a couple of restaurants ... I want to be taken seriously* (I want people to recognise my ability) *there won't be many people prepared to take me on* (hire me) *unless I have some idea of the language.*

TEST TWO

p.48–49 PAPER 1 Part 1

1   **C:** *I was from the wrong class and went to the wrong university ... You resign yourself to working at the local factory.* Sarah is saying that her social background and education would not help her career in the UK.

2   **D:** *'People at work were far too competitive for my liking.'* Lucy is saying that she didn't like the competetive behaviour of her colleagues.

3   **B:** *it would ... have been harder to break into this kind of field ... it may have taken longer in the US.* Jenny is stating that she has achieved success in New Zealand more quickly than would have been possible in the USA.

4   **D:** *Sometimes it bothers me that we're so remote – you can feel a bit cut of from ... the rest of the world...* Lucy is saying that at times she is bothered / frustrated by the fact that New Zealand is a long distance from anywhere else and that she doesn't always know what is happening in other countries.

5   **C:** *if you want to do something here, you just go for it, which is an attitude I admire beyond belief.* Sarah is saying that New Zealanders are ambitious, and are not afraid of taking risks.

6   **A:** *she's mourning for a country she once called home ... but I do miss it.* We usually use the verb *mourn* when someone has died: *Everybody mourned* (felt and showed sadness) *when our great-grandfather died.* The writer suggests that Nicky thinks she has 'lost' her country.

7   **D:** *Another thing that impresses me is that you can leave your stuff in a café and it'll still be there ... later. People are ... trustworthy.* Lucy is saying that if a person accidentally leaves something in a café / restaurant, etc., it will not be stolen. People are honest.

8   **A:** *I'm so glad I have the opportunity to leave my stamp on my new country.* The word *glad* corresponds to 'happy'; *stamp* corresponds to 'impression'.

9   **B:** *'I'm from Alabama, but no, we didn't run around barefoot and my father didn't play the banjo!' she jokes, in anticipation of my preconceptions.* Jenny believes that the writer may imagine she is from a poor, uneducated background because of the writer's wrong ideas about people from Alabama.

10 **A:** *I just love the tranquillity and the fact you can lead a safe and ordinary life.* Tranquil corresponds to 'calm' and *ordinary life* corresponds to 'normality'.

11 **A:** *I have to take great heed of earthquakes, which isn't an issue in South Africa.* To take great heed of means 'to consider carefully'.

12 **B:** *worked in corporate design for ten years in the USA ... a job with an Auckland design firm, where she was able to gain experience in an unfamiliar but challenging area of design – packaging.* Jenny had worked in corporate design in the USA but worked on the design of packaging in New Zealand.

13 **C:** *Being a foreigner certainly works in her favour ... respondents tend to see me as impartial and open-minded and are ... willing to share their lives with me.* Sarah says that because she's English and wasn't brought up in New Zealand, people feel that she can be more objective and fairer about local situations.

14 **B:** *opposing views are what make strategies, concepts and designs better.* Jenny feels that differences of opinion and discussion will finally lead to better results.

15 **C:** *I wish New Zealanders could see their country as I do ... it saddens me that they don't think they're good enough on the global stage.* Sarah is suggesting that she sees many positive things about New Zealand that New Zealanders don't see for themselves.

16 **D:** *... my ... colleagues are ... easy-going* (relaxed). *A good atmosphere more than makes up for* (is more important than) *... salary.* Lucy is saying that she now enjoys working in a friendly, co-operative environment.

p.50–52 PAPER 1 Part 2

Key to test and further practice

17 **E:** *There's less excuse for… explorers, scholars and philosophers who … were more naïve.* Other people should have been able to recognise whether they were looking at real wool or not.

18 **D:** *too* suggests that the option must contain a similar description: *when the fruits ripened … to reveal tiny lambs.* The words referring to *tales* and *stories* are *in some versions.*

19 **B:** *he … had heard this from reliable sources. Reliable sources* means in this context 'people you can trust'.

20 **G:** *Still it eluded them* refers to *lamb* (singular) and *travellers* (plural). The word in the first line of that option which means 'to avoid being found' is *elude*. In the phrase *And so it went on*, the word *it* refers to the idea in option G that people who doubted the lamb-plant's existence were then persuaded it did exist. The idea continues in the text: *As soon as anyone voiced doubts …* (there was) *new evidence.*

21 **C:** This option contains a 'singular' reference: *a curious object … a sort of toy animal.*

22 **A:** This option contains a reference to *the case: And so it was … for 180 years.* In other words, the case was closed for 180 years. The text under 22 also mentions 'Henry Lee' by introducing him as *a little known naturalist.*

p.53–54 PAPER 1 Part 3

23 **D:** The writer says that *if you think (humans) are the only creatures with a moral sense … you're in good company.* This simply means that many people believe this to be true. The writer is not saying he agrees. He also disagrees with *most experts* by saying *yet I'm convinced that many animals can distinguish right from wrong.* A *misconception* means 'a wrong belief which many people have'.

24 **A:** The writer says *Biologists have had real problems trying to explain why people are frequently inexplicably nice to each other … Perhaps we expect a payback somewhere down the line, or maybe our good deeds are directed only towards kin.* The word *inexplicably* means 'impossible to explain'. The use of *perhaps* and *maybe* also suggest a lack of certainty.

25 **C:** The writer states *… on the rare occasions when an animal says 'Let's play' and then beats up an unsuspecting animal, the culprit usually finds itself ostracised by its former playmates.* 'Let's play' suggests the animal wants to engage in non-aggressive social play. To *beat up* in this context means 'to attack aggressively' – so the animal is not following the rules of social play. To be *ostracised* means that an individual is ignored or excluded by others.

26 **D:** The writer says *If I'm right, morality evolved because it is adaptive. It helps many animals, including humans, to survive and flourish in their particular social environment.* In the writer's opinion, there is no 'universal' code of morality. Different moral codes or rules depend on the situation in which groups live.

27 **D:** The writer says that *… provided virtue is rewarded by a greater number of offspring, then any genes associated with good behaviour are bound to accumulate in subsequent generations.* A simpler way of saying this is if good behaviour results in a greater number of 'children', then any genes connected to good behaviour will probably increase in future generations.

28 **B:** The writer says *First, we didn't invent virtue – its origins are much more ancient than our own. Secondly, we should stop seeing ourselves as morally superior to other animals.* He is suggesting that people should not believe humans invented moral behaviour nor believe that we are morally better than animals.

p.55–59 PAPER 1 Part 4

FURTHER PRACTICE AND GUIDANCE (p.58–59)

1 b **2** b **3** a **4** a **5** a **6** b **7** b **8** b **9** b **10** a **11** b **12** a **13** a **14** b **15** a **16** b

p.55–57 PAPER 1 Part 4 (TEST)

29 **E:** The answer comes from *On an average week, the entertainment guide … lists around 50 Latin dance nights … Meanwhile, traditional dance schools too have started to report significant attendance rises …*

30 **D:** The writer states *'We can delight in all the accessories – the glittery hair and the extravagant costumes.'* He is saying that the dancers' appearances may make us laugh, but in a positive way.

31 **A:** The answer comes from *… dancing is an instinctive celebration of physical existence … understood by everyone. Beyond speech, learnt behaviour, or even conscious thought.*

32 **H:** The answer comes from *… DJ Vic Jones … fumed:* (said angrily) *'… I resent them gatecrashing and taking up all the dance floor. There is nothing worse than dancing round the floor and bumping into people doing a line dance. It stops your rhythm.'*

33 **G:** The answer comes from *Clubbing, with its deafening music, solo dancing and heavy competitiveness, provides less and less social contact, and becomes an avoidance activity* (avoiding contact / communication with other people).

34 **B:** The answer comes from *More and more of us are returning home* (from holidays) *… with glowing memories of cultures in which dance is a vital part of life.*

35 **G:** *… social dancing offers … opportunities to encounter a range of partners, in a forum* (place / situation) *where ability and enthusiasm transcend* (are more important than) *age, gender and class.*

36 **C:** *… pop music … consigned* (sent) *ballroom, Latin and rock'n roll to the laughably middle-class scrapheap* (rubbish pile). In other words, when people became interested in pop music, they thought that the old forms of social dancing were ridiculous middle-class activities and laughed at them. The writer also says that *dancing with … partners, was broadly perceived* (regarded) *… as a slightly bizarre* (strange) *cultural quirk practised by eccentric people in shiny, spangly outfits.*

37 **D:** *There's also the boredom with the loud unfriendliness of modern dance clubs.*

38 **A:** The answer comes from *Who really doesn't like dancing? Can even the most bad-tempered dance-floor-avoider last an entire lifetime without a … display at a wedding … after the birth of a child – or a particularly good goal – or refrain from a secret shuffle around the privacy of their living room?* The writer is saying that even people who usually hate dancing will, at some point, be unable to stop themselves dancing.

39 **E:** *An evening's dancing is as good for you as a three-hour hike. It pumps blood up your legs, so it's good for your heart, and it helps posture and breathing.*

40 **F:** The answer comes from *Dance is also good therapy too, busting stress, promoting relaxation and … self-confidence and a sense of achievement.* The writer also says *All humans need tactile contact. The touch of another person affirms that we are real, that we are alive.*

41 **B:** The writer says that *as a nation, our reputation as dancers has historically earned us no points and no recognition.*

42 **D:** The answer comes from *Lyndon Wainwright … lays the decline of social dancing squarely at the fast feet of the actor John Travolta.* The expression 'to lay something at somebody's feet' means to say that they are responsible. Wainwright is saying that John Travolta's character, Tony Manero, in the film *Saturday Night Fever* made people want to dance alone.

43 **A:** The answer comes from *Dance can take many forms: whether it comes as an impulsive* (spontaneous) *release of energy and emotion, or within a skilful display of practised* (rehearsed) *artistry.*

p.61–63 PAPER 2 Part 2

FURTHER PRACTICE AND GUIDANCE (p.62–63)

Content
The answer needs to refer to changes the Internet has brought about in your country – not across the world. You can write about the effects the Internet has had on business and/or on education and/or on home life. The sample answer has focused on business and education.

Effect on the target reader
The purpose of this article is to provide general information about the effects of the Internet. The reader would be informed about the general effects of the Internet in the writer's country.

Register
The register should be informative and factual.

Format
An eye-catching title is important, and clearly separated paragraphs for each point.

Organisation and cohesion
Paragraph 1: A general introduction
Paragraph 2: Examples of how the Internet has affected the business world.
Paragraph 3: Examples of how the Internet has affected education.
Paragraph 4: A summary or conclusion.

Linking words/phrases
even, unless, indeed, similarly, for instance.

Range of vocabulary and structure
Adjectives: *competitive* (companies), *increasing* (number), *greater* (number), *vast* (opportunities), *latest* (research).
Adverbs: *dramatically* (increased), *simply* (through)
Tenses:
• Present perfect simple (*has increased, has revolutionised, it's become, have done*)
• Present continuous (*are using, are relying*)
• Future simple (*will have, will be able*)
Passive: *can be used, may be published, has been estimated*

Accuracy
The errors are:
the trend continues to grow ~~up~~.
contact ~~with~~ our friends
has ~~the~~ access to the Internet
are using this opportunity ~~for~~ to research
can provide ~~us~~ are vast
~~researches~~ (uncountable)

Mark: *Band 4*
The writer has responded to the question appropriately and the answer would inform the target reader. The answer has been written in a suitably informative style and is well organised and laid out. There is a good range of tenses, cohesive devices and vocabulary. There are a number of basic errors but these do not impede communication. The errors bring the mark down to 4.

p.64–68 PAPER 3 Part 1

FURTHER PRACTICE AND GUIDANCE (p.66–68)

0   a convinced   b determined   c converted   d persuaded/convinced
1   a suggest   b convey/suggest   c bear   d transfer
2   a attracting   b causing   c devoting   d paying
3   a exact   b specialised   c detailed   d specific
4   a divided   b split   c detached   d separated
5   a appear   b draw   c move   d approach
6   a assists   b informs   c enables   d facilitates
7   a fits   b ties   c corresponds   d complements
8   a succession   b sequence   c system   d progression
9   a presented   b tempted   c demonstrated   d shown
10   a view   b sight   c notice   d perception
11   a Surely   b Presumably   c likely   d predictably
12   a expectations   b suspicions   c calculations   d estimates
13   a related   b connected   c descended   d evolved
14   a look into/work out   b work out   c think over   d take in
15   a partners   b allies   c defenders   d helpers

p.64–65 PAPER 3 Part 1 (TEST)

1 B   **2** B   **3** A   **4** C   **5** D   **6** C   **7** A   **8** A   **9** C   **10** D   **11** B   **12** D
13 A   **14** B   **15** C

p.69 PAPER 3 Part 2

0   **past/last:** In this context, over a period of time these adjectives are synonyms.

16   **into:** The verb *force* takes the preposition *into*, e.g. to force someone into a decision.

17   **only/just:** The structure *not only/just … but* is used to show addition, e.g. *Tony is not only generous with his money but with his time* (Tony is generous with both his time and money).

18   **What:** *What* can be used to refer forward in a sentence, e.g. *What amazes me is how much money he spends every month!*

19   **until:** *up until* is another way of saying *until* and is mainly used to describe past duration, e.g. *I lived there up until I was married.*

20   **hardly:** *hardly anyone* means the same as 'almost no one', e.g. *Sarah was upset because hardly anyone remembered her birthday.*

21   **one/them:** Both are grammatically correct but *one* is better because it emphasizes how rare bananas used to be.

22   **with:** *to meet with failure* is a fixed expression.

23   **However:** *However* is used to contrast this sentence with the previous one. *However* always has a comma immediately after it when used as a conjunction.

24   **this:** *this* refers back to the problem of rotting bananas on long ship voyages.

25   **now:** *then, as now* compares the past to the present and suggests that a situation hasn't changed, e.g. *Then, as now, I spent my holidays with my aunt and uncle in Sicily.*

26   **were:** We need *were* to form the passive of the past simple.

27   **which:** *which* refers back to *enthusiasm.* Compare: *It was an experience **which** he never recovered **from**,* to *It was an experience **from which** he never recovered* (more formal/written).

28   **with:** *It is packed with energy* means the same as 'It is full of energy'.

29   **so:** *so* shows the connection between the health benefits of the banana and its popularity. In other words, it is popular because of its health benefits.

30 not: Bananas are so good for our health that we should not be suprised that people like them.

p.70 PAPER 3 Part 3

0 some, : A sentence beginning with *Although* requires a comma after the first clause.

00 necessary

000 ✔

31 August, the: *the month Madrid shuts down,* is extra information and requires a comma on both sides.

32 ✔

33 their: Be careful – sometimes a word may be spelt correctly but does not fit in with the sense of the text.

34 apartments

35 four weeks': We need to use the apostrophe to show the possessive aspect. Compare *a four-week holiday* (a noun phrase) to *in four weeks' time.*

36 breaks: The word *breaks* is the plural of *breaks*. We do not use apostrophes to indicate plurals.

37 require

38 ✔

39 silence, : We only need to put a comma between *silence* and *foreign backpackers* because commas are used to separate nouns in lists, e.g. *I've been to Turkey, Egypt, France and Germany.*

40 here, however, : Within a sentence, *however* needs a comma on both sides.

41 unwritten: *Writing* has one *t, written* has two.

42 ✔

43 ✔

44 leisurely

45 'There's: It is important that you read the whole sentence – not just a line in this test. *'There's no one here to take your call.'* is part of the recorded phone message.

46 answering

p.71–72 PAPER 3 Part 4

47 global
48 upcoming / forthcoming
49 renew
50 membership
51 recipient
52 Additional
53 payment
54 equivalent
55 likelihood
56 Endangered
57 extensive
58 extinction
59 shortage
60 survival
61 threatened

p.73 PAPER 3 Part 5

62 (appropriately / correctly / suitably) dressed
63 be allowed / permitted
64 circumstances
65 requested / required
66 later than
67 promptly / punctually

68 to inform
69 preferably
70 absences
71 obtained
72 aware of
73 (immediate) attention
74 cooperation

p.74–75 PAPER 3 Part 6

Key to test and further practice

75 I   76 E   77 B   78 H   79 D   80 C

p.76 PAPER 4 Part 1

1 7 million
2 a decade / an entire decade
3 sand dunes
4 perfectly / well preserved / in good condition
5 hope of life
6 double
7 (surprisingly) primitive / advanced
8 advanced / primitive
9 flat
10 human-like

p.77 PAPER 4 Part 2

11 (more) frequent
12 excellent connections
13 15
14 express services
15 a supplement
16 reserve seats
17 youth hostels
18 transport / carry silk

p.78–80 PAPER 4 Part 3

FURTHER PRACTICE AND GUIDANCE (p.79–80)

Question 19
1 fairly unusual
2 facing danger
3 wrong with her
4 not a career path

Sentences **3 + 4** contain the answer. Although Sarah mentions the fact that travel was dangerous and it was an unusual occupation for a woman, she says that Isabella believed she was a very ill person and had never imagined she would be well enough to travel.

Question 20
5 do her good
6 worth seeing, interesting people
7 remarkable career

Sentence **5** contains the answer. Although Isabella says there is nothing worth seeing and no interesting people, her reason for going was to improve her health. Her friend has suggested the climate would be beneficial to her. Sarah mentions that Isabella's career is about to begin, but that is not her reason for going to Australia.

Question 21
8 raise her head
9 cut off by snow
10 huge elephant, black horse
11 social standing

Sentence **8** contains the answer. Sarah suggests that Isabella spent a lot of time on her sofa, feeling ill and tired. Therefore, it would be surprising for someone like her to enjoy an active life of travelling. She doesn't say that Isabella has never experienced extreme temperatures or that she is afraid of animals. She says that Sarah comes from a good social background (*her social standing*) but she doesn't say that Isabella enjoyed socialising and going to parties.

Question 22

12 remained unseen
13 the content
14 extreme detail
15 understatement

Sentence **15** contains the answer. Sarah does not say the letters should have been published earlier – she just states the fact that they weren't. She says that the content of the letters was later used to help write her newspaper articles – not that the newspaper articles helped her write the letters. Sarah says that Isabella often provided too much detail. She says she cannot be accused of *understatement*, which means that Isabella often exaggerated or went into too much detail about what she saw.

Question 23

16 inherited
17 sparkles, shines
18 bravest rider
19 compatible

Sentence **17** contains the answer. Although Isabella has inherited her father's strictness, this isn't an unusual thing. There is no suggestion that she wasn't brave and was never actually ill. Sarah says that Isabella *sparkles and shines* when she's under pressure; in other words, she seems happy and bright.

Question 24

20 destroyed
21 doubt about, influence
22 cynical
23 adventure, newness

Sentence **21** contains the answer. Sarah mentions that many modern writers are too *cynical* and seem to prefer their home country. Perhaps these writers have had bad experiences, but Sarah doesn't suggest that Isabella had bad experiences or should have written about them. Although she says some of the letters were destroyed, she doesn't say this made the book less interesting or less worth reading. Sarah says that it is unclear what Isabella has edited and what the editor has edited.

p.78 PAPER 4 Part 3 (TEST)

19 B   20 C   21 A   22 C   23 B   24 A

p.81 PAPER 4 Part 4

Speaker 1: 25 B 30 B
The first speaker is talking about his favourite pop group when he was a teenager. He mentions his friend Simon, but does not say that Simon influenced him. We can understand that he is talking about a pop group / pop star from *they weren't that well known … (then) … they got pretty big* (became successful). *It wasn't just the* (music) *albums … I wanted to play* (guitar) *like the lead* (guitar player) *… But I never learnt a single chord* (I didn't learn how to play music). We can guess that he is a parent from *And my kids … I've got no idea who it is on the posters …* (who the singers / groups are).

Speaker 2: 26 F 31 G
The second speaker is talking about her interest in writing when she was a child. We know she is a writer from *I was a voracious reader* (I read a lot) *but I never used anyone else's ideas in my work* (I never used ideas from other authors' books in my books) and *when I first got published.* We can guess she is talking about her teacher from *It was Mrs Shelly that encouraged me … she read out one of my essays …* By saying <u>Mrs</u> Shelly, we can tell that she had a formal relationship with the person who influenced her. An *essay* is a piece of writing you produce in school.

Speaker 3: 27D 32 E
The third speaker is talking about how her father was a very honest and direct man. We can understand that she is talking about her father from *Mum never got used to it. She'd be after* (she wanted) *some compliment … and he'd tell her 'No love, it's wrong on you'* and *I'd like to think I take after him* (inherited his qualities / personality). We can understand that the speaker is a politician from *I've been accused by other people in my* (political) *party of being too outspoken* (too honest) *… but … the public need to trust you.*

Speaker 4: 28 G 33 H
The fourth speaker starts by talking about his life as a journalist now and how he often remembers his childhood friend, James. He says that James was a very interesting person and that it was James who originally intended to become a journalist. We can understand that the speaker is talking about journalism from *when the* (news)*paper has sent me overseas … I'm sitting with … the cameraman* and *he was the one who was planning on reporting from far-off regions but it turned out to be me instead.* We can understand that he is describing a childhood friend from *I was a miserable teenager … James moved in next door and I was allowed to go round there* (to visit him).

Speaker 5: 29 E 34 D
The fifth speaker is talking about a TV star and the way he and his classmates used to copy the TV star's *moves* (the way he used to fight). We can tell he is talking about a TV star from *he was on* (appearing on the TV) *every Thursday night at 5 o'clock … I'd grab the remote control.* We can understand that he is a teacher from … *now it's me who's telling the kids* (the school children) *to calm down and leave each other alone* (stop fighting). *Sometimes you have to leave half the group* (the class) *with something to get on with* (work to do) *while you're taking* (them) *to the* (school) *nurse.*

TEST THREE

p.84–85 PAPER 1 Part 1

1 **D:** *It is an immensely entertaining and illuminating novel.*

2 **B:** *for every published page, there are six that John McGahern discarded.* The writer is saying that the author wrote many pages, but re-wrote and reduced a lot of the book to produce a better one.

3 **A:** The answer comes from *Peripheral* (not as important as the main) *portraits are skilfully drawn.* The writer says that the young child's dialogue is moving but not overly sentimental. Kate's in-laws are also genuinely funny.

4 **C:** *The combination of serious theme and comic description is so appealing that you hardly care when big chunks of the book start to crumble in the last 50 pages or so.* The writer is saying that in general, this fascinating book has been well written and so the occasionally weak writing and plot in the last 50 pages doesn't matter.

5 **B:** *We are never quite sure when the novel's events take place and McGahern has indicated that the novel's dating is deliberately vague.*

6 **C:** It has been written in a way that the reader will not find confusing. The answer comes from *it's not hard to follow, since the structure reveals itself in stages.*

7 **B:** *We randomly assemble a picture of others in the community.* The writer is saying that there seems to be no order or pattern to how the characters are presented to us.

8 **D:** *Always interesting, if only intermittently well written.*

9 **A:** The answer comes from *These are plot lines familiar to all of us … What distinguishes … Crow Lake is that she* (the author) *combines these plots with a twist* (something unexpected).

10 **C:** *You keep laughing out loud, losing your place, starting again, then stopping because you're tempted to call your friends and read them long sections of Foer's assured, hilarious prose.* The writer is saying that the book is so funny that it constantly makes you laugh and makes you want to read sections of it to other people.

11 **C:** *one of the book's attractions is its writer's high degree of faith in the reader's intelligence.* The writer is saying that the author believes that his readers will be able to understand the serious themes in his book.

12 **B:** *… it is a difficult novel to get into since one cannot immediately locate the centre of the narrative.*

13 **A:** *the necessary solemnity of the heroine-narrator is a somewhat stifling influence.* This means that the heroine/narrator speaks in a very serious way so it takes the reader a while to follow what she is saying.

14 **C:** *a whole series of themes so weighty that any one of them would be enough for an ordinary novel.*

15 **B:** *this initially demanding but ultimately rewarding novel.*

16 **D:** *This claim … hinges on the authenticity of Crafts' manuscript, a subject all but laid to rest in Gates' long introduction to the book. Although Gates never manages to identify Hannah Crafts … he presents a formidable array of evidence authenticating her story.* The writer is saying that Henry Gates has mostly proved that the story was true, but that he has not been able to find out exactly who it was really about.

17 **A:** *… in its earnest determination to make Kate and Luke and their choices credible.*

p.86–89 PAPER 1 Part 2

FURTHER PRACTICE AND GUIDANCE (p.88–89)

1 a 2 b 3 b 4 c 5 a 6 b 7 c 8 b 9 c 10 b 11 c 12 a
13 a 14 b 15 c 16 c 17 a

p.86–87 PAPER 1 Part 2 (TEST)

18 **H:** The connection between the text above 18 and H is *this seemed more like a military operation* and *But that, however, was exactly what it was.* The writer is saying that in reality, this expedition <u>was</u> a real military operation. It also mentions in H that the writer was not a soldier and in the text below H, the writer says that Mark, the leader, would not be responsible for him – because he is a civilian, and not a soldier.

19 **D:** In the text above 19, Mark promises not to let the writer fall, in other words, he will keep him safe. D begins with *Despite that welcome reassurance.* To 'reassure someone' means to promise a person something in order to remove anxiety or fear.

20 **F:** In the text above 20, Mark explains all the reasons why climbing Mont Blanc is a dangerous challenge. F begins with *To add to my apprehension, it was this same route that had beaten me the last time around.* The writer suggests that travelling on the same route is an additional fear to others that Mark has already mentioned. F also connects to the text under 20: the writer says that the soldiers did not appear *too fit.* Then he says that *looks* (appearances) *can be deceptive.* He is saying that he was wrong about the fitness of the soldiers.

21 **A:** In the text above 21, the writer says that he had *turned back* or given up on the route up the Col two years ago. Option A begins with *This time … I was having better luck.* He is saying that he is having more success on the same route on this expedition. A also connects with the text under 21: the writer says that *everyone was suffering and slowing down.* The next piece of text begins with *Even digging snow pits for the tents was a real struggle.* Digging the snow pits was extremely difficult because everyone was suffering from exhaustion.

22 **E:** This paragraph finishes with the writer believing *at least the worst was over.* The text under 22 says *I couldn't have been more wrong* and continues *the descent made everything that had gone before seem easy.* The writer is admitting that he made a mistake – that the ascent to the top of the mountain had been easier than the descent to the bottom.

23 **B:** This paragraph begins with *It looked like the decision had been made for us.* This refers back to the previous text that mentions that the soldiers were forced to change direction because a large piece of ice was blocking their route. B finishes with the writer mentioning how easy it is to make a mistake. The text under 23 then says that he slipped and was unable to stop himself from falling.

24 **G:** This paragraph begins with *Despite my humiliation…* The writer is referring to his embarrassment and shame at being unable to stop himself from falling. He also mentions that there were *many further stumbles* – meaning that he continued to slip and almost fall.

p.90–91 PAPER 1 Part 3

25 **D:** The answer comes from *At one time the notion of a career on stage may have been frowned upon.* 'To frown upon something' means 'to disapprove of it'.
A: It was usual for comedians only to receive free drinks and sandwiches.
B: There is no mention of awards that were offered in the past.
C: The text only says that *stand-up comedian(s) would have to*

endure years on the circuit of small-time venues. This means that comedians were forced to give many performances in places that only attracted a small audience. They did this as they hoped it would lead to a successful career, but this was not always the case.

26 B: The answer comes from *five comedy awards that are regarded in the industry as one long audition for lucrative TV work.* So, comedians take part in the festival in order to show their level of ability to TV producers or *a top agent.*
A: There is no mention of comedians wanting to 'revolutionise' comedy. The *revolution* which is mentioned refers to the growing interest in watching comedians.
C: Although the number of people watching comedy is growing, a *wide audience* suggests 'people from different social or cultural backgrounds'. There is no mention of comedians hoping to be seen by a wide audience.
D: There is no mention of a cash prize, only the possibility of future work in Melbourne or Montreal, where the comedians may receive a salary, not a prize.

27 A: The answer comes from *it's not all milk and honey for those seeking fame and fortune. Milk and honey* are a metaphor for the good things in life. The answer can also be found in *There are many, many comedians who have been around for years without a breakthrough.* This means they have tried for a long time to become successful, but have failed.
B: Although Burdett-Coutts refers to three cities where opportunities are limited, he does not say that comedians should not try to work there or in other cities. Perhaps some comedians will succeed.
C: Burdett-Coutts only says there are many comedians looking for success. He doesn't refer to how talented they may or may not be.
D: Burdett-Coutts *maintains that there's room for another comedy festival in a seemingly overcrowded market.* This means that he believes that the market is not really overcrowded and that another festival is possible.

28 A: *What you have these days is a concern with the comic's creative potential. They may think someone … has a talent that could be put to better use coming up with ideas for sketches in established TV shows or even for editing scripts.* This means that TV producers are looking for comedians who can write jokes for other people.
B: The text says *Not so long ago, TV producers would want to see someone up there performing live…* This is not the key because it refers to a past situation.
C: *and audience reaction was the bottom line.* This means that how the audiences responded to a comedian was the most important thing, but again, it is referring to a past situation.
D: The text says *Despite the risk of obscurity.* This means that there is a chance that the comedian will never become well known or successful. However, there is no reference to the comedian's attitude towards this.

29 C: Lisa says *It certainly helps in terms of knowing whether a joke is 'sayable' or if the timing's right when they go into writing or production.* This means that new comedians can test their material and their act on live audiences before later going on to work as writers.
A: The text states that if a new comedian wins an award, afterwards this will lead to work opportunities where he or she can practise their act.
B: Lisa *believes they are hardly an automatic guarantee of well-paid comedy life.* This means she thinks the awards do not necessarily lead to success.
D: There is no mention of this in the text. There is a reference to *the industry shop window* which means that TV producers and agents are able to see a lot of different comedians perform, but it does not refer to a choice that comedians make.

30 D: The answer comes from *I couldn't face starting over, doing try-out sessions … my heart sank at the thought.* Whelans had already had a successful career with a comedy partner. When this partnership finished, he did not want to start from the beginning again, trying to create a solo act. *I couldn't face* and *my heart sank* both refer to his lack of enthusiasm.
A: This is untrue. Whelans says that *there are hundreds of competent, blandish, slightly uninteresting stand-ups who I would be up against.* This suggests that he regards many other comedians as 'average' or having little talent. He did not want to waste time taking part in events in order to prove his ability.
B: Whelans says that people in the industry can earn a lot, but this is not the same as what his expectations were regarding his own salary when he became a writer.
C: The text says that his comedy act with a partner finished, but there is no reference as to why this happened. It does not say that Whelans found team work difficult.

p.92–94 PAPER 1 Part 4

31 D: *I was over the moon to actually win something.*

32 C: *You've got to be aware of what is happening all the time, you can't switch off* (stop concentrating) *about anything.*

33 E: *I love caving but I wouldn't class* (consider) *myself as a* (real / professional) *caver.*

34 C: The answer comes from *I am now more involved in scheduling other drivers, so I don't spend as much time on the river as I did.*

35 B: *I just wanted to settle down and find a base.*

36/37 A/C: (A) *The volcano was throwing bits and pieces at us … That kind of thing appeals to me;* (C) *There are cut-off points* (situations which would be too dangerous) *that we believe are not safe to operate above, but mostly we try our hardest to get the trekkers out by boat.*

38 D: The photographer says, *And filing photos is not my strong point. It's the most tedious part …*

39 A: *Unfortunately, there isn't currently a way around having enough flexibility in the programme.* He is saying that unfortunately there is no possibility at the moment to make his programme / course more flexible.

40 A: *The best aspect is the quality of the students.* In other words, the students who he teaches are very capable and skilled.

41/42 B/E: (B) *without a guide it would be beyond most people's ability* (most people couldn't go climbing / trekking alone), *and it's rewarding to know they appreciate that fact;* (E) *Occasionally some people get scared stiff and I get a lot out of* (a lot of satisfaction) *helping someone overcome that.*

43 B: *To go through this training and have other people look at your work and get their input is invaluable.* The mountain guide is saying that he thinks the comments that more experienced guides make about his work / ability is very useful.

44 C: The jet-boat driver says *every day is a highlight … on a day-to-day basis, it's just the varying nature of the area we operate in.*

45 A: *What does bother me* (annoy me) *are the endless meetings and things to do within the polytechnic system.*

46/47 C/D: (C) *For commercial driving it's learning as you go* (you learn through experience); (D) *All my training for this career has been completely hands-on* (practical / not theoretical).

48/49 B/E: (B) *Dealing with some of the older dilapidated* (in bad condition) *shelters is not always pleasant, especially having to clean up after irresponsible previous occupants;* (E) *I could do without* (I would prefer not to experience) *the freezing cold in the middle of winter when getting into a wetsuit can be a bit of a torture.*

50/51 D/E: (D) *waiting on payment from people you work with is a frustration you have to put up with* (tolerate / accept); (E) *I used to get really offended, but now I'm resigned to it* (I don't like it but I accept it).

52 E: The answer comes from *One of the best things is ... you get to see them at their highs and lows.*

p.95–97 PAPER 2 Part 1

FURTHER PRACTICE AND GUIDANCE (p.96–97)

Sample answer

1 **Five content points:** the showers need to be improved; the changing rooms need decorating; new TV screens need to be installed; the health club needs to open earlier; the health club should hire two new staff: a physiotherapist and a nutritionist.

2 **Writer:** an employee at the health club.
Target audience: the employee's manager / a senior person.
Effect/register: He's writing to someone in a senior position – someone who can influence his chances of promotion and pay rises, etc. Therefore his suggestions need to be constructive, helpful and polite rather than negative and critical.

3 **'Expanded' points:** *members are happy with staff and the service they provide; the showers were renovated only three years ago;* (music screens) *would increase their motivation as many people find exercising very repetitive;* (extending opening hours) *We could do this for a trial period, of say, two months, and see what effect on membership it has.*

4 **Organisation:** the report is divided into clear sections with the content points sensibly divided between each of them. You could also use sub-headings in a report, e.g.
Showers and Changing Rooms:
The condition of these facilities was generally considered to be poor.

Mark: *Band 5*
The writer has covered all the content points and expanded on them – providing more detail where appropriate. The report has a heading and is logically divided into paragraphs that deal with each main content point. The content of each paragraph is also clearly marked by use of cohesive linkers such as *Firstly, Secondly, Finally,* etc. There is a wide range of vocabulary, e.g. *considerable dissatisfaction, strongly recommend, considerable expenditure.* The target reader would be fully informed and would be able to take action based on this report.

FURTHER PRACTICE (p.97)

1a 2a 3b 4b 5a 6b 7a 8b

- The past continuous of *to hope, to think,* and *to wonder* is used to make diplomatic or tentative suggestions in English.
- *Perhaps* is a more formal way to say *Maybe.*
- Using the passive makes the action more important, i.e. *It should be done ...* . In an active sentence, i.e. *You should do it,* this can sound rather aggressive or accusatory.
- The second conditional, i.e. *If we did this, there would be ...* makes the suggestion sound more tentative. The first conditional, i.e. *If we do this, there will be ...* can sound too direct.

p.99–100 PAPER 3 Part 1

1 **C:** *to go* is the only verb that collocates with *ahead* in this context.

2 **B:** You can *raise a bridge or barrier, erect a building, install equipment* and *lift an object off the ground/table,* etc.

3 **A:** *to threaten* is the only verb that is followed by the infinitive, e.g. *threaten to cover the city / to hurt someone; endanger* is often used in the context of an animal species and is followed by the object, e.g. *Cutting down the rainforest endangers many species; to risk* is followed by *-ing; to jeopardise* also means to put something at risk, and is followed by the object, e.g. *His inexperience is jeopardising the project.*

4 **B:** We use *to sink* when an object / area is going deeper into the water; old food, a civilisation or a dead body *decays;* a building could *collapse* onto the ground if it was old or if there was an earthquake.

5 **A:** *to erode* means 'to gradually destroy the surface of something through the action of the wind or rain'; material and clothes can become *worn* (old / thin / in bad condition); a person can be *corrupted* if they accept money to do something immoral or illegal; we usually use *broken* for simple objects or machinery.

6 **D:** *stood* can be used for geographical features, e.g. *The city stood on the hill / the forest stood at the foot of the mountain;* we can use *faced* to mean 'to be opposite to', e.g. *the bank faced the supermarket;* we use *occurred* for events, e.g. *The festival occurs every summer;* we use *featured* to mean 'to include', e.g. *This month's magazine features an interview with the actor.*

7 **C:** *to assault* means 'to attack a place or person'; we use *to offend* when somebody is impolite, e.g. *She offended him when she said she didn't like his cooking; to crash* takes the preposition *into; to oppose someone* means 'to strongly disagree with someone'.

8 **A:** *the building of a barrier* is the only construction that is grammatically correct; you need to say *someone's intention is to ...* . You would need to change the sentence to *there are fears about what the 'result' of such a barrier might be.*

9 **C:** The verb *to restrict* means 'to limit or stop something'. In this case, the movement of the water; we say *to impose a rule* and *to delay something from arriving.*

10 **D:** We use *stagnant* to describe the water in a non-moving, bad-smelling river or canal; we could use *motionless* to describe a person or animal that isn't moving because it is frightened or hiding, *stationary* for traffic, and *inactive* for a lazy person or a machine not being used.

11 **B:** If there is an emergency and extra help is required, we say that someone is *brought in; to ask someone over* means to 'invite someone to your house'; young men or women are *called up* to join the army; *to take someone on* means 'to give someone a job'.

12 **A:** Although *victim* usually describes a person, a city can also be *a victim of global warming / pollution* and a company can be the *victim* of a bad economy; we use *target* to show that a person has deliberately chosen someone else / something to be attacked; *sufferer* is used in the context of disease or illness.

13 **C:** *expected* is the only verb that fits in grammatically when we want to talk about the future in a passive way. Another example would be *Crime is expected to increase in the next five years.*

14 **D:** *the situation is deteriorating* is a collocation meaning that 'the situation is getting worse'; we use *destabilise* to mean 'to make a country / system or government less successful'; *the rain detracted from our enjoyment of the picnic* (made our enjoyment less); *to deflate* is often used to mean 'to remove air', e.g. *Someone deflated his car tyres.*

15 **B:** *the whole process* is a collocation. You need to say *all the water* and *all the damage.* It is possible to say *whole event* but this sounds too positive in a situation where we are talking about flooding.

p.101 PAPER 3 Part 2

0 would: In direct speech, the writer said *'I will not be able to teach myself.'* In reported speech, *will not* becomes *would not*.

16 there: *there* introduces the clause that follows.

17 unless: The writer is saying that he doesn't believe there were any more ways that he could fall over *unless* another skier crashed into him – then that would be another way.

18 be: We need *be* to form the passive of *going to*.

19 what: We can use *what* to refer forward.

20 which: *which* refers back to the moment the writer's friend speaks.

21 other: The writer is saying that he put his skis under one arm and then put them under the other (arm).

22 Despite: *despite* is followed by a noun phrase.

23 with: *with no co-ordination* means 'without co-ordination'.

24 this: *this disability* refers back to the disability of having no co-ordination.

25 between: *difference* takes the preposition *between*.

26 an/the: *ability* is a noun and requires a determiner. We can use *an* to introduce an ability we haven't mentioned before, or *the* to emphasize the importance of this specific ability.

27 cannot (not *can't* which would be counted as two words): The writer is saying that if you cannot learn to *snowplough*, (position your skis in a way that slows you down), you will not be able to stop.

28 it: *it* refers forward to the action of *turning my feet*.

29 did: *did* is used here for emphasis.

30 so: *so* goes in front of an adjective which is followed by a consequence, e.g. *It was so hot (that) all the plants died! The book was so expensive (that) I decided not to buy it.*

p.102 PAPER 3 Part 3

0 its: *is by necessity* is a fixed expression.

00 ✔

31 their: The noun *feedback* does not take a possessive pronoun when used in the general sense.

32 not: The writer is trying to say that it is satisfying to read positive reviews from critics but these reviews don't tell him what ordinary people think. *Not* does not make sense in the context.

33 ✔

34 do: The sentence beginning *While it may not be true … ordinary people think of your work* is not a question and doesn't need the auxiliary *do*.

35 own: It is possible to use a possessive pronoun in front of *own* but not an article (*an/the*).

36 ✔

37 of: We can say *Most of the writers who* and *Most writers who* but not *Most of writers*.

38 there: *to send in* means 'to send something in response to a request': *After a public appeal, many people send in food and clothes* (to the appeal / not to a place).

39 ✔

40 such: The writer has not yet mentioned an unkind review, so it is wrong to use *such*.

41 feelings: You could say *to shield your feelings* or *to shield you* but not *to shield you feelings*.

42 too: *too* is in the wrong position here. You could say *but there are those* (reviewers) *who write essays which are too long …* or *there are those who write long, strangely formal essays, too*.

43 which: In order to make *which* correct, you would need to write *contain* not *containing*.

44 on: *to impress* does not take a preposition when it means 'to make someone admire you'.

45 to: *suggest* is followed by a pronoun and bare infinitive, e.g. *I suggest you try a different approach*.

46 ✔

p.104–105 PAPER 3 Part 4

47 reliable
48 succeed
49 recruitment
50 vacancies
51 preference
52 applicants
53 relocate
54 priority
55 reduction
56 healthy
57 spokesman / spokesperson
58 mishear
59 unbearably
60 ensuring
61 quieten

p.106–108 PAPER 3 Part 5

FURTHER PRACTICE AND GUIDANCE (p.107–108)

Letter 1
1 would like
2 enquire
3 whether
4 vacancy
5 currently
6 large
7 considerable
8 grateful

Letter 2
1 confirm
2 However,
3 contact
4 convenient
5 reconfirm
6 in advance
7 Should
8 require
9 further

p.106 PAPER 3 Part 5 (TEST)

62 acceptance
63 raise
64 be used
65 equipment
66 are planning
67 to reach
68 arranged
69 minimal / small charge
70 donate items / goods
71 very good / good / positive / excellent
72 wondering
73 be kind
74 express our

p.109 PAPER 3 Part 6

0 J: The first sentence *introduces a strange pattern in a British wheat field … in the late 1970s.* The key is J because the writer uses the word *strange* to show this was a surprising event *but at this point* (the early 1970s) *nobody paid much attention.* J also connects to the following sentence *However …* .

75 D: The writer says that more patterns appeared by the early 1980s. They were getting larger and sometimes six or more patterns had been made in the same field during the night.

76 E: The writer says that mystics (people who claim to have spiritual powers) believed that the patterns were created by cosmic energy or UFOs and that scientists believed the patterns were created by unusual weather conditions. The writer says that both scientists and mystics agreed that the patterns couldn't be created by humans.

77 **B:** The writer is saying that the scientists and mystics didn't believe the patterns were man-made because it would have been too difficult for humans to produce them in just one night.

78 **G:** The writer is saying that the patterns began to attract tourists, and the local farmers used this situation to make money (by making people pay money to get access to the fields).

79 **C:** The writer says that two elderly men claimed to have made the first pattern in 1978 and that they had continued to make further patterns during the next 13 years.

80 **A:** The writer explains how the reporter believes the elderly men's story but that other people *thought there was more to it*: this means that other people thought this was not the whole or truthful answer to the mystery.

p.110 PAPER 4 Part 1

1 Sunday
2 (spectacular) stunts
3 40,000
4 (the latest) equipment
5 (live) music festival
6 unique atmosphere
7 new sports
8 fine
9 Channel 4

p.111 PAPER 4 Part 2

10 Indian curry
11 1.7 billion
12 oriental
13 cosmopolitan
14 different/various countries
15 chains
16 coffee shops
17 12 days
18 loss (in profits)

p.112 PAPER 4 Part 3

19 don't change
20 grey market/over-50s
21 affected
22 TV advertising/adverts/commercials
23 biggest section
24 low proportion
25 fashionable
26 comfortable
27 social responsibility
28 make the advertisements/are in charge of advertising/run advertising companies

p.113–114 PAPER 4 Part 4

FURTHER PRACTICE AND GUIDANCE (p.114)

Speaker 1: 1 T 2 T 3 F 4 T 5 T 6 T 7 F

Speaker 2: 8 F 9 T 10 T 11 F 12 T

Speaker 3: 13 T 14 T 15 T 16 F

Speaker 4: 17 F 18 F 19 T 20 F

Speaker 5: 21 F 22 F 23 T 24 F

p.113 PAPER 4 Part 4 (Test)

Speaker 1: 29E 34G
The first speaker is talking about her lifestyle as a flight attendant. She says that when she was growing up, it was her dream to be a flight attendant, but now she doesn't find the job very satisfying. We can understand that she is a flight attendant from (I don't see) *much of the world except for hotel rooms ... the hours are bad ... jet lag... it's the same old routine...* She also mentions that she has to deal with complaints when people are served with food they don't like. We can understand that she is disappointed from *It's all I wanted to be when I was growing up* and *If I'd known it was going to be like this ... I would have chosen another career.*

Speaker 2: 30G 35A
The second speaker is talking about the problem of airplane delays and how this affects her job. She says that people arrive at her hotel very late and that she has to work overtime. We can tell she is a hotel receptionist from *...we're still around to check them* (the guests) *in* (to the hotel) *when they arrive.* We can understand that she is irritated from *there's one thing that really winds me up* (irritates me) and *the most annoying thing is...*

Speaker 3: 31H 36 E
The third speaker is talking about his work as a travel agent and describing the type of customers he has to deal with. He says that some customers are very decisive about the holiday they want, but others cannot make up their minds and take a long time to reach a decision. We can understand that he is a travel agent from *there's a lot more destinations we need to know about ... you can get down every brochure, call up all the tour operators...* and *most people only get one holiday a year.* We can understand that he is accepting about the customers' indecision from *I don't blame them ... You have to be patient. It's part of the job.*

Speaker 4: 32 C 37 D
The fourth speaker is talking about his future job working in Greece. We can understand that he is a tour guide from *I've got to start reading up on the history so I know what I'm talking about* (he needs to be able to talk about Greek history to holidaymakers). He also says *I've got three weeks ... before I'm having to explain it all ... I can always refer to my notes.* We can understand that he is curious from *I've always been fascinated by the language, the customs, just the whole culture ... I've got a lot to learn.*

Speaker 5: 33 F 38 B
The fifth speaker is a tourist who is talking about where the other people in his group want to go. His friends want to visit an art gallery and go sightseeing. He says *It's* (the art gallery) *about the last place on Earth I'd choose to go to* and *I'd rather just sit and have a drink ... than ... looking at a lot of old monuments.* He concludes that all statues look the same to him – *once you've seen one old statue, you've seen them all.* We can understand from this that he is unenthusiastic about art and sightseeing.

TEST FOUR

p.117–118 PAPER 1 Part 1

1   **C:** *There is a great tradition of isolation literature and there are multiple isolations here … but it is what Pi reflects upon which is uniquely engrossing.*

2   **D:** *…the pacing is frustratingly slow at times as Carter indulges his delight in character construction.*

3   **B:** *Such a varied plate of ideas and situations can be partaken of at leisure, but … it can be consumed in one go without a touch of indigestion.*

4   **D:** *Carter's … ability to sketch a state of mind, or a dilemma.*

5   **B:** *There are spooky and wry tales, sad and bleak … the cute and touching ones.*

6   **C:** *This … novel … has enjoyed great critical acclaim.*

7   **A:** *Structurally, this novel has its challenges. We're expected to keep track of a plethora of characters.*

8   **B:** *The backstory of the characters … is revealed in just a few words.*

9   **D:** *the common ground between all the players, is … loneliness.*

10   **C:** *The witty narrative engages from the start.*

11   **A:** *This stems partly from the desire to maintain suspense.*

12   **B:** *Little is wasted on precise geographic location.*

13   **A:** *Tate has the knack of articulating the awkwardness of social intercourse when difficult decisions are made or when conversation fails.*

14   **C:** *Readers will no doubt find 'Life of Pi' to be a highly readable and a pleasingly troublesome book that irritates as often as it brings a smile.*

15   **A:** *Tate's portrayal of Monica … struck me as inconsistent.*

16   **D:** *The pages teem with … subplots … and you can't afford to ignore any of them.*

17   **C:** *Pi questions the nature of existence … But Pi/Martel also questions more mundane precepts.*

18   **A:** *If the words 'Halfway to Africa' conjure up visions of the exotic, forget it. It's a metaphor for where most of us are in our lives.*

p.119–120 PAPER 1 Part 2

19   **D:** In the text above 19, the writer says that she doubted the truth of what the doctor was saying. The doctor believed that baby talk is meaningless. Paragraph D begins with *it is science that is having second thoughts.* This means that scientists are starting to doubt the traditional theory too. D also includes *If they smile, it may well be because they recognise your voice. When they babble, they are probably not speaking nonsense.* This language for 'possibility' connects to the first line of the text under 19, *This is not just hopeful theorising* (guessing).

20   **G:** The text above 20 mentions *the traditional understanding of early language development, which holds* (believes) *that babies must develop motor skills before they can … connect sounds to meanings.* Paragraph G begins with *Petitto and her team take a different view.* This means that they disagree with the traditional theory.

21   **C:** The text above 21 mentions the research done on three different groups of babies from France, England and Spain. Paragraph C starts with *The results showed uniformity in all cases.* This means that the results were the same in every case. There was no difference between how the French, English or Spanish babies were using their facial muscles to smile or produce sounds.

22   **A:** Most of the text above 22 is Petitto's explanation of how the brain controls facial muscles for different functions. Paragraph A begins with *What this tells us… . What* refers back to the explanation that has just been given. The text above 22 also mentions *smiling* and *babbling* (an attempt at speech). There is a connection between these words and *a purely physical response* (smiling) and *an oral one* (babbling) in paragraph A. There is another connection between *the brain* in the final sentence of paragraph A and *that is not all it can do* in the text below.

23   **E:** The text above 23 states that (babies) *can tell the difference between happy features and sad features* (on a face). Paragraph E begins with *This is borne out* (proven) *by the fact that they* (babies) *can imitate these same expressions* (happy / sad faces). Paragraph E finishes by saying *This means they* (babies) *can learn how to use things just by watching people.* The text under 23 says *They can grasp* (understand) *simple arithmetic by using the same capacity* (ability). This means that they can learn how to use things and understand simple maths because they watch people or things carefully.

24   **F:** Paragraph F finishes with *It appears that our brains all start out with the same approach to learning and development.* In the final piece of text it compares the brain of a baby and what it knows instinctively with a computer program. The writer then says that it depends what babies do with their brains and what they learn that leads to a difference between babies later on. In other words, everyone is born with the same potential for learning, but we develop according to how much stimulation the brain receives.

p.121–122 PAPER 1 Part 3

25   **D:** The answer comes from *There might be those* (people) *who quietly slip away to foreign lands for nothing other than pure pleasure, but it will be a secretive and frowned upon activity. No one will want to own up to being 'one of those'.* This means that people will not admit to going on traditional holidays because other people will disapprove.
A: The text says that a few countries have banned tourists from certain areas, but that does not suggest that tourists will only be able to go to a few places in the future.
B: There is no reference to the cost of holidays. The writer says that tourists have been accused of *(charged with)* only bringing money, in other words, they contribute nothing else to the country they visit.
C: The writer only says that the term or word *tourist* will not exist.

26   **A:** *The challenge to forcibly curtail more than a billion tourists from going where they want is immense. It is so immense as to be futile.* This means that it is impossible and pointless to try and stop tourism.
B: There is no reference to countries which rely on tourism. *Economically empowered* refers to tourists meaning that they have enough money for holidays.
C: *there will be 1.56 billion tourists travelling at any one time.* This is a prediction about the number of tourists travelling by 2020, but there is no mention of the tourism industry's ability to handle this number.
D: The writer says that tourism can only be stopped if you convince people *that only the truly malicious, utterly selfish and totally irresponsible would ever even consider doing it.* However, she then says that *This is clearly absurd*, in other words, ridiculous.

27   **B:** The writer uses the whole of paragraph 3 to suggest ways in which travellers are deceived. She says that tour operators have replaced the word *tourist* with *volunteer, field worker*, etc, that *brochures* are now called *pamphlets*, that *holidays* are called *cultural experiences*, etc. A person who believes they have volunteered to help others is under the same illusion as Victorian travellers – that they are 'doing good' rather than enjoying the experience of travelling.

A: There is no reference to travellers' skills. The writer only says that the *volunteers* think they have the same *ethos* (moral attitudes) as the people in the areas they visit.
C: Although tour operators who advertise 'un-tourism' holidays may point out some harmful effects of mass tourism, their real intention is to sell their own holidays.
D: Again, the tour operators may say that their type of holidays bring benefits to local communities, but they use this strategy to sell their holidays.

28 C: The answer comes from *The re-packaging of tourism as meaningful, self-sacrificing travel is liberating. It allows you to go to all sorts of places that would be ethically out of bounds to a regular tourist.* This means that if you believe your intention is to help people, rather than enjoy yourself, you can go to places that normal tourists are discouraged from going to.
A: The writer does not suggest that normal tourists are not interested in environmental issues, just that 'un-tourists' believe they are helping the environment.
B: The writer says that 'un-tourists' feel uncomfortable or embarrassed about paying, perhaps because they believe money is part of the 'capitalist world' and not part of the 'moral world' they feel they belong to.
D: The writer says *the theory behind un-tourism relies upon exclusivity; it is all about preventing other people travelling in order that you might legitimise your own travels.* This means that un-tourists do not want normal tourists to go to the same areas as them. By staying separate, un-tourists can *legitimise* (make something seem acceptable) their own travel.

29 A: The writer says that un-tourists believe third world cultures will be disturbed / harmed by tourists. We can understand that the writer disagrees when she says *This is despite the fact that these cultures are more rooted* (stable), *ancient and have survived far longer.*
B: The writer says *respect for local culture also concerns the un-tourist* and this *respect for local culture is based on a presumed innate inability within that culture to understand that there are other ways of living to their own.* The writer is saying that the un-tourist believes people from third world cultures do not have the ability to understand other cultures.
C: Again, it is the un-tourist that believes this, not the writer.
D: *Meaningful contact and respect for local culture* might suggest that visitors should integrate rather than behave differently, but it is the un-tourist who believes this.

30 C: The answer comes from *We aren't interested in saving leisure time abroad for the majority of people. We're interested in making ourselves feel good. That's why we've succumbed to* (failed to resist) *the re-branding of our enjoyment, and refuse to take up a term we believe to be tainted* (dirty). *How many times have you owned up to* (admitted to) *being a tourist?* In these lines the writer is saying that people like her, who are interested in the debate about tourism versus un-tourism, are probably the kind of people who are un-tourists themselves, and don't want to admit it.
A: There is no reference to this. When the writer says *We aren't interested in saving leisure time abroad for the majority of people*, she means that she is not worried whether or not most tourists can continue to enjoy foreign holidays.
B: The writer only says that some *tourist developments* (tourist resorts) have not treated the environment correctly and that they should be *challenged* (punished or made to do something about it).
D: *There is no difference between them – they are just being packaged as something different.* This refers to the traveller, not the holiday.

p.123–125 PAPER 1 Part 4

31 D: *Deadlines* (time constaints) *are not as fast paced as newspapers of course, but to stay at our standard we have to work for it. It's often heads down* (we need to concentrate) *and getting on with it.*

32 A: *Only in my wildest dreams (I never really believed / imagined) did I think I would end up* (become) *as an editor.*

33 D: *While the editor of 'International' is on maternity leave Gillian Rolland … the deputy editor, has stepped into her shoes* (taken over her position) *and has taken on what she calls a 'caretaking role'.* The meaning of *caretaker* in this context is someone who looks after a company while the usual manager is absent.

34 C: *people move around a lot in this industry and I am more likely to look for people who have done this.* The editor is saying that journalists usually work for many different magazines and that she is more interested in hiring these people.

35 B: *She says the perception* (general belief) *of women's magazines being competitive environments is unfounded* (untrue). In other words, the editor disagrees with the idea that people who work on women's magazines are competitive.

36 D: *The features team will have to go out to parties and have fun as part of their job, but likewise they can end up at fundraisers for charities we are working with.* The editor is saying that sometimes journalists go to parties and have fun but they also have to take part in raising money for charity – the more serious side.

37 B: *Her enthusiasm* (interest and passion) *for her current job and the team of people working with her is overwhelming* (very strong).

38 C: *Karen Goss, 46, says her love for the job has not diminished* (become less). Karen is saying that she has always liked her job – she still likes it.

39 A: *I can always tell* (understand / recognise) *who will do well. It's the young woman or man willing to do anything – not those who think they should be writing a feature on the first day.* The editor is saying that she prefers new writers who are happy to do any kind of work, and she dislikes writers who believe they are capable of writing an important feature / article as soon as they start work.

40 B: *She started her career… but had no idea of what her ultimate aim* (final ambition) *was.*

41 A: *She was told at the interview by both the lecturers present that she didn't have what it takes.* The writer is saying that the lecturers who interviewed Jayne told her that she wasn't good enough to become a writer.

42 C: The people she admires are *those who … have re-trained in an attempt to enter the industry … The sheer hard work it takes to re-train is a serious undertaking.* The editor is saying that re-training to become a journalist requires a lot of hard work and commitment – she appreciates and admires people who are prepared to do this.

43 A: *I learned to type – no one should underestimate the importance of this skill – and that enabled me to get work temping. After landing a job as a PA in the editor's office at City magazine, Jayne … took on other roles including feature writing.* Jayne is saying that her typing skills were extremely important – they allowed her to get temporary work as a personal assistant to an editor. From here, she then began to write features herself.

44 C: *Some people come into magazines thinking they will be able to have flexible working hours … But … they need to remember that it takes time to make a name* (establish a reputation) *for yourself.*

45 B: *With fashion, for example, you can't teach someone about it. I think people are probably born with it.* The editor is saying that only a few people with an instinctive understanding of fashion should work on fashion features.

46 C: *but if someone stands out* (is exceptional / is really good), *as one applicant did recently, they can get in* (get a job).

47 A: *I had such brilliant training … but most of it was on the job.* The editor is saying that she was trained through practical experience – by writing features herself.

48 D: *I trained as a newspaper journalist but always aspired* (hoped) *to work on a glossy magazine.* The editor started writing for newspapers but always wanted to work for a glossy magazine.

49 B: *In my experience, so long as someone believes in themselves … they can go for* (do / try) *whatever they want.* The editor is saying that self-confidence allows people to do anything they want.

p.126–127 PAPER 2 Part 1

FURTHER PRACTICE AND GUIDANCE (p.127)

1 **dealing:** In this sentence, *used to* is an adjective and preposition. It means the same as 'I am familiar with'. Remember that after a preposition, the verb takes the *-ing* form.

2 **have been:** We use the Present perfect simple to show an activity or situation started in the past which continues up to the present.

3 **for, position:** *apply* takes the preposition *for. Position* is more formal than *job*.

4 **feel, suitable candidate:** *feel* and *suitable candidate* both sound polite. *I know* and *I am the right person* sound a bit aggressive – if you were very confident, you might say this in an interview, but not a letter.

5 **worked:** You use the Past simple to show a finished activity or situation in the past. You only use the Past perfect *had worked* if the Past simple also occurs in the same sentence, i.e. *Before I became a software analyst for TechSystems in March 2002, I had spent five years as a computer programmer.*

6 **with:** *familiar* takes the preposition *with*.

7 **from:** *graduate* takes the preposition *from* + university, or *in* + Maths / Science, etc.

8 **manner:** *telephone manner* is a fixed collocation.

9 **qualifications, experience, relevant:** *diplomas* are pieces of paper that show the qualifications you have; *experience* is used to show what you have achieved at work. *Experiences* refer to different things you have done in life (*I had some strange experiences when I was travelling round Europe!*); *relevant* takes the preposition *to*.

10 **involve, liaising, setting:** *consist* requires the preposition *of; discussing* requires an object, e.g. problems / ideas; *to set up a meeting* means to organise it.

p.128–130 PAPER 2 Part 2

FURTHER PRACTICE AND GUIDANCE (p.129–130)

Content
The answer mentions *a wide range of delicious sandwiches, continental snacks and hot meals* and *excellent coffee*. It says the café is conveniently located in the centre of the city and provides an address. The friendly service, reading material and internet facilities would also attract customers.

Effect on the target reader
Because of the persuasive language, the clear layout and the content, this leaflet would probably have a positive effect on the reader.

Range of vocabulary and structure
Adjective-noun collocations: *good cup of coffee, warm atmosphere, friendly service, conveniently located, wide range, reasonable prices, extensive selection.*

Format
The leaflet is eye-catching because of the clear spacing, the sub-headings, underlining and bullet points (•).

Register
Each sub-heading is a question and uses a question mark (?). The use of questions in advertising is a typical way to get the reader's attention. The leaflet also uses exclamation marks to make an emphatic point (!). You can also use hyphens (–) in leaflets, unlike in more formal writing.

Accuracy
Corrected spelling mistakes: *appreciate, conveniently, delicious, excellent, recommend, reasonable, travel, access, definitely, practising.*

Mark: *Band 4*
The writer has answered the question appropriately by addressing all the content points. The wide range of adjective-noun collocations, the informal and friendly register and the eye-catching layout would have a positive effect on the target reader. There are a number of spelling mistakes which do not impede communication but which are fairly basic for CAE level. The spelling mistakes bring the mark down to 4.

p.132–133 PAPER 3 Part 1

1 **D:** *To seek* means 'to look for' and is not followed by a preposition; *to search* requires the preposition *for*; the other two options mean 'to ask about' and do not fit in with the sense of the sentence.

2 **C:** *get along with* is a fixed expression and means 'to have a good relationship with'.

3 **C:** *ranged* is followed by *from; consisted* is followed by *in* or *of; covered* is followed by *with*.

4 **B:** *the management world* is a fixed expression.

5 **A:** Children *grow up* but are *brought up* by parents or someone else.

6 **D:** *fooled by* means *tricked* and is the only option which makes sense here.

7 **A:** *management tool* is a fixed expression.

8 **C:** *eager* is the only option followed by the infinitive form and which makes sense here; *enthusiastic* and *excited* are followed by *about* and the *-ing* form.

9 **D:** *dedicating* is the only option which collocates with *themselves*.

10 **C:** *meet the demand* is a fixed expression.

11 **B:** *help* collocates with *from; assist* is followed by *with; aid* is followed by *in; support* is followed by *in*.

12 **C:** *to mean in reality* is a fixed expression.

13 **A:** *joining* is the only option which fits here; *participating* needs *in; entering* does not collocate with *session*.

14 **D:** *firms* cannot be *symbolised, demonstrated* or *illustrated*.

15 **D:** The focus here is on the workplace, so *work* is the only option that fits.

p.134 PAPER 3 Part 2

0 **with:** *with time on your hands* is a fixed expression which means 'you have some spare time'.

16 **but:** The writer is saying 'perhaps you wanted to be a model *but* you never had the confidence'.

17 **this/now:** *this* and *now* both refer to *the right time.*

18 **Neither:** We use *neither* to show addition. It is used together with *nor. She has neither brother nor sister* means 'She doesn't have a brother or a sister'.

19 **in:** (not **on**) You appear *in* a programme / film / advertisement.

20 **are:** We need *are* to form the passive of the present simple.

21 **Unless:** The writer is saying that you will not earn a lot if you aren't very lucky.

22 **as:** *as some may hope* means 'as some people may hope'.

23 **however:** *however* marks a contrast and can occur between two commas as here.

24 **As/Because/Since:** All these words are synonyms in this context and they are all followed by a reason.

25 **long:** *as long as* means 'providing that' or 'if'.

26 **at:** *at short notice* is a fixed expression which means 'with little time for preparation'.

27 **your:** *to come your/my/his way* means that something 'comes in your direction'.

28 **more:** the writer uses *more* to compare modelling to acting in the earlier sentences.

29 **how:** *how* goes with *much*, e.g. *It was amazing how much money I spent on holiday!*

30 **for:** The noun *demand* takes the preposition *for.*

p.135 PAPER 3 Part 3

0 ✔

00 **destruction**

000 **Diggers:** *Diggers* is the plural form of *a digger.* Apostrophes are not used to indicate plurals.

31 **textiles**

32 **sails:** Be careful – sometimes a word may be spelled correctly but does not fit in with the sense of the text.

33 ✔

34 **South:** *South, North, East* and *West* take a capital letter when they are part of a name.

35 ✔

36 **steel:** Another example of where a word may be spelt correctly but does not make sense in the text.

37 **campaign**

38 **disassemble, record**

39 ✔

40 **ambitious**

41 **visitors**

42 **through:** Another example of where a word may be spelt correctly but does not make sense in the text.

43 **conserved,':** We use a comma at the end of direct speech.

44 ✔

45 **than:** *than* is needed in a comparative sentence, not *then.*

46 **it's:** We use the apostrophe to show *it is*; without the apostrophe, *its* is a possessive pronoun.

p.136–137 PAPER 3 Part 4

47 resident
48 visual
49 entitled
50 nearby
51 hypnotic
52 historically
53 admission
54 entry
55 understandably
56 worthless
57 irreplaceable
58 theft
59 precautions
60 reliable
61 presence

p.138 PAPER 3 Part 5

62 gained
63 telephone reservations
64 enthusiastically
65 was promoted
66 dealing
67 organising
68 lack of / limited
69 leave
70 successful completion
71 assistant to
72 has proved
73 accept
74 no hesitation

p.139 PAPER 3 Part 6

0 **J:** The writer is saying that the festival week in Buñol is filled with festivities and filled with even greater anticipation for (excitement about) the battle (fight) at the end of the week.

75 **A:** The writer is saying that since the original fight, the local people have continued the tradition every year and this year they expect more people than ever before to attend the festival.

76 **G:** The writer is saying that the point of the festival nowadays is to have fun, so it doesn't really matter what the reason for the original fight was.

77 **D:** The writer is saying that the festival is held for two reasons: one reason is to get more tourists to come to Buñol and the other reason is that these tourists can be used as targets for the tomato throwers.

78 **I:** The writer is saying that the night before the fight, the tomatoes are presented in a much more appealing / attractive way. He explains that they are used to make *paella*, a traditional Spanish dish.

79 **B:** The writer is saying that the trucks arrive in the town square and they are cheered / welcomed by the people in the crowd.

80 **C:** The writer is saying that people throw tomatoes at the truck drivers, each other, and any other person who comes close enough.

p.140 PAPER 4 Part 1

1 Presenting your Proposal
2 convincing characters
3 (The) conservatory
4 Objective Editing
5 Twist in the Tale
6 (the) library
7 1.50–4pm
8 print your name
9 second choice

p.141 PAPER 4 Part 2

10 manor house
11 (original) stone foundations
12 two (huge) fireplaces
13 six towers
14 fire
15 (magnificent) palace
16 1.6 million
17 lake
18 wooden carvings

p.142 PAPER 4 Part 3

19 tough
20 exaggerate
21 relevant
22 (unique) qualities
23 society
24 by hand
25 first impression
26 enthusiastic, flexible
27 spent usefully / usefully spent

p.143 PAPER 4 Part 4

Speaker 1: 28 E   33 A
The first speaker is talking about her memories of living in Cornwall. She remembers the *big open spaces, the beach, the long walks in the countryside...* We can understand that she is a parent/mother from *where I'm bringing my lot* (my children) *up*, and *when they built these flats, I don't think they had kids in mind* – in other words, the people who designed and built the place where she lives did not consider what children would like or need. We can understand that she is talking about a lack of green spaces from her memories of Cornwall compared to her description of her current home: *there's nowhere for them* (the children) *to play ... it's all concrete and not a bit of grass...* and *you need a bit of colour* (flowers/plants), *something growing to make you feel better.*

Speaker 2: 29 G   34 E
The second speaker is complaining about the loud music that his neighbours play. He talks about *the walls, the floor, the bed* which suggest he is talking about his home, but the last sentence makes it clear that he is a homeowner: *I'd be happy to move only* (but) *we just bought the place* (this house) *eighteen months ago.* We can understand that he is unhappy with his noisy neighbours from *I'm ... in a really deep sleep when it* (the music) *starts ... you can hear it through the walls, really loud ... and it's not just the sound ... we've asked them* (the neighbours) *to turn it down.*

Speaker 3: 30 A   35 C
The third speaker is complaining about the increase in traffic. He starts by saying *It wasn't as bad as this when I started out* (when I started my job). We can understand that he is a taxi driver from *You could get from A* (the first place) *to B* (the second place) *in 20 minutes.* He also mentions *the mirror* and *the passengers ... they can see they're going to have to pay more.* He also talks about restrictions on car drivers and says that this will be good for his business (those drivers will have to take a taxi instead). Finally, he says *I do my best to get* (drive/take) *people to where they want to go.* We can understand that he is talking about heavy traffic from *now it* (the journey) *takes twice as long...* and *if there's a* (traffic) *jam.*

Speaker 4: 31 H   36 G
The fourth speaker is complaining about the number of people who use cars to travel and the pollution that these cars produce. We can understand that she is a cyclist from *I find myself behind a car, trying to get past* (overtake)... *sometimes I tap* (knock lightly) *on the window and say something ... and other times I just want to get by and into some fresh ... air.* The speaker must either be riding a bicycle (or motorbike) if she wants to overtake a car and can also manage to tap on the window. We can understand that she is talking about pollution from *air quality ... you can't breathe ... what you've been wearing is ... filthy* (very dirty). *I wear a mask ... lethal fumes* and *fresh air.*

Speaker 5: 32 C   37 H
The fifth speaker is talking about his life as a policeman in the countryside compared to his current job as a policeman in the city. We can understand that he is a policeman from *I'd had all that training ... when I was stationed* (working as a policeman) *in the village, all I had to deal with was a few bicycle thefts.* We can understand that he is talking about loneliness from *it's not like we* (my colleagues and I) *socialise after work ... I can't say I've made many real friends ... I spend my free time on my own ... you can still feel isolated.*

LISTENING SCRIPTS

TEST ONE Part 1

Well, before I let you all go in for dinner – I know it's been a long day already and in two days' time, of course, it's going to be the longest day of the year, at least here in Finland – I'd just like to tell you a bit about tomorrow's itinerary and a bit about the customs here.

As some of you might know, the Finnish festivities for midsummer are called 'Johannus'. They do actually go back to pagan times, but nowadays people tend to think of them as connected to the Christian feast of St John that's on June 24th.

It's quite common for people here to go back to the countryside for midsummer, to their ancestral homes, leaving towns and cities almost deserted. We'll be following them all first thing in the morning. The coach'll take us to Elk Channel, that's Hirvensalmi in Finnish. It's about three hours from Helsinki, but it'll take us through some really beautiful, some really dense forests. Elk Channel is a lovely little village in the Finnish lake district that nowadays only comes to life during the summer holiday season. At other times, there's … it's pretty much deserted.

The main celebrations for midsummer take place the evening before, just as they do here for the other annual celebrations of Christmas, New Year and May Day. With the sun not setting until just before midnight, there is plenty of time for a long evening of outdoor entertainment which is this fantastic and traditional local dance organised on a lakeside stage. Again, it all takes place with the forest surrounding you, so it really is a 'back-to-nature' experience. The dancing is accompanied by some old-fashioned accordion music …well, the dances *are* the old ones – different types of waltzes, polkas and tangos, that kind of thing.

When it gets closer to midnight, you'll see a bonfire built on a raft of logs set alight … and then pushed out into the lake, that'll actually be when the sun is going down even though it's midnight. People often get a little bit sad at this point, since at least in terms of daylight, this is the best it ever gets. The nights will be drawing in from now on, during the descent back into the next long, gloomy winter.

The next day is more about visiting relatives and recovering from the night before. Well, it'll be a beautiful place for you to simply explore and wander around, but if anyone's interested, you can always hire a man to take you out on the lake for a leisurely row and a spot of fishing. You'll need to be wearing several layers, though. Even though the sun is shining, it's still really chilly…

TEST ONE Part 2

Thank you for coming, everybody. And thanks to Sheila for getting everyone together – for making the phone calls. Shall we get straight down to business? I'll try not to take up too much of your time as this is an unscheduled meeting. Erm, as I think Sheila told you all … when she spoke to you … there's been a couple of, well, a few changes we need to think about.

First of all, we've been told that the church hall isn't actually available for rehearsals on Saturday afternoon. As you know, we thought Saturday would be best for everyone, but it's turned out, in fact, that it's already been booked by another group… something to do with a photography club or something. We thought about the school gym instead but it's turned out it's being redecorated. So, if it's OK, erm, the committee is proposing we do Tuesday evening in the church hall? Can I have a show of hands? Is Tuesday OK? Is Thursday any good? It looks like a majority for Tuesday. From seven? OK, we'll go with that.

Now secondly, we hoped to be getting a donation from Winton Arts Council, and we are, but not the amount we'd reckoned on. It'll be sufficient to cover costume costs and the sets, but it won't go as far as sorting out the lighting we need. Dave and Trisha managed to keep the equipment going for eight years … but some of it's pretty unreliable now. I think this means we'll need to be doing some fund-raising ourselves, and any ideas for suitable events or activities would be more than welcome.

What else? Oh yes, changes to a couple of cast members. John Roberts was going to be the lead, but you've possibly already heard on the grapevine that he's had to pull out. I'm not actually sure why, as such, but it's something to do with family commitments. So we need a replacement pretty urgently. And Sue Cook has also pulled out, so that leaves the part of 'third witch' open. So – if anyone wants to audition for the part of Macbeth or Sue's old part, the auditions will be held first thing on Thursday.

We've also been thinking about the advertising … I know the first live performance is a long way off but it's always good to promote things in advance, so we need to think about the cost. We don't want the price to be prohibitive … but we need to meet costs, too. It's been suggested that tickets go for £4.50 each, meaning a relatively small increase of 50p, or a discount on a group of five, say seventeen pounds fifty. We'll print those up if everyone's agreed. And we'll be using the *Winton Gazette* as usual, an ad in there, and for the first time, the production and tickets for it will be available on-line – everyone got a pen? – at www.wintondrama…that's one word…dot.co.dot.uk. That's www.wintondrama.dot.co.dot.uk.

TEST ONE Part 3

Presenter: It's an amazing fact that Amelia Bryant took up kayaking only two years ago, yet she is the only British woman to have competed in Norway's gruelling Arctic Sea Kayak Race, otherwise known as the ASKR. It demands both exceptional fitness and superb navigational skills. It covers an incredible 45 kilometres and takes up to four days, including a test of paddling endurance and ending with the ocean marathon world championship, which Amelia won at the first attempt. Amelia, that's an incredible feat. How did you get into kayaking in the first place?

Amelia: Working in London stuck in an office, I decided I needed a change of scene. I got into rock-climbing through my boyfriend, and becoming quite accomplished at that gave me the confidence to try new things. I eventually got round to trying kayaking and knew straight away it was the sport for me.

Presenter: I see, but your 2001 marathon title came after only a few years in the sport. What made you enter the world championship?

Amelia: I'm on the river all the time with my work, and I'd completed a 10-day kayak tour of the Outer Hebrides about two months before the event, averaging about 30 kilometres a day. While the ASKR is very prestigious in sea-kayaking, I knew I had the fitness, and so once I'd entered it was simply a question of pulling together a suitable training regime.

Presenter: And why do you think you are the only British woman to have competed in the ASKR?

Amelia: I can only assume it's because the race is seen as too extreme. When I arrived in Norway last year, I was surprised at how many more men than women there were, and I have to admit I was quite intimidated. I began to wonder if there might be a reason, but once the race got under way it was fine. While the women do paddle some way behind the men, there is a lot of mutual respect. Sea-kayaking is a popular hobby for both men and women in Britain, and so hopefully we'll see more Brits at the world championships soon.

Presenter: How is marathon training different from regular workouts and does sea-kayaking require a special technique?

Amelia: Paddling on rivers every week is great for general fitness, but for long-distance sea-kayaking you need to make sure the muscles you work are the ones you'll actually need. This involves lots of gym work on the upper back, shoulders and arms. To develop core stability in trunk muscles such as the abdominals, I do about 100 sit-ups a day, as well as interval sprint training on a local reservoir every other day and about 60 kilometres at sea on weekends. As for technique, the main difference is paddling style. Most people naturally adopt a 'touring style' when they first sit in a kayak, digging each blade into the water and pulling back with the arm. The distances involved in sea-kayaking mean this will eventually put strain on the back, and so I use a 'forward' paddling style to prevent this. Rotating at the wrist for each stroke, you aim to put pressure on your right foot as you plant the left blade and vice versa.

Presenter: And what other skills are important? What do other potential champions need to know?

Amelia: Given that race organisers only tell competitors where to go and not how, your navigational skills need to be pretty hot, and you must be able to read the water. The ASKR takes place during the Scandinavian summer, and while it's light 24 hours a day, the race coincides with the tides. About half the race is on open sea, where you have to take account of the wind, and the rest is island-hopping, where you must be aware of black eddies – swirling pools of water which can measure up to two kilometres in diameter. Crossing an eddy line in the wrong place might mean you're battling against the tide, but getting it right can get the tide behind you and save time.

Presenter: Would you say that mental toughness was important? I imagine that's a big part of it.

Amelia: Bearing in mind you can be racing up to six kilometres from land, you need to have confidence in both your fitness and ability, but it's often closer to shore that you experience problems. During the ASKR, competitors paddle between islands in swells of over three metres – that's the equivalent of sitting in your kayak on the ground and looking to the top of a telegraph pole … that's how high the water is above you. In that situation, when the water's too rough even for the rescue boats, I just tell myself to paddle as if I'm on the river and that tends to settle my nerves.

Presenter: And what happens if … if the worst happens … if you capsize – if your boat gets turned over?

Amelia: Competitors who capsize are just allowed help from other paddlers and not from the rescue crews. There's usually somebody around to load you back into your kayak and set you on your way. Because of the potential dangers of the racing environment, anybody losing time going to the aid of someone in trouble is automatically awarded the same time as the person finishing first. Which, by the way, is not how I won my title.

TEST ONE Part 4

1 The thing I hate … and I always used to get myself into this situation – fortunately I've got a strategy now – but when I'm supposed to be showing foreign clients round, I can never remember names. My mind just goes blank. It's pretty poor, really. I mean, it doesn't exactly come across as professional for someone in my position. I'm supposed to be setting an example but I'd find myself saying things like 'Have you met…?' and hoped people would get on with it themselves. I became really aware that I was getting a reputation for it. My assistant actually suggested I rehearse the whole thing with her beforehand so that's what I do now. We actually role-play the whole thing. I'd be lost without her.

2 Well, I'm not exactly the maternal type. Maybe that's got something to do with it. They come along and I'm setting up the equipment and they're beaming with pride and of course you're expected to make all the right noises and comments, but it's not really me. And recently I've found myself in this situation a couple of times. I've managed to come out with 'What's *his* name, then?' or 'Have you got a name yet for…?' and then my voice just trails off and I just hide behind

the lens. And they've noticed, of course. They feel offended and they're paying money to have their kid's portrait taken. It's not exactly good for business or personal recommendations.

3 I don't have much self-confidence in general but I really feel exposed when we've gone out to eat after work. It's usually the others who decide because, you know, I'm the new girl in the department and I haven't been in the area long either, and it's always somewhere posh and foreign. I usually get one of them to order or I just say 'the same' so I don't have to repeat it. I wish I'd studied foreign languages at school. They all seem to know exactly what they're ordering, or they pretend they do. I think I'm going to get a phrase book – one that shows you the meaning and the pronunciation nice and clearly. I'm fed up with them all looking down on me. It makes me feel really small at times.

4 I didn't spend a lot of time there, a couple of terms I think. My father was working as a foreign correspondent so we were always relocating. But I *was* in the same dormitory as Peter Hayward and we got on from the absolute start. Really nice guy, Peter, and we've always kept in contact. It was his idea … in fact, I think he organised the whole thing. I really didn't want to go – I knew exactly what it'd be like – but he went on and on and eventually I gave in. And when I turned up, it was worse than I could possibly have imagined. Nobody had much to say to anybody and the few conversations we had were utterly contrived. What do you expect after a gap of 20-odd years? Nothing in common except most of us had ended up in banking and everybody remembered hating the physics teacher.

5 My brother was working on the island as a diving instructor. It's a good lifestyle. My grandmother was Greek and used to make us repeat certain phrases but I can hardly remember a thing, so I flicked through this pocket dictionary on the way over just to have a few ideas. Anyway, my brother took me to meet some people and I was speaking to one owner in English but I thought it might make more of an impact if I could show I knew a bit of the language. I came out with a couple of phrases I'd memorised … or thought I had. Obviously not well enough judging by his face. He just collapsed laughing. I'm going out there again in a month's time and showing my CV to a couple

of restaurants. At least my catering skills are alright … but first I'm going to get myself some private tuition … I mean, I want to be taken seriously. There won't be many people prepared to take me on unless I have some idea of the language.

TEST TWO Part 1

Erm, I'll start by showing some slides … if someone could dim the lights, yes, thank you. Very well, this is the first one … a skull in incredible condition considering its age. And the label, as you can see, says 'Toumai' – that's the name the researchers have given it. As you're probably aware, this discovery is one of the most important in the search for human origins in living memory. At 7 million years old, this is certainly now the oldest fossilized skull that we've ever seen, and it certainly took the French team who found it a considerably long time to do so. Fossil hunters Michel Brunet from the University of Poitiers and some very dedicated colleagues spent an entire decade in Chad. Chad is located on the southern fringes of the Sahara – and when the skull's owner lived, the area was a very green, a very lush part of a northern extension of Lake Chad – but still the sand dunes were never far away. Now today, the lake has receded far to the south, the dunes cover everything, and the landscape, it has to be said, is among the least comfortable research environments outside Antarctica. Researchers coming out of the field look like they've been sand-blasted – the wind and sand just tear into them, but these conditions are ideal for fossils. The fossils in the region have been almost perfectly preserved. They show us that there was apparently an abundance of animals large and small – from elephants to aardvarks – that once lived in the area. Not to mention the prize itself – this amazing skull, which the researchers have nicknamed 'Toumai'. This is a local name for a baby born just before the dry season, with fate stacked against it. Toumai in fact translates as 'hope of life'.

So why is Toumai so important? One reason is simply that it is the earliest known surviving piece of a hominid – a member of the group of creatures more closely related to human beings than to any other animals. It is also double the age of the earliest known skull. The previous record-holder, from Kenya, is around 3.3 million years old.

So what does Toumai look like? It is a mixture of primitive and surprisingly advanced characteristics. The braincase has the same size and shape as a chimpanzee's. The face, though, is where the interest lies. Rather than having a projecting snout with large canine teeth, the face is flat and the teeth are very small and human-like. Strangest of all are the enormous brow-ridges. These are usually associated with our own species, and are not otherwise seen in anything older than about 2 million years. Well, let's look at the next slide…

TEST TWO Part 2

…and we've received a letter from a Mrs Theresa King from Edinburgh whose daughter's currently on a one-year student exchange in Strasbourg. Mrs King says she's going over to meet her daughter and they plan to spend four weeks travelling around Europe together. She's asked, 'What's the best way to travel round?' and 'Where can we stay cheaply?' Well, Mrs King, we've been checking out the options for you.

First of all, most people I'm sure will agree that travelling by train around Europe is preferable to taking the bus. Trains tend to be faster, more frequent and more comfortable and tend to have excellent connections. So, as long as you're sticking to the west of Europe, a Europass would be your best bet. It covers France, Germany, Italy, Spain and Switzerland and for five travel days, costs around £300; for a maximum of 15 travel days, it's around £500.

If your daughter has been in France for more than six months, I'm afraid she is not entitled to buy a Europass but she could buy an Inter-Rail pass, which is aimed at the under-26s. Be aware that for fast trains or express services you may have to pay a supplement. If travelling at peak times or if you require a sleeper, try to reserve seats ahead of your journey.

For places to stay, youth hostels would be the cheapest option, unless you're prepared to lug tents around and stay at campgrounds. As for sightseeing – we can certainly tell you what the absolute must-sees are. First of all, save your appetite for Lyons – it's renowned as one of France's gastronomic centres. And underneath the city, there's also a maze of secret passageways. Some of them date from Roman times and others were made by silk weavers in the 19th century so they could transport their silk around town during rainy weather. Sounds like a very sensible idea…

TEST TWO Part 3

Interviewer: So, Sarah, this week's book is entitled *Letters to Henrietta* but I believe the book is actually about a woman called Isabella Bird. So, who was Isabella and who was Henrietta?

Sarah: Well, Isabella Bird was a remarkable 19th century woman, and Henrietta was her sister. The book is pretty much composed of Isabella's letters home – hence the title.

Interviewer: And what was so remarkable? I have to say, I'm afraid I haven't heard of Isabella Bird before.

Sarah: Actually, in her day, Isabella was a renowned travel writer. This was fairly unusual for a woman. It was usually men going off on expeditions – out into the unknown and facing danger. We're certainly more familiar with famous male travel writers. The irony of it all is that she was a complete hypochondriac – I mean she always had this idea there was something wrong with her and you can see a fair bit of evidence of this in her diary entries. Here – 8th November 1872 – she reports she's suffering from 'terrible headaches, pain in my bones, exhaustion, inflamed eyes, sore throat' and so on – you get the picture. But when it came to other people, she couldn't see it at all. She had very little time for tea and sympathy when friends or acquaintances complained of *their* problems. So anyway, what with all her supposed suffering, it was probably not a career path she'd ever imagined for herself.

Interviewer: And where was she when she penned that entry?

Sarah: Hmm, Melbourne, I think. She'd gone there, apparently on the advice of a friend who thought the climate would do her good – but when she got there, she found she loathed Australia. She thought there was nothing worth seeing and no interesting people. What was incredible is that it was at this point that this 40-year-old woman was on the brink of a remarkable career that was going to take her to the remotest parts of the world and bring her considerable fame at the time. Imagine – someone who could scarcely raise her head from the sofa at home in Scotland would then be climbing up Mauna Loa in the Pacific, surviving being cut off by snow on a ranch in Colorado, riding a huge elephant through the Malayan jungle, and even at the age of 70, crossing the Atlas mountains alone, on a fierce black horse. It was definitely unusual for someone of her social standing.

Interviewer: I'm just wondering about the equipment. It can't have compared to what's available today. Did, did Isabella work for a newspaper?

Sarah: She did have articles published quite regularly, but the book, you see, contains these diary letters that she wrote to her sister – most of which have until now remained unseen. She used those letters – or the content – to provide much of the raw material for her other work. I'm afraid it's not always … well … an editor now would probably ask her to exercise a little more control over the adjectives. She goes into particular detail – I mean *extreme* detail – especially when describing dramatic landscapes, like for example when she's having the time of her life in Hawaii. She was riding up incredibly steep mountain passes to get to their camp – she writes – 'companioned only by stars' beside 'a black lake from which rise fountains of fire' and so on. She certainly can't be accused of understatement.

Interviewer: You certainly seem to admire her.

Sarah: Yes. She has – at least to my mind and I'm sure any reader will feel the same – she has a very contradictory character and it's this that keeps you hooked. Her father was a preacher. He was strict and frowned upon 'fun' and you can see she's inherited that aspect. She rarely – in fact, she hates, to admit that she enjoys all her adventures, but when under pressure, all her imagined illnesses magically vanish and she just positively sparkles and shines. She boasts about her riding about in Colorado – saying that others are describing her as the bravest rider they've seen. This image isn't really compatible with the poor woman suffering from those ghastly headaches! Anyway, as I said, it *is* pretty amazing but – as for the book itself – I do have one small reservation. I mean, the book isn't quite what it seems.

Interviewer: In what way?

Sarah: Well, Isabella herself destroyed or heavily edited many letters – so maybe you're not always reading what you think was an original viewpoint or observation. And then, you see, the editor has also been editing, of course. What you're left with is doubt about who's edited what – what did Isabella write or cut, and how much influence has the editor had? Anyway – I do *utterly* recommend it. A lot of travel writing comes across as quite cynical or leaves you with the impression that the writer would prefer the country they're visiting to be a bit more like home. In *Letters to Henrietta*, you're getting a real glimpse of what it was like to be travelling at a time when there was still a sense of adventure and 'newness'. All of Isabella's stories are full of drama and full of interest.

Interviewer: Thank you, Sarah.

TEST TWO Part 4

1   When I was a kid, well, a teenager I suppose, they weren't that well known, not at the start, although, you know, they got pretty big afterwards. But me and my mate Simon, we were really into them and we used to … just be glued to the TV set whenever they were on, and I'd be doing all these extra jobs round the house just for the pocket money so I could afford all the stuff. It wasn't just the albums – it was T-shirts, posters, magazines, the lot. I had this massive poster on the wall. I really wanted to play like the lead. He was my absolute idol. But I never learnt a single chord. And my kids – they're doing the same thing now but if I ever look in their rooms, I don't know who it is on the posters.

2   It was about the only thing I was interested in. I wasn't much good at anything else. I still can't add up and I've completely lost anything to do with all that biology stuff. I was quite a voracious reader but I had my own ideas too. I've never used anyone else's ideas in my work – not consciously – although there's probably no idea that's absolutely unique. Anyway, I suspected I had a talent for it but I was too shy to show anyone my stories. Certainly not my mum. She's never read a book in her life unless you count cookery books. It was Mrs Shelly that encouraged me. She read out one of my essays. It was one of the proudest moments I ever had the whole time I was there. I reckon it was her who started me off. In fact, when I first got published, it was Mrs Shelly I dedicated it to.

3   There's one thing I can say for him, he was honest. He said what he thought – no politeness, no deference, no hesitation – just 'this is how I see it'. He was the same with everyone. Friends, strangers, the men he worked with, his bosses. Not everyone liked that but at least they knew where they stood. Mum never got used to it. She'd be after some compliment about her new dress or her new hair-do, and he'd tell her straight out. 'No love, it's wrong on you.' It *was* a bit much at times, but I'd like to think I take after him in that way. I've been accused by other people in my party of being too outspoken, but in my view, the public need to trust you. If you even slip up once, you'll never get that trust back.

4   Sometimes, when the paper has sent me overseas on an assignment, and it could be in the middle of gunfire or I'm just sitting on a rock at the side of the road with the cameraman 'cos the jeep's broken down, or just crashed out in my hotel room even, I have this sudden flashback to the first time we met. I was a miserable teenager – no interests to speak of – quite introverted actually. And I was probably going to be following my dad into the factory. Then James moved in next door and I was allowed to go round there. He was interested in just about everything – his room was full of unfinished science projects and weird pets, but what I really liked were his books. Books with stories and photos from all round the world. They were a real eye-opener. In fact, he was the one who was planning on reporting from far-off regions but it turned out to be me instead.

5   He was brilliant. All the kids in my class loved him! As soon as the bell went, all of us – well, not the girls of course – we'd all rush into the playground and do all the moves on each other. It was probably quite dangerous – come to think of it, there were definitely more than a few black eyes and bruises. But he was our hero! He looked so cool and of course, he always beat all the bad guys. He was on every Thursday night at 5 o'clock. My dad would collect me and as soon as I got out of the car I'd run in and grab the remote control off my sister. Things haven't changed much except now it's me who's telling the kids to calm down and leave each other alone. Sometimes you have to leave half the group with something to get on with while you're taking little Johnny – or Sarah, these days – to the nurse.

TEST THREE Part 1

On this week's *Sports Review* we're taking a look at a fairly new, yet one of the biggest extreme-sports festivals in Europe – The National Adventure Sports Show. If you're not entirely sure what an extreme-sport is, you'll be able to see for yourself when the three-day event is televised next weekend. It takes place in Somerset in Britain and on Friday afternoon, the cream of the Continent's skateboarders, BMX riders, snowboarders and all manner of other athletes, not to mention thousands of their fans, will turn up for high-speed thrills and spectacular stunts.

If you're under 30 and a fan, you'll probably already know that the Sports Show is, for many, the highlight of the extreme-sports calendar. The event has grown dramatically since it started in 1999, and this year 40,000 people are expected. The success of the show seems to be due to a combination of factors. First, there's the fact that it's not only the biggest exhibition of its type – you can buy or just gaze enviously at the huge range of sportswear and the latest equipment on offer – but it also provides the setting for a number of major national and international extreme-sport competitions, and, on top of all that, there's a massive live music festival as well.

A lot of the young competitors I met this week while they were practising say the Sports Show in Britain is one of their favourites – one of the best in the world. And the fans were equally enthusiastic. The fact that they can mix with their heroes and bring along their own bike or board and have a go, too – this is what they say gives the event 'a unique atmosphere'.

One of the main aims of the show, according to the organisers, is to introduce new sports from abroad, some more successfully so than others. They told me about a particular enthusiast from Holland who'd attached a windsurf sail to his skates and was managing speeds of up to 70 kilometers per hour. Unfortunately for him, they said, the wind died on the second day and that was the end of that. So, for anyone planning on introducing a new sport this weekend, bear in mind the local conditions. The forecast is apparently for fine, sunny weather, so let's hope that's what most of the competitors want, rather than high winds!

And if you needed further proof of the event's success, you only have to look at the dramatic increase in publicity it's getting. A few years ago, television coverage was largely limited to a mere ten minutes after most people had gone to bed. Now it's promoted by a major organisation and if you prefer to watch sport from the comfort of your own home, the whole event is being screened by Channel 4. So, even if you can't make it along this year, you'll certainly be able to get the whole picture – what the extreme-sports scene is all about.

TEST THREE Part 2

What's the number one take-away food in Britain? Go on – have a guess. Well, it may or may not come as a surprise to you to know that Britons like Chinese food even more than we love our old favourite, Indian curry. How can we know this for certain? Well, researchers have just carried out the most comprehensive survey ever of British dining habits and the results show that we ate a staggering 1.7 billion meals in restaurants last year – that's about 30 meals a year for one person.

The survey also shows chicken tikka masala may no longer be our national dish. There are more oriental restaurants, 5,410 of them in total, than Indian –

around 5,200. And by comparison, far more meals were eaten in Italian restaurants than in what the survey calls cosmopolitan restaurants, a category that includes fusion cuisine. Fusion cuisine is, as you probably know, food that takes something from the menu of one country and combines it with another's. And while restaurants have always been thought of as small family business, the survey reveals a spreading corporate culture: in fact as many as 40 per cent of restaurants are now part of chains.

The figures come from the first study conducted solely into the restaurant business – that's excluding takeaways or coffee shops – the first study by the Restaurant Association. The report, they say, reflects the growing part that eating out plays in our modern lives and shows that over the last 20 years there's been a real revolution in dining habits. While dining out used to be a rare treat, it has now become something we all do on a regular basis. According to the new figures – we eat out on average once every 12 days, and I think I'd go along with that.

Another thing the report suggests is that while the restaurant industry is growing, this doesn't necessarily mean all is well. More than 30% of restaurants last year reported a loss in profits, and many high street chains are actually selling off their branches. But despite this, despite the difficulties and the hard work, it seems that most people at some time say they want to own a restaurant. But, of course, you have to know what you're doing … a lot of people think…

TEST THREE Part 3

Interviewer: Advertising. These days it seems to be inescapable. We're constantly bombarded by an endless stream of images and messages. And those on the TV, the ones interrupting your favourite programme – well, some of them are certainly well made and clever, some are quite entertaining, and some simply irritating. But are any of them actually effective? Darren Conway – a researcher for a leading advertising agency – is here in the studio with us, today. Darren, what do you say to that question?

Darren: Well, Murray, the answer is 'yes' and 'no'. Judging by the results of a study we've just done, I'd say it depends on the consumer group you're aiming at. What we've found out – and I can't say everyone in the industry is happy about this – is that after the age of 35 – the spending choices of consumers don't change. And it doesn't matter how much money we spend on coming up with the ultimate commercial …

nothing will actually convince them to try new products.

Interviewer: You mean old habits die hard?

Darren: Exactly. It's probably true that we throw away billions of pounds each year designing commercials for the so-called 'grey market' – that's the over fifties – when many of us have in fact 'cemented' our spending choices once we approach middle age.

Interviewer: I think you're absolutely right there, Darren. Even the ads that I like, the clever ones, I still wouldn't go out and buy a new product just because it was on TV.

Darren: Yeah, most people of your … er … age group wouldn't. By the time people are 35 they're often increasingly happy with their lives and the choices they've made. And we've found that married couples or people in long-term relationships are unaffected by new trends, whereas teenagers and people in their twenties are interested in anything they might see or hear about. And here's another issue for advertisers – they spend around £16 billion a year in Britain alone, a quarter of it on television, and that can cost up to £80,000 for 30 seconds – and up till now, a lot of it's been aimed at attracting older consumers because that's potentially – statistically – the biggest section of the market. In a country like the UK, or the States, or France, where there's a low proportion of young people in the population – you want to be able to target the high proportion of older people. But it doesn't really seem to work.

Interviewer: So is there a particular reason for people's 'stubbornness' – if you like? I mean, 35-year-olds usually have more spending power than younger people and it can't be true that they're 100% content with what they've got.

Darren: True, true, but usually at that age, people have stopped being interested in being fashionable. The people in the study – most of them told us that they don't like new experiences or they can't cope with new technology or that they don't need to show off any more. There isn't that sense of pressure to keep up with the trends that there is when you're younger. When you're 35 and upwards – it seems to be – being comfortable – that matters.

Interviewer: So, does the advertising industry have an answer to this dilemma?

Darren: Well, perhaps one change we'll see is a shift in the type of adverts that are directed at the older

market. What you'll most likely see are advertisements that focus more on perceptions of quality and social responsibility. And you've noticed already, I'm sure, the increasingly common use of old pop songs. You know, when the big companies are attempting to persuade middle-aged consumers to recapture the spirit of their youth.

Interviewer: You don't sound very optimistic.

Darren: I think perhaps it's not just about the target groups … I think the big advertising companies need to look at who's designing their ads and what ads they decide to put out. Even capturing the youth market is becoming more difficult for them. If you consider who's at the top … I mean the people who control the purse strings, the budget … they're middle aged and older themselves. Even if they've got teenage children, their way of looking at things is often a million miles away from the teenage perspective. They just don't understand what teenagers want.

Interviewer: I think any parent listening will identify with that, Darren. Thanks very much for coming in today.

TEST THREE Part 4

1   It's hard work, you know. People still have this image that it's a glamorous lifestyle but it's not. I was the same. It's all I wanted to be when I was growing up. Never wanted to be anything else. And here I am. Not exactly seeing much of the world except for hotel rooms and if I'm lucky, the hotel swimming pool. The hours are bad. It's not the jet lag – you get used to that. But it's trying to have a social life when all your friends have regular jobs … or at least jobs with normal working hours. And a lot of the job, well most of it, is the same old routine every time. And you always have to keep a smile on your face, even if you're absolutely fed up and there's four or five people all complaining that they ordered a vegetarian meal and where is it? If I'd known it was going to be like this, I guess I would have chosen another career instead.

2   On the whole, I quite like what I do, but there's one thing that really winds me up. Delayed night flights. They have this chain effect. Of course it starts with the people waiting in the airport, you know, they're really excited about their holiday, and then they find out they've got to wait another 5 or 6 hours. By the time they get over here, they're exhausted and in a bad mood and they take it out

on you. What they don't realise is that we've had to work longer shifts so we're still around to check them in when they arrive. And the most annoying thing is that we often find out at the last minute. You think you're finishing at 8.30 and then one of the couriers calls from the airport and tells you it's going to be another three hours before they all arrive.

3   I've been in the job for quite a while now. There's been a lot of changes, mostly to do with the technology side and there's a lot more destinations we need to know about – but the customers don't change. There are certain types. Some of them come in knowing exactly where they want to go and then it's simply a matter of finding something at the right price and time. Then there's the other type who you can spend hours and hours with and still they're hesitating about it. You can get down every brochure, call up all the tour operators … and still they're saying, 'Maybe … I'm not sure … can we think about it?' I don't blame them. It's a lot of money to pay out and most people only get one holiday a year. You have to be patient with them. It's part of the job.

4   This year I'm off to Greece. I've never even been there myself before, so it's going to be a bit of a challenge. I've got to start reading up on the history so I sound like I know what I'm talking about. Before I was working in St Lucia and Antigua – really different – so this really is a big jump. But I'm looking forward to it. I've always been fascinated by the language, the customs … just the whole culture. Yeah, I've got a lot to learn and I've got about three weeks to make a start before I'm having to explain it all. Anyway, I can always refer to my notes or ask one of the others.

5   You know where we're off tomorrow? An art gallery. It's about the last place on Earth I'd choose to go but then, you see, it isn't my choice. That's the problem when you go with a group of people … they're all different. It was supposed to be just the three of us at first and then … I don't know … it ended up there's eight. It's impossible. I don't know. Maybe I'll go off and do my own thing, but then you get accused of being anti-social. And the day after, they want to drive around and go sightseeing. I tried to tell them about the traffic but they won't listen. I'd rather just sit and have a drink than be driving round looking at a lot of old monuments. I mean, once you've seen one old statue you've seen them all.

TEST FOUR Part 1

Organiser: Well, I hope everyone enjoyed the seminars they attended today. I'd like to thank all the speakers for putting them together and for sharing the benefit of their experience with us. I know there's a lot of talent here in the room, and that bit of extra guidance can mean all the difference. OK, the programme for Sunday afternoon – erm, for any new writers here, you'll probably be interested in Eliza Stirling's talk 'Presenting your Proposal' – that's really about the layout or format that agents expect from you when you submit your script or synopsis. That'll be in room 5 on the first floor. Then Elaine Johnson's session is, as you can see, 'Three-Dimensional Heroes and Heroines'. She'll be giving tips on how to make sure your characters are convincing, rather than seem like stereotypes, which is why so many first time script writers fail to impress. Elaine's talk will be here, in the conservatory. In room 9, which is on the second floor, I think some of you were in there today for Michael John's seminar, you can attend a talk by Terry Hunt on 'Objective Editing'. The title speaks for itself. We all know how hard this can be. It's easy to get so wrapped up in your own plot and characters that you can't see it from an outsider's point of view. So, if this is one of your tendencies, then 'Objective Editing' might be the seminar for you. And last but not least, if the endings in your stories come as no surprise to anyone, you would be well advised to go along to Ian Walter's seminar in the library, which he's called 'Twist in the Tale'. A good twist is one of the key features of a successful script, something that makes the whole story – or tale – memorable. So we have four very useful, very practical seminars tomorrow: 'Presenting your Proposal', 'Three-Dimensional Heroes and Heroines', 'Objective Editing' and 'Twist in the Tale'. Oh yes – and all the seminars will be running from 1.50 to 4pm – a slightly earlier start than today, but it means we'll have time for a quick tea break. Our speakers will tell you it's thirsty work, giving a talk for two hours. Now you need to decide which seminar you want to attend before going into dinner tonight so remember you'll need to print your name – no signatures, please – on the booking form which will be … I think we're leaving it here in the conservatory, actually. Obviously – unfortunately – not everyone can go to their first choice, but I'm sure whatever you go to, you'll find it very, very informative, so we'd appreciate it if you'd put your second choice up, too. Hopefully you'll get to see your first choice, but we'll see how it goes.

TEST FOUR Part 2

Tour guide: Have we got everyone … are you with the group? Good, well, welcome to Dereham Palace. It has a long history and it's seen a number of architectural changes. Of course, it didn't start out as a palace. The original building was a Saxon manor house belonging to the Royal Family. The stone foundations of this room – you can't see them now because the wooden floor is covering them up – were laid over a thousand years ago, in 863 AD. And apart from the foundations nothing else remains of the original manor house. From the records we have, we know that this was the main hall. There used to be two huge fireplaces – one there on the western wall, and another on the east side. They needed two fires – just think how much heat was required to make the room temperature even moderately comfortable. The castle was built on the same site and in 1258 AD, it passed into the hands of a powerful landowner, who took it upon himself to carry out extensive improvements. Two of these improvements were the six towers that were built as part of the castle's defences and the moat. I'm afraid the towers have long since disappeared but still, if you use your imagination – and have a look at the first two plans on your leaflet – you can see how much bigger the castle was than the original manor house. The castle remained in that form for just over seventy years, until it burnt down in 1324. The land was eventually granted to Charles Dereham in 1329 who had been an ally to the king. Dereham had an ambitious plan in mind for the site and set about building a magnificent palace. It took over twenty years to complete and in the process, actually bankrupted him. It cost £32,945 to build, which is the modern day equivalent of £1.6 million. Fortunately, Dereham managed to marry a rich heiress and this put him back on his feet. It was his wife, Catherine Dereham, who had the lake extended and drew up a design for the gardens. Now, we'll go and have a look at the chapel Catherine also had built and what you might find amazing is some of the beautiful wooden carvings in the ceiling that have managed to survive. Let's head for the exit on the west side.

TEST FOUR Part 3

Presenter: Susan Shepherd is a careers adviser who deals with job seekers from all walks of life and with all kinds of experience. Today she's here to talk about CV writing, and specifically for young people who've just graduated from university. Susan, of course there's an incredible amount of competition for jobs nowadays and I imagine it's a particular challenge for new graduates.

Susan: Yes, there are far more young people going to university nowadays and thousands all graduating and looking for employment at the same time. Because of the tough competition, I'm afraid you often find that some candidates are tempted to exaggerate their experience, or worse, lie on their CVs just to get an interview. Don't be tempted. You'll be found out. If you get found out, the company have the right to get rid of you. Nowadays selection procedures are very sophisticated and interviewers tend to be better trained. That means that any lies or distortions of the truth are likely to emerge at some stage. If you don't have much work experience, you can still turn your weaknesses into strengths without resorting to complete fabrication. The main weakness for new graduates is that the information on their CVs is often neither interesting nor particularly relevant to the position they're applying for. Because they've been studying, most of them can't refer to any real or substantial work experience, so they should pinpoint any unique qualities and skills that they have and use these as selling points. That doesn't mean you have to be the brightest or the best in your class. Often it's quite small things like taking a role in a club or some kind of society or developing a skill or ability that is different from your peers that'll make you stand out.

Presenter: And any tips for presentation?

Susan: To be honest, this is quite basic – it's going to be the most straightforward part of your CV. At least 10%, possibly 20% of applicants do not put enough attention into how it looks. Of course it should be done on a word processor but keep it simple. Also, employers will immediately discard anything that looks even a little messy so no handwritten CVs, please, and don't write too much. A maximum of two sides is usually perfectly sufficient. Your CV is the first impression potential employers have of you, so you need to make it look professional.

Presenter: Yes, I've seen CVs that have been sent here, on pink paper or emailed CVs where the person's name is flashing at the top. You're just not going to take them seriously. Susan, what else can you recommend?

Susan: As well as only having little or no experience, graduates often have a lack of knowledge, especially if they've taken a general degree in literature or an arts course. What's important here, then, is that they emphasise transferable skills such as enthusiasm and flexibility. Employers are often looking for the right attitude as much as practical experience or knowledge. Someone with the right attitude and qualities can always learn the job. They might have to start at the bottom of the career ladder, but they'll soon work their way up.

Presenter: What about those graduates who delay the job hunt for a while – who go off travelling? Will this reflect badly on them – if there's a gap between graduation and applying for work?

Susan: Not at all … well, within reason. If you've just gone backpacking for three months, that's fine. There's no need to mention it. But if it's for longer, then I suggest you do make reference to it, otherwise an employer will be left in doubt as to what you've been up to. So, if you have been travelling round the world for six months say, you need to show it was spent usefully. Any new skills you've acquired, such as learning to scuba-dive, put them down. Or that you learnt some of the language of the place you went to. It shows a willingness to learn – to improve yourself.

TEST FOUR Part 4

1 We moved up here from Cornwall when I was a kid, when I was about 10 years old. So I was old enough to remember what it was like, in Cornwall. Big open spaces, the beach, the long walks in the countryside. I seem to remember you could walk and walk and not meet another living soul. Maybe that's just how I remember it, but, you see, where I'm bringing my lot up, there's nowhere for them to really play. Nowhere for them to kick a ball or run about. When they built these flats, I don't think they had kids in mind. We're all squashed up together and it's all concrete and not a bit of grass in sight. It gets you down. You need a bit of colour, something growing to make you feel better.

2 It drives me crazy. It's the same every night – well, every afternoon actually. You see, I work nights, so I really, really do need my sleep during the day. I get home about 8.00 a.m. – and I see my wife for about 30 minutes before she goes off to work, and maybe I'll have a bit of food – and then I'll get to sleep about 11 a.m. I'm just about in a really deep sleep when it starts. You can hear it through the walls, really loud. And it's not just the sound – the walls, the floor, the bed, they actually vibrate because of how loud it is. We've asked them to turn it down and they do for a day or two and then it's back to square one. I'd be happy to move, only we just bought the place eighteen months ago.

3 It wasn't as bad as this when I started out. You could get from A to B in 20 minutes, no problem. Now it takes twice as long and, what's worse, because you can see it going on in the mirror, the passengers are sitting there in the back, fuming because they can see they're going to have to pay more. I'm not saying I know what the solution is. The government are talking about restricting access to the city centre – not letting private vehicles in – but how do they expect people to get here if they don't use their cars? I mean, it'd probably be good business for me but there aren't enough of us to cope with the extra demand, and the buses and trains are already overcrowded. I do my best to get people to where they want to go in the shortest possible time, but if there's a jam, there's not much I can do.

4 There's no need for it. People are just lazy. Our society has just become completely reliant on the private car, and it's not necessary. OK, maybe if you're a mother and you need to get to the supermarket with your two kids – maybe you need your car. But most people don't. Everyone's complaining about air quality – you can't breathe – you get home and what you've been wearing is absolutely filthy. I cope because I wear a mask but I shouldn't have to. I find myself behind a car, trying to get past, and it's just chucking out these lethal fumes. It makes me furious. Sometimes I tap on the window and say something and other times I just want to get by and into some fresh – well – slightly fresher air.

5 When I got my transfer to the city, I was thinking great – I'm finally going to be doing something useful. I'd had all that training and when I was stationed in the village, all I had to deal with was a few bicycle thefts and lost dogs. So when they told me I was coming here, I was certainly pleased about it but … to be honest … life in the city isn't all it's cracked up to be. I've got some good colleagues … people I trust … they do a good job, but it's not like we really socialise after work. Maybe it's my fault – I'm often really exhausted and just go home, but I can't say I've made many real friends. I seem to spend my free time on my own. It's a massive city with a huge population but you can still feel isolated.